Things Might Go Right

Things Might Go Right

❖

Prospects for Peace and a Better Life in an Age of Globalization and Specialization

W. Phillips Davison

iUniverse, Inc.
New York   Lincoln   Shanghai

Things Might Go Right
Prospects for Peace and a Better Life in an Age of Globalization and Specialization

All Rights Reserved © 2004 by W. Phillips Davison

No part of this book may be reproduced or transmitted in any form or by any means, graphic, electronic, or mechanical, including photocopying, recording, taping, or by any information storage retrieval system, without the written permission of the publisher.

iUniverse, Inc.

For information address:
iUniverse, Inc.
2021 Pine Lake Road, Suite 100
Lincoln, NE 68512
www.iuniverse.com

ISBN: 0-595-32933-0

Printed in the United States of America

To my former associates in Columbia University's Department of Sociology and Graduate School of Journalism—good friends and cantankerous colleagues—this volume is nostalgically dedicated.

Contents

Part I

CHAPTER 1 Introduction—and Brief Summary 3
To Start at the Beginning
Thesis to be Developed
A Few Practical and Impractical Applications

CHAPTER 2 Functional Groups Enable People to Exist 34
How People Cooperate
Diverse Groups Must be Compatible
Successful Groups are Works of Art

CHAPTER 3 The Process of Group Formation 51
A Case History from World War II
The Role of Ideas in Group Formation
Communication Channels: Another Basic Requirement
Personnel: Education and Training
Placement: Ensuring That Necessary Roles are Filled

CHAPTER 4 Why Good Organizations May Perform Badly 99
Motivation and Morale
Rules and Principles Governing Interpersonal Behavior
Intergroup Dependency and Patterns of Intergroup Conflict
Public Opinion

CHAPTER 5 Adaptation to Environmental Changes 125
Characteristics That Favor Adaptation
Style of Governance and Adaptability

Chapter 6   A Peaceful and Democratic World Society?.... 148
Indicators of the Developing World Society
Prospects for Peace and Democracy
Threats to Democracy and Peace
Probability of a More Democratic and Peaceful World

Part II   *Practical and Impractical Applications*

Chapter 7   Everyone Can Affect the Shape of Tomorrow 191
Building Infrastructures for Functional Groups of All Kinds
A Second Universal Task: Critiquing Established Groups

Chapter 8   Implications for Governmental Operations.... 222
What Should be Expected from Democratic Governments
Some Examples: Immigration, Taxation, and Terrorism

Chapter 9   Education and Placement 253
Emphasis on Diversity and Cooperation
The Vital Role of Communication in Education

Chapter 10   Notes on the Individual's Pursuit of Happiness............................. 266
Making Better Use of Functional Groups
What Nearly Everyone Wants Out of Life
Education as a Lifelong Preoccupation

Chapter 11   Where do We Go from Here?.............. 295
Thinking about Households (and Other Collectivities)
Defining, Evaluating, and Reconciling Behavioral Codes
Functional Group Interrelationships

References and Further Reading..................... 315
Index 327

Acknowledgements

In Chapter X of this essay, the following passage appears:

> …everyone with whom we come in contact has not only a unique supply of information and misinformation but also has memories of unique experiences. You will get more out of life if you can learn from other people's knowledge and experiences, as well as from your own.
> The trick is to somehow identify the specialized knowledge each person has, and then persuade him or her to talk about it. That is not always easy. Some of us seem to have an inborn talent for drawing others out, but we all can develop this skill to at least some extent.
> One way to improve your ability for this kind of informal interviewing is to watch how the experts do it. The most important thing is not to regard participation in a discussion as an opportunity to hear yourself talk.

Soon after writing the above, I came across a quotation from the English philosopher Francis Bacon, who lived from 1561 to 1626, which expressed much the same idea in fewer words:

> "He that questioneth much shall learn much,…but especially if he apply his questions to the skill of the person whom he asketh; for he shall give them occasion to please themselves in speaking, and himself shall continually gather knowledge. But let his questions not be troublesome, for that is fit for a poser; and let him be sure to leave other men their time to speak."

Although I wish I could say the above quotation came to my attention while reading Bacon's complete works, the fact is that I became aware of it because it is incorporated in one of Dorothy Sayers' charming detective stories—namely, *Gaudy Night*. It is quite possible that classicists and historians could point to similar passages in the literature of many cultures.

The reason for this digression—if I can digress even before addressing the subjects with which this essay is concerned—is that I want to acknowledge indebtedness not only to the writers to whose work there are references in the following pages but also to hundreds of other students whose ideas have become widely accepted and are no longer associated with specific names. These familiar ideas may, however, have a new significance when incorporated in a new context. Thus, while I am indebted to many nameless writers for thoughts that constitute important building blocks of this essay, I believe that the resulting structure is an original one. I hope that readers will feel rewarded if they take time to walk through it.

More specific acknowledgements are due friends, relatives, and colleagues who have kindly read portions of the book's manuscript at my request or have contributed suggestions and ideas that influenced the book's content. In particular, I would like to extend hearty thanks to Marguerite Cairns, Albert H. Cantril, Robert L. Cohen, Herbert J. Gans, George Ihlefeldt, Emily Jones, Sylvia Lindsay, Edwin H. Martin, Hermann Richter, Bernard Roshco (who is responsible for the removal of many malapropisms), Paul Salisbury, Carla Sykes and Gresham Sykes. Langdon Gilkey generously agreed to read the chapter that relies heavily on his fascinating work, *Shantung Compound*, thus helping me avoid inaccuracies. I should emphasize that none of those who did so much to improve the book's content bear any responsibility for the facts or opinions incorporated in it. I'm sure all of them will find notions with which they differ.

Richard Rowson has given me the benefit of his long experience as a publisher to shepherd me through the complex process of creating a book manuscript. And many thanks are due Ken Lindsay, who photographed and then digitalized "life's winding road," which is shown on the cover. Without the help of my son, Stowell W. Davison, and grandson, Phillips B. Wolf, both of whom understand the care and feeding of computers, various sections of the manuscript would long since have disappeared into cyberspace. My wife, Emma-Rose Martin has, with loving fortitude, put up with the author's anti-social behavior, and has been good enough to review the whole project not once but several times. I am happy to report that she seems to have not only survived these exhausting experiences but still plays a fast game of tennis at the age of 84.

Part I

1

Introduction—and Brief Summary

One conclusion emerging from this discussion of changing patterns of social organization is that violence and coercion, whether on a small or large scale, are becoming less and less likely to enable individuals, organizations, and nations to get what they want. Instead, the future will be a happier one for everybody if we can learn how to make the fullest possible use of each human being's capabilities, how to coordinate the efforts of diverse peoples more smoothly, and how to solve differences more satisfactorily. Those who are the most skillful in building formal and informal groups to help achieve their goals, whether these groups are composed of individuals, other groups of various sizes, or national states, are most likely to prosper in the world of today and tomorrow.

A related conclusion is that recent developments in communication, combined with the growth of knowledge and increased educational opportunities for more people, have created a situation where more and more of the world's population can benefit from new cooperative relationships. Individual computer owners, entrepreneurs in business, and political leaders all can take advantage of the expanding possibilities to form productive or rewarding groups, whether in the neighborhood, the nation, or the world. A major question facing the 21st century is how best to exploit the new environment for everyone's benefit. Increasing scientific knowledge and changing social patterns present both opportunities and problems. Although there is still much to be learned about the processes of cooperation, we are not making the best use even of what we already know. Governments, in particular, should be devoting far greater efforts to involving as many people as possible in this search for a better life. Unless it is demonstrated that significant improvements are possible through cooperation, terrorism will continue to flourish.

During previous periods in human history, various forms of violence and compulsion, including slavery, the caste system, absolute authority of the family patriarch, and military conquest, were often rational (whether or not moral) means by which certain individuals and groups, and sometimes many members of a whole society, could acquire wealth, power, and other values. Indeed, the use of raw power might be the only way a society could survive. There are still occasions when violence and coercion turn out to be rational choices for action by individuals or groups, including nations, but these occasions occur more and more rarely. Under present conditions, it is more likely that everybody will lose when they become involved in violent conflict.

This change in social dynamics started thousands of years ago, when people learned that they often could get more of what they wanted by cultivating good relations with members of their families and their neighbors, rather than by beating or intimidating them. Voluntary cooperation became increasingly likely to prove profitable, with ups and downs, during the following millennia. This was true for individuals as well as groups, and in both international and domestic affairs. The trend in this direction speeded up tremendously during the 20th century.

Among reasons for the rapid growth of cooperative relationships during the 20th century are the emergence of a worldwide network for instant communication and the sudden increase in capabilities for fast transportation everywhere. In addition, interdependence among individuals, organizations, and nations continued to increase during the century at an accelerated pace, and has played a major role in promoting cooperative relationships. Interdependence has been stimulated by the fact that more and more of the things people everywhere want—including not only material objects such as computers and automobiles, but also non-material values such as security, affection, self-respect, good health, and justice—depend increasingly on voluntary cooperation of many diverse individuals and groups, both at home and abroad.

We are now at a stage where we can take advantage of this novel situation to improve the quality of life for all the world's populations. Or, we can slip back to conditions similar to those that existed in the past, leaving to future generations the possibility of finding better ways to realize human aspirations. This is why we should be making special efforts to strengthen our capacities for working together with as many other people as possible—whether they are like us or are very different—in families, in associations of all kinds, and on the national and international level.

The above sweeping assertions are based on a review of many small and large transactions of daily life, as well as on more general observations about social organization and world affairs.

To Start at the Beginning. As a small boy growing up in the 1920's, the first sound I usually heard in the morning was the clip-clop of the horse that pulled the milk wagon. Sometimes I could also hear the footfall of the milkman as he left three quarts of milk on the back porch. Rich, golden cream occupied the top quarter of each bottle. Shortly after that, except during the summer months, there would be bangs and clangs from the cellar, as my father shook the dead ashes from the furnace, opened the draft, and shoveled new coal on the embers that had survived the night. Then, as the first suggestions of heat began to penetrate the chilly house, there were noises from the kitchen, where my mother was starting the oatmeal in a double boiler. It took about an hour to cook.

Breakfast was a formal occasion. My brother and I had to be in our places by 7 o'clock. Conversation was discouraged until everyone had finished eating. This was partly because my father liked to scan the morning newspaper while at the table. In addition, my mother had been raised in days when, as an old adage puts it, "children should be seen and not heard"—especially early in the morning. She had also inherited a rule about conversation which, fortunately, she did not enforce strictly. Before saying anything, one should be prepared to answer three questions in the affirmative—Is it true? Is it kind? Is it necessary? The first two questions were tough enough, but the third was a real stopper!

When everyone had finished his or her cereal, we recited a psalm together, or my father read a passage from another part of the Bible. Finally, if there was still enough time before my brother and I had to leave for school, one of our parents would read a chapter from some book that was likely to be of interest to all age groups. Many of the books were really too difficult for the smallest of us (namely, me), but I learned to enjoy them, especially *Pickwick Papers*, long before I had mastered more than a fraction of Charles Dickens' formidable vocabulary.

The walk to the neighborhood public school was sometimes like running a gantlet. This was especially likely in winter, when we were often pelted with snowballs by members of a rival gang, members of which lived along the route we took. Actually, to use the word "gang" today is inappropriate. Its meaning has changed. We used it then to describe almost any male play group. Members of these groups in our neighborhood were mostly between six and twelve years of age, none of them carried weapons as far as I know, and property destruction was minor and occasional. Gang warfare was usually confined to throwing snow balls, shouting insults, and shoving those who belonged to rival aggregations off sidewalks and into the gutter.

At the school, boys and girls entered by separate doors. In the classroom, children of both sexes sat at small desks that were arranged in rigid ranks and bolted firmly to the floor. Sometimes, children who had done the best in recent tests were seated in front, and less impressive students in the rear. Most of the teachers seemed very strict to me.

Although physical punishment was rarely meted out, all students were aware that it could occur. Some teachers were likely to spank small boys who were egregiously insolent or uncooperative. When it came to strictness, Miss Barnes, the second grade teacher, outdid other members of the instructional staff. She required not only that books, papers, pencils and erasers in each desk be stored according to a prescribed pattern, but she was known to send children home if they were not dressed according to her demanding specifications. Another teacher, whose name I can't remember, insisted that I learn to write with my right hand, although I was clearly left handed. Fortunately, a third grade teacher, Mrs. Stock, allowed me to revert to the left hand and to print my letters rather than to use cursive writing.

There is nothing extraordinary in these recollections. Similar memories are shared by many who were growing up in the United States during the early years of the 20th century. My reason for devoting a few paragraphs to them is to illustrate several common sense propositions that are relevant to the focus of this book. The first of these propositions is that from the time of our birth the satisfaction of nearly all our basic needs, and many of our desires, is made possible by groups of people who work together to deliver particular gratifications and services—in addition to sometimes causing annoyances and frustrations. Of these groups, the family is the most ubiquitous and indispensable. Businesses, schools, informal neighborhood organizations, governments, and other institutions and associations also play an important part. Members of these groups—including parents, employees of companies that provide food and fuel, other children, policemen at school crossings, and teachers—all affect our lives, starting at an early age.

A second proposition, equally obvious, is that the quality of our lives, however we may perceive or define quality, is determined in large part by how well such groups satisfy our needs and desires, and by the compatibility of the various groups with each other. Unkind or incompetent parents and teachers may make our lives miserable and have unpleasant long-term effects. And if the family and school don't cooperate, the child is likely to suffer.

Also unsurprising is that most of us tend to take existing institutions for granted. We assume the good institutions will always be there when we want them; the bad ones we will always have to avoid if possible. We feel that we have a right to loving care, enough food, safe streets, and an education, but we usually assume that it is someone else's responsibility to provide these gratifications. When we think about it, we may acknowledge that we receive benefits from families, schools, businesses, and governments, but it is easy to ignore our collective responsibility for organizing and maintaining, or cooperating with, these institutions. The idea that people must work together in many kinds of groups to provide benefits we all want does not come as a shock, but it is a notion that doesn't get much day-to-day attention, except when we are reminded of it by spokespersons for such institutions as religious bodies, athletic teams, or employers.

As a child, I rarely thought about institutions at all. Good things, as well as threats and annoyances, were associated with individuals. Mother provided breakfast and many other necessities; the milkman (not the company he worked for) was responsible for the milk; and there were good and bad teachers, neighborhood children, and policemen—not good and bad schools, neighborhoods, and governments.

A final self-evident point illustrated by the above smattering of recollections is that many of the organized groups affecting our lives behave differently as time goes on and environments change. Few families now conduct breakfast with such formality, and the previously clear distinction between what is women's work and what is men's work has become blurred. Milk is no longer delivered with the aid of a horse; indeed, it is rarely delivered. Schools are less likely to allow corporal punishment. Teachers are more permissive, and in most cases left-handed children are allowed to write with whichever hand they or their parents wish. Such changes have been occasioned by developments in public opinion, new scientific knowledge, changing educational theories, and many other factors. The environment of 2000 is thus quite different from that of 1920, at least in most parts of the globe, and many of the groups that help to satisfy our wants and needs have adapted to changed circumstances.

One small mystery is why there is no single term designating the groups of people, like families, schools, businesses, governments, and informal gatherings of friends and neighbors, on which we depend to satisfy most of our needs and many of our wants. (At least, I am not aware of any such expression in English.) Therefore, I have adopted a somewhat cumbersome term, namely, "functional group" to refer to all such human collectivities. As used here, the word "functional" carries none of the special meanings sometimes assigned to it by sociologists, economists, or political scientists. It is employed in conformity with one of its dictionary definitions: "intended to be useful." Some groups that we encounter frequently are *not* intended to be useful—such as crowds and traffic jams—and we are only indirectly concerned with these here. The "functional group" term will be explained more fully in Chapter I, below, for the benefit of readers who skip egocentric introductions and brief summaries.

Some twenty years after the period of childhood described above, I began to specialize in the academic study of communication, public opinion, and the mass media. This was partly the result of my assignment as a private soldier to the Psychological Warfare Division of the Allied Forces in Europe during World War II. Research and writing in the field of communication gradually led me to the realization (which should have come much earlier) that to understand what happens when people exchange information and emotions with each other, whether in person or through mass or point-to-point media, it is necessary to have a conception of how societies work. What part does meaning conveyed by communications from other people play in the lives of different individuals and in the behavior of organizations? How do the mass media and other channels of communication help or hinder the human groupings that make up a society to become organized, operate, change, and relate to each other? Such questions redirected my attention back to the family, schools, governments, and other social organisms that serve human wants and needs.

My attempts to construct pictures of societies that, I hoped, would lead to a better understanding of the role of communication in our lives metamorphosed many times during the following decades. With each revision these efforts became more focused on functional groups. Communication was increasingly treated as one of several processes that made it possible for these groups to become organized, operate, and thus affect our lives. Pictures of societies that resulted from this project had little to say directly (although a lot indirectly) about the distribution of wealth or power in any given society, but they did help to explain differences in the quality of life in societies throughout the world and to relate these differences to various forms of governance.

Even with their many shortcomings, I have found these models of society useful in my own thinking. They have provided guidance with respect to voting, contributing to "good causes," writing letters to editors and government officials, choosing subjects to study, and deciding how to spend my time in general. They also make each day's news more interesting and understandable. I gradually came to believe that this approach to studying social organization might prove useful, or at least interesting, to others who are involved in both academic and non-academic pursuits. Therefore, I have done my best to describe it in the following pages, and to do so in non-technical language.

I hope that those who dip into this essay will find it possible to expand and correct its content in the light of their own knowledge and experience, and that at least a few who pick up the book will be motivated to do further research on questions that are raised. Advancing age has limited what I can do myself. It is not a project that one should undertake in the ninth decade of his or her life, but I came to this realization somewhat late in the game. The models of society presented here could be elaborated, clarified, and probably made more interesting by incorporating in them additional factual and illustrative materials, and also by relating them to more of the existing body of social research. If it had been possible, I would have liked to devote at least several additional years to developing the themes that are outlined below.

But to take more time in preparation did not appear to be a viable option. I was faced with what looked like a "go" or "no go" decision. A former Columbia University colleague, Professor John Hohenberg, used to tell his journalism students that, when confronted by a deadline, "You've got to go with what you've got." Well, age imposes its own deadlines, so I'm taking his advice.

What I have done is to set forth some ideas about social organization that I think are helpful in understanding today's world and in deciding what to do about tomorrow's world. Implications of these ideas and various conclusions that grow out of them are illustrated and supported by data from a variety of sources. Some of the books that I found relevant are listed, and a few are annotated, in the "References and Further Readings" section at the end of this volume. Others, which should be there, are not included because I no longer remember titles and authors of books I read many years ago or because I have not found time to read new books that probably would be relevant.

In addition to making use of scholarly works, I have incorporated information from the news media—especially the *New York Times, Washington Post,* and *Economist*—that bears on the phenomena being discussed. When available sources fail to provide appropriate examples to illustrate these phenomena, hypothetical examples are sometimes used. It is likely that many readers will be able to supplement some of these hypothetical examples with real ones if they consult their own experience, and I hope they will do this. Everyone has his or her own mental picture of the world, and we all have a lot of information about social organization. We have to, since we need this knowledge in our day-to-day activities.

Thesis to be Developed. The argument presented in the following chapters is based on the premise that the satisfaction of most human wants and needs, both material and nonmaterial, is made possible by groups of people who, willingly or unwillingly, coordinate their actions in order to achieve anticipated ends. Functional groups provide most of the necessary coordinating mechanisms, and members of these functional groups follow certain specified rules that guide what they do. All of us belong to such groups and, in addition, we derive both benefits and deprivations from the activities of many other human collectivities to which we do not belong.

This is not to say that the solitary human being is totally helpless, that such a person cannot satisfy many of his or her desires without the cooperation of others, or that decisions made by a single individual are not important. We can choose when to eat, assuming that food is available, and can select a book to read, if there is a library, and can do our job well or badly, if we have a job. The point is that to survive for more than a relatively brief period and, even more, to prosper, everyone needs the assistance of other people. And the extent to which others assist us often depends on whether they are members of a caring family, a business on which we rely, a school's staff, a card-playing club, or some other association that helps to satisfy one or more of our many desires.

Even the shipwrecked mariner on a desert island depends heavily on the work performed by functional groups in the past. He uses his factory-produced pocket knife, some of the skills previously learned from schools and on-the-job training, and supplies washed ashore from his ship. He is sustained especially by memories of his family and loved ones. But if he gets sick, or is attacked by wild animals, there is no one to help him. He is unlikely to survive for long.

The dependence of individuals on each other is most obvious at birth, when family members, or their surrogates, must ensure that the infant is somehow fed, protected, and taught. Dependence continues as we grow older, especially as we develop new desires and interests, some of which can be satisfied only by other people with specialized talents and training, such as musicians, automobile mechanics, and gourmet chefs. Many of us who are alive today can thank scientific researchers, medical schools, doctors, and hospitals for our continued existence.

Whole societies, which can be thought of as populations that are able to satisfy all, or nearly all, of their basic needs without assistance from the outside,[1] are dependent for their survival on the ability of their members to provide essential goods and services. Although societies may prosper or fail for many reasons, some continue to exist today, and some afford their members a better quality of life than others, because the surviving and prospering peoples have made superior use of their available human resources. They have organized their members in such a way that the living space of the society can be defended, adverse climatic conditions can be overcome, and adequate food and shelter can be found. Less successful societies, the individual members of which may have been equally strong and intelligent, have succumbed to natural disasters, including disease, or were killed off or assimilated by larger, more warlike, more fecund, or more enterprising peoples. Nations and groups have often disappeared because their individual members were not organized in such a way as to surmount hardships and compete successfully with other peoples or groups.

Nobody knows how many societies, of the total that ever existed, have flourished, or struggled, at one time or another in various parts of

---

1. Just how self-sufficient a population must be in order to be considered a separate society is a matter of opinion. A tribe that is isolated in a rain forest or on an island is a completely self-sufficient society. National states that can satisfy most of their own basic needs for more than a brief period are also usually considered societies, especially if their citizens share a common language and customs and identify themselves as members of a given tribe or state. But there are many borderline cases. Some political entities, especially in areas where colonial powers formerly drew political boundaries—as in Africa—may include several relatively self-sufficient societies. Later in this essay there are references to a "world society," of which national societies are members. Thus, some people may consider themselves to belong to both a national society and the world society.

the world. We do know that the proportion of societies surviving into the present era is miniscule—probably smaller than one in many hundred. Even in the 21st century, the last traces of little societies become fainter every year. One indication of this constant winnowing process is the decline of languages that once served to link together members of tribes or bands. Some of these languages, while they cease to be used in daily life, are preserved in documents or on stone tablets. Others are lost completely. A recent estimate by British anthropologist William J. Sutherland is that there are still some 7,000 languages in use throughout the world, but that over 350 of these are now spoken by 50 or fewer individuals. Other estimates put the number of spoken languages at closer to 6,000, but agree that a large proportion of these will die out during the current century. A contemporary researcher, looking for remnants of the Yagnob tribe, which dominated parts of central Asia 1500 years ago, could find only a single village where Yagnobi was still spoken. "Now it was actually very difficult to find Yagnob living in their ancient land. You might find cab drivers or cleaners in the capital who came from this region, but...the Yagnob had largely decamped..." (Wells, 2003, p. 187)

Anthropologists have observed numerous tribes, which at one time probably were fairly independent societies, in the process of dissolution. In one of these tribes, composed of the Ik people who lived in the mountains of East Africa, social organization had deteriorated to such an extent that even members of the same nuclear family often failed to help each other in emergencies. For example, a man who obtained medicine from the government for his sick wife decided to sell the medicine rather than administer it to his ailing spouse. When no close relationship was involved, lack of cooperation might be even greater. A blind man, trying to get edible meat from the body of a dead hyena, fell on a rough mountain path and was unable to get up. Other members of his tribe, who were also seeking food, left him bruised and bleeding on the roadside. The researcher observes: "While they still retain the quaint old-fashioned notion that man should share with his fellows, they place the individual good above all else and almost demand that each get away with as much as he can without his fellows knowing." (Turnbull, 1972, p. 101) Even after the rains came, and food was plentiful, the Ik were unable to cooperate sufficiently to harvest the crops and repair buildings in which to store the grain. (*Ibid.*, p. 269)

While societies that failed to organize their members in such a way as to take care of each other have tended to disappear, the numbers, categories and complexity of functional groups *within* major surviving societies has increased tremendously. Most of this increase came only after human societies had existed for many thousands of years. Anthropologists and sociologists point out that until about 10,000 years ago nearly all human beings who were able to do so had to spend almost full time finding food. But when the cultivation of crops and domestication of formerly wild animals led to the emergence of settled villages a "new class of people—albeit a small class—who did not have to produce food for their own survival" came into existence. (Massey, 2002, p. 10) These people were able to explore more aspects of the world around them and to learn new ways of satisfying human desires.

The curiosity and enterprise of this new category of individuals led to experimentation and to more knowledge about subjects such as building materials, food sources, medicine, weapons, and navigation. New or revised functional groups resulted from this process. These groups made more comfortable lives possible for more people, and the numbers of those with disposable time became larger. Groups of people devoted to manufactures and trade, the arts, music, amusements, and the growth of knowledge in general, increased in numbers, size, and activity. Further investigation and experimentation led to even more specialization. There have been periods in history when the numbers of specialists in some societies have declined, but the secular trend has been up. Modern societies have become enormously complex.

This circular process, which has been especially lively during the past 500 years, has enabled many people in "modern" societies (as distinguished from traditional societies) to enjoy goods, services, and nonmaterial satisfactions that only a few generations ago were unimaginable. Populations in less developed areas increasingly demand similar benefits. Large numbers of people in both industrialized and more primitive societies want their lives to become more comfortable (however they define this) in the future. The current flood of migrants from less developed areas into cities and into industrialized nations testifies to the intensity of these demands.

Pressures for increases in the capabilities of functional groups and for the organization of new ones raise numerous questions. How can both modern and more traditional societies develop efficient new functional groups, and revise old ones, fast enough to keep up with rapidly changing environments and growing expectations? How can these new and revised groups complement each other, or at least avoid destructive conflicts with each other and with traditional social organisms? How can the best possible use of available human talents be made in operating the myriad of specialized organizations that enable modern societies to function? These are some of the subjects addressed in the following essay.

One conclusion is that continuing proliferation of highly complex functional groups makes it increasingly desirable that individuals learn how to get along with those who are different from themselves. Many of the new social entities have to be staffed by people with widely differing talents and values, and often are dependent on individuals and other groups in distant geographical areas. Modern societies thus have to give more attention to the advantages and problems resulting from diversity among people and social groups. If handled correctly, diversity can be a great advantage. But what is "correctly?" International businesses, families, and religious bodies are searching for answers, as are governments of countries that receive immigrants from many parts of the world.

In general, the ability to adapt and adjust has become a more and more valuable asset in today's world. Each person is dependent on a diverse assortment of other individuals, some of whom are hard to get along with. It is more important than it once was to know how to cooperate with others who are different from the self. Skills in adaptation, conflict avoidance, and conflict resolution, which increasingly are being taught in schools and families, become even more useful than before.

Growing numbers and complexity of functional groups in modern societies cause further new demands to be imposed on individuals. Choosing an occupation used to be a fairly simple task for most people; now there are many more possibilities than there were even a generation ago. Young people increasingly have difficulty deciding among different careers. They also have more choices when it comes to marriage, recreational activities, and religious affiliations. The quality of life they experience depends heavily on the answers they find to questions about group affiliation. They need more help in making decisions about the roles they play in life.

Whole nations and societies, as well as individuals, are affected by radical changes in the ways human needs and wants are being satisfied. It used to be that nearly all countries had official religions; now there are far fewer. Older democracies have for some time stressed that they welcome people with differing religious traditions, and some newer nations now do so also. In 2003 Kazakhstan, a country with a Muslim majority, sponsored a meeting of leaders from 18 faiths at which a Congress of World and Traditional Religions was founded. Press reports noted on the occasion of this conference that, during a visit two years earlier, Pope John Paul II had called Kazakhstan an "example of harmony between men and women of different origins and beliefs." (*New York Times,* Sept. 25, 2003; *Washington Post,* Sept. 30, 2003) A somewhat similar sentiment, which a *New York Times* reporter labeled "retrospective utopianism," has been voiced by officials in Spain, who have praised the "spirit of tolerance with which Jews, Christians and Muslims created a premodern renaissance" in 10th century Spain. Whether or not reports from various parts of the world about current and past tolerance are overdrawn, it is apparent that religious diversity is increasingly regarded positively—not as a weakness.

There are also indications that another basic shift in attitudes is taking place. As has already been mentioned, war is less often regarded as a useful instrument of foreign policy. For thousands of years, tribes and states could gain wealth and power by seizing territory from other ethnic groups, forcing them to pay tribute, or enslaving their members. Just as arguments among individuals could be settled by murder or other forms of violence, disputes among peoples could be resolved by genocide. An evolutionary biologist, drawing on anthropology and related disciplines, has noted that with the rise of political units that were too large to allow widespread mutual acquaintance, some 7500 years ago, "people had to learn for the first time in history, how to encounter strangers regularly without attempting to kill them." (Diamond, Jared, 1999, p. 273) Another social scientist, describing tribal behavior on North America's west coast in the pre-colonial period, writes that "aggression was a way to obtain land or slaves or women, or just to do some quick plundering. (Wright, 2001, p. 57)

Despite the fact that in later historical periods strangers were less often routinely murdered or mistreated and casual attacks occurred more seldom, war and large scale violence continued to offer good chances of profitability until fairly recent times. European invaders killed large numbers of the early inhabitants of both North and South America in the 16th, 17th and 18th centuries, and even more Native Americans died as a result of diseases the Europeans brought with them. The invaders thus gained possession of enormous territories. As late as 1835, the warlike Maori tribe exterminated the peaceful Moriori people of the Chatham Islands in the South Pacific, taking over their lands and villages. A Maori conqueror has been quoted as saying: "We took possession…in accordance with our customs and we caught all the people. Not one escaped. Some ran away from us, these we killed, and others we killed—but what of that? It was in accordance with our custom." (Diamond, Jared, 1999, pp 53-54) Following similar traditions, Hutu warriors killed thousands of the Tutsi people in Rwanda during the last decade of the 20th century.

Although such practices thus persist, genocide, tribute, and slavery are now unlikely to seen as legitimate instruments of policy by major world powers. In fact, these behaviors are frequently denounced—even though more subtle means are sometimes used to achieve similar ends.

The idea that war and violence are no longer cost effective has been voiced more and more frequently during the past century. According to this view, wars may sometimes be unavoidable, but everybody loses. The two world wars of the 20th century are often cited as having brought misery to most of the victors as well as to the vanquished. As a political scientist describes the situation, in 1900 governments and people in major nations considered war to be a necessary instrument of policy. One hundred years later, he notes, war had become "morally dubious and politically pointless.... It was the two world wars, combined with the development of nuclear weapons that did the most to bring the ancient practice of organized warfare into disrepute..." (Mandelbaum, 2002, p. 383) Similar judgments by academicians and public figures can often be seen in the mass media. The Dalai Lama has been quoted as saying that "the very concept of war is out of date." And a journalist who conducted a survey of social scientists studying warfare and aggression reported: "Researchers argue that one need not be a Pollyanna, or even an aging hippie, to imagine a human future in which war is rare and universally condemned." (Angier, 2003) She also cites an estimate by a University of Illinois anthropologist, Professor Lawrence Keeley, to support the idea that the world is gradually becoming more peaceful, even though the past century saw two world wars: "...if the proportion of casualties in the modern era were to equal that seen in many conflicts among preindustrial groups, then perhaps two billion people would have died." (*Ibid.*)

Although war is now more frequently recognized by people in modern societies as an inefficient way to promote prosperity and happiness, and it is often agreed that every other alternative should be considered first, these relatively new ideas have gained less ground in several parts of the world. Military adventurers continue to raise armed forces and to seize power, or attempt to do so. Similarly, there are a few governments that, in effect, wage war on their own citizens in order to gain space or other advantages for certain favored groups. Nevertheless, this use of force is now more often condemned, rather than being accepted as a normal course of events. In several cases, the United Nations has intervened in attempts to prevent or contain hostilities.

On the international level, the major holdouts as of the end of the 20th century—North Korea and Iraq—can serve as exceptions that prove the rule. Both countries had the human resources to develop an excellent quality of life for their citizens during the last half of the century. Nevertheless, their dictatorial governments tried to increase their wealth and power by the ancient formula of stealing from neighbors—in one case from South Korea and in the other case from Iran and then Kuwait. These aggressions failed, but the dictators who controlled North Korea and Iraq apparently learned nothing. Life for the great majority of people in both countries became increasingly difficult, while small elites prospered.

At the same time, cooperation is increasingly regarded as the most reliable avenue to wealth, as well as to nonmaterial benefits, such as respect, knowledge, and security. Violence and compulsion now play a less important role in private spheres, including families and schools, as well as in political affairs, although they have not disappeared. The survey by Natalie Angier, cited above, notes that: "In laboratories around the world, researchers have found that participants implement the mutually beneficial strategy, in which cooperators are rewarded and noncooperators are punished." Nor does there appear to be any innate biological reason why conflicts are inevitable. (*Ibid.*)

A related trend is that a world society is gradually emerging as a result of increased interdependence among peoples and new opportunities for international cooperation. To a greater extent than ever before, what happens in any corner of the globe is now likely to be relevant to those who live in other parts of the world. No major society is now a world to itself. Thomas Friedman, in his *New York Times* column, points this out when he refers to "a world without walls." (May 28, 2003) The cover of the magazine *Foreign Affairs,* for September/October 2003, reflects a growing emphasis on interdependence by highlighting three articles in bold headlines: "Why the U.S. Needs the UN," "Why Arab Opinion Matters," and "Why Failing States Endanger America."

Indications of this trend toward a world society are frequent not only in political and economic affairs, but also in cultural affairs, education, and other fields. Africa, until recently largely ignored by many economists and political scientists—and sometimes labeled as irrelevant—now receives much more attention from both faculties and students in American universities. A *New York Times* survey (November 12, 2003) found that the number of Americans studying in Africa more than doubled between 1990 and 2001, and that Princeton University faculty members who specialized in African studies increased from 12 to 20 during roughly the same period. Professor Jeffrey Sachs of Columbia University was quoted in this article as saying that Africa was the most challenging area of the world as far as economic development was concerned. Frequent commentaries in the daily press suggest, and sometimes state explicitly, that as long as violence and misery dominate major areas of the earth people everywhere will enjoy less peace of mind and less security.

Among other indicators that a world society is developing are the numbers, size and importance of international political organizations, multinational corporations, and associations of all kinds that draw their personnel from several nations. Increasing incidence of dual citizenship, international and interethnic marriages, and international legal mechanisms contribute to the trend. The World Wide Web and other technological innovations make it feasible for the first time in history for millions in any part of the globe to communicate directly with people in other countries. There are also nearly 4,000 new international listings in the 2003 edition of the *Gale Directory of Publications and Broadcast Media*. The volume of international trade, often cited as one index of "globalization," although not necessarily the most meaningful, tends to fluctuate in response to both economic and political events, but over the long-term the trend is up. Current developments suggest that, increasingly, interdependence among various nations will continue to grow and that most or even all countries will become part of a world society.

Another conclusion of this essay is that, under present conditions, democracies are better able to develop and operate functional groups that are responsive to human needs and desires than are major alternative systems—namely, authoritarian or traditional governance. One reason for this is that functional groups in democracies can more easily adapt to major environmental changes. Democratic systems tend to offer more latitude to people who come up with new or deviant ideas, are more likely to emphasize freedom of communication both at home and across borders, and usually provide more educational opportunities in more different areas of knowledge. In addition, democracies generally allow and sometimes encourage criticism of ideas and organizations, whether old or new, thus making it more likely that functional groups will deliver benefits people want.

More opportunities for experimentation are usually present under democratic systems, too. The fact that one group of leaders can usually be voted out and another group voted in gives democracies the benefits of political competition by making it possible to try out different policies. In this connection, it is significant that many democracies also attempt to avoid prepublication censorship, even though they may punish those whose communications can be shown (after the fact) to have resulted in harm to others. Thus, in democracies more ideas can be presented for consideration, even though some of these ideas may later be rejected. Further, individuals in democratic states are less likely to be arrested because they *might commit* a crime. This means that new ideas for functional groups can more easily be tried out before they are either generally condemned or widely accepted.

One of many possibly controversial hypotheses suggested by this essay is that as long as a substantial proportion of people everywhere want more material and non-material benefits they probably will tolerate and even support those who actively demand freedom of thought and information. That is, even though majorities may not care much about creativity, accurate news, or freedom for anyone but themselves, they will support democratic governments as long as they believe that these governments can provide them with what they regard as a happier life. And democracies, in spite of their limitations, have a better record than competing forms of government when it comes to improving the quality of life for the population in general. Authoritarian governance and traditional governance have both demonstrated their ability to provide comfortable or even opulent life styles for relatively small groups of leaders and security personnel but most members of the population in these societies usually have to live more simply.

If, however, more of the world's inhabitants become willing to accept lower standards of living, perhaps because they believe that deprivations in this life are necessary in order to gain bountiful rewards after death, then chances for authoritarian and traditional polities to survive and prosper are much better. Ironically, the freedom of philosophers and theologians to speculate, and of scientists to investigate, may be hostage to the desires of millions for computers, television sets, and theme parks. Democratic institutions, such as independent news media and honest elections, will have little significance if a population as a whole willingly accepts domination by a traditional aristocracy or by authoritarian religious leaders.

It is conceivable, too, that even mature democracies could lose their superior ability to organize and operate the functional groups that can provide masses of people with what they regard as a better life. There are several ways in which this could occur. Major wars and increasing terrorism could deprive these democracies of the necessary resources and freedom to produce increasingly attractive environments, whether of a material or non-material nature. (At the present moment, the policy of terrorist groups in Iraq seems designed to achieve precisely these ends.) Or, excessive greed and dishonesty on the part of political and corporate officials in complex industrialized societies could undermine the mutual trust that is needed if people are to cooperate in producing both wealth and more elusive values such as security and justice. (Again, it is easy to find examples.) Or, continuing and severe population imbalances in both industrialized and traditional societies could result in either too few qualified people to operate complex functional groups, or to situations in which very high birth rates outstrip abilities to form essential functional groups and lead to ever-increasing protests by deprived masses. These gruesome possibilities are spelled out in more detail in Chapter VI.

As an optimist, I do not believe that any of these threats to democracy will be determining. Rather, it is more likely that the democratic advantage will grow, although there will of course be temporary dips in the rising curve. Some countries that are now experimenting with democratic forms of government will temporarily revert to authoritarianism; a few might even succumb to traditionalism for a generation or two.

Nevertheless, most people will not give up their hopes and expectations for a more comfortable life and will gradually recognize that some form of democracy is likely to be more successful when it comes to building a prosperous complex society. At the same time, a stubborn minority of idealists and public spirited activists will continue their efforts to find ways in which greater numbers and proportions of people everywhere can make use of their individual talents, indulge their personal tastes, and enjoy life more fully. The gradual emergence of an increasingly peaceful and democratic world society will be accompanied by rising demands and expectations among nearly all human populations, and by the development of functional groups that are more numerous, specialized, and complex.

A Few Practical and Impractical Applications. The argument summarized above outlines a number of goals toward which those who wish to do so can work. It also suggests ways in which we might come closer to realizing some of these goals. Such suggestions are presented in more detail in Part II of this essay. A few can be mentioned here by way of example.

Most significantly, almost everyone can help to make their own society more hospitable to the development and operation of functional groups that are more responsive to human needs and desires. We can all show more respect for both creative personalities and carping critics, welcome new ideas and experimentation, help to make sure that communication channels are open to both innovators and defenders of the existing order, and support the best possible educational facilities. Leaders in government, business, education, and religion can do the most to create and preserve conditions that favor efficient functional groups, but we all play a part when we defend freedom of the press, pay attention to both friendly and unfriendly critics, insist on due process for those who are regarded as trouble makers, and vote for an adequate budget for public schools. None of these observations is new or surprising.

This analysis reminds us also that all societies need mechanisms to eliminate or contain functional groups that prove to be damaging. A group that serves its members well, such as a lucrative organized crime syndicate, may have to be eliminated because it interferes with the operation of other groups that provide benefits to much larger numbers or violates accepted moral standards. Each society has its own ways of determining what activities have net negative effects. In some instances, authoritative persons or groups decide, in others an elected body will make the determination, and in many cases public opinion will be a major factor. Each society also faces a two-fold problem. First, how to find the best ways of determining whether or not to treat any given functional group as a threat and, second, how to eliminate or control groups that are adjudged criminal, or selfish, or wasteful. Damage control facilities may include such mechanisms as legislatures, courts, police departments, neighborhood busybodies, and a watchdog press. We can all play a role in shaping and supporting damage control facilities.

The model of democracy presented here may be able to help us decide which groups, public or private, are useful and which should be reorganized or discouraged. It also can be useful in identifying the activities that are most essential for democratic governments to undertake, and also activities that might more appropriately be carried on by non-official functional groups. In general, those activities that require communication channels to all or nearly all adult population members—such as defense, public order, and tax collection—are governmental functions; other activities, especially those sensitive to rapid environmental changes—such as production of food and consumer goods—are better performed by private groups. Foreign policy falls in the first group, on the premise (even though often false) that a government speaks for all citizens when conducting international relations.

A further responsibility of governments, whether democratic or not, is to settle disputes among private functional groups and, in general, to do what they can to minimize friction and promote cooperation among all functional groups that are judged to be beneficial to the society.

Other suggestions, some of them more specific and more controversial, regarding such governmental activities as taxation, immigration control, and foreign relations are also advanced in Part II. As far as paying taxes is concerned, it is unlikely ever to become a popular activity, but could be made much more palatable than it now is by emphasizing its virtues as a surrogate for more burdensome forms of cooperation. For example, few home owners stop to think that they no longer have to take pick and shovel in hand to repair the roads in front of their homes because the taxes they pay make it possible for professionals to do the job. With regard to immigration policies, industrialized democracies should give far more consideration than is now the case to protecting essential functional groups in their own societies—especially schools, neighborhoods, and political organisms. This does not necessarily mean reducing immigration quotas, but rather suggests taking measures to ensure that efficient functional groups, which may have taken years or generations to develop, are not overwhelmed.

In both their domestic and foreign policies, governments of all nations would do well to emphasize that, increasingly, improved cooperation among peoples with diverse characteristics is the most reliable avenue to wealth, security, mutual respect, and cultural achievement. Governments should actively seek ways to make sure that steadily growing opportunities for communication and cooperation both at home and among men and women in all parts of the world are used to promote productive cooperation. A major goal of every country's foreign policy should be to work toward a situation where all the world's inhabitants can find roles for themselves in functional groups that produce material and nonmaterial values that contribute to more satisfying lives. Many of the new functional groups that result from these efforts are likely to be nongovernmental, such as small businesses, adult education programs, artistic organizations, and scientific activities.

The importance of working toward increased cooperation among human beings everywhere is emphasized by the fact that millions of people still believe that they can achieve a better life for their own tribes or nations by murdering members of other ethnic groups, participating in guerrilla armies, and persecuting those with differing religious beliefs. While worldwide developments, especially during the past century, have made it more and more unlikely that national or tribal interests can be served by military aggression, or by other kinds of force, many individuals and a disturbing number of government officials and tribal leaders adhere to the older doctrine—that violence can be a rewarding instrument of policy. This doctrine is all the more convincing to many because, as has been noted above, in previous eras it was likely to be true. It can be controverted most effectively by demonstrating that in the present world environment violence is less and less likely to be an efficient tool.

If one accepts this reasoning, it follows that the Bush administration in the United States made a serious mistake when it decided to use military force in Iraq instead of supporting continued and extended efforts in the United Nations to contain Saddam Hussein. The use of military power before other policy instruments had been exhausted did substantial damage to the cause of a more peaceful and prosperous world in the long run. Whatever short run benefits may have been realized, the United States action tended to undermine confidence in the efficacy of cooperation and collective action, while supporting traditional but increasingly outmoded beliefs in the utility of violence. An excellent opportunity to refine and promote greater acceptance of non-violent methods of settling disputes was lost.

To the extent that more people everywhere come to realize that their interests are better served by cooperation than by violence, the threat of terrorism will be reduced. Terrorist activities can be carried out by small groups that are not deterred by large-scale armaments and are difficult for police to prevent. These activities can, however, be minimized and perhaps even eliminated if enough people in all sectors of a society are willing to help the authorities control them. But why should people take the risk of becoming whistle blowers if they have no personal stake in preserving the peace? Those to whom peace is no more than continuation of a miserable existence have little reason to oppose violence.

What is required is not only propaganda and publicity, official and private, that emphasize the importance of peace and democracy as necessary conditions for producing both wealth and nonmaterial values. Even more important are policies and programs that involve as many people as possible in functional groups that help them satisfy their desires for a better life or at least give them hope for the future. Both public and private bodies have had considerable success in making small loans to people in very poor areas who have ideas for the establishment of their own businesses. There are numerous instances in which both official and nonofficial bodies in less developed countries have been able to improve local living conditions by forming groups of residents to discuss priorities and methods. Some of these efforts are described in Chapter VIII. For example, if industrialized nations could be persuaded to limit or abolish subsidies to their own agricultural sectors, this would provide a golden opportunity to encourage farmers in poor countries to get together and explore how to take advantage of the new situation. People throughout the world who are involved in such groups are likely to see peace and democracy as avenues to a better life rather than as slogans used by prosperous and industrialized nations to protect their own advantages.

Government policies should be directed especially at stimulating private programs aimed at finding new opportunities for cooperation in such fields as business, education, and the arts. People who can be persuaded to take part in the hunt for additional ways of working together for the benefit of all parties involved already have a stake in a more peaceful world.

Education is another important area in which the increasing significance of highly specialized functional groups in modern societies suggests new emphases not only by governments but even more by private educational institutions. The ability of tomorrow's functional groups to satisfy a wider range of desires will depend in part on the ability of schools to identify and cultivate more and more different abilities among their students. Traditionally, teachers have tried to see that we all acquire a common body of skills and knowledge, thus facilitating cooperation among large numbers of people from the same society. Most children, also, have traditionally valued uniformity—to want to be like their peers and not to be seen as peculiar. Now, schools are beginning to look for ways they can help children appreciate the desirability of diversity, and to emphasize that it is fortunate—not a calamity—that we do not all have the same abilities and interests. The more schools can do to teach skills in cooperation and conflict resolution, so that these diverse talents will be more appreciated and used more efficiently, the more they will contribute toward a better life for everyone.

Educational institutions are being called upon also to give more attention to placement—to offer students more help in finding the jobs for which they are best suited, and also in locating the most appropriate roles in other specialized functional groups of many kinds, whether formal or informal, income producing, or recreational. Educators should do as much as they can to help each individual identify his or her special abilities, and also deficiencies, and to encourage all of us to make the most of the former while compensating for the latter. Greater use can be made of psychological testing techniques, as well as of techniques for evaluating communication skills, which include sharpness of hearing, clarity of speech, and ability to put two and two together. The goal should be to make it possible for the student to match both inherited abilities (such as keen hearing or vision) and acquired skills with roles in different kinds of jobs, families, recreational activities, hobbies, and neighborhoods. Specialists in education are already aware of the growing importance of this goal in modern, complex societies. The discussion in Part II suggests additional ways of matching capabilities with opportunities.

Government and education are only two of the many areas that are impacted by current trends toward specialization and complexity. All functional groups share some of the same properties. Discoveries about ways to improve schools or official agencies often apply to other social organisms as well. My hope is that this discussion will help to stimulate ideas that are relevant also to families, businesses, religious bodies, and other organizations, including informal groups such as neighborhoods and gatherings of friends. Many of us, although we often don't realize it, play "governmental" and "educational" roles in organizations to which we belong. We can help these groups develop and adapt to changed conditions.

Nor is the discussion in the following chapters directed only to those who are interested in finding ways to organize and operate more efficient functional groups. Some of the ideas presented here may be useful also to individuals who feel a need to enrich their personal lives. Relationships between social organization and a good life are as relevant to each individual as they are to the society in which he or she lives. In this respect, knowledge about social processes is similar to knowledge about the psychological characteristics that affect our own behavior and the behavior of others. Both kinds of information help us get more of what we want out of life. We are unlikely to enjoy much security, well-being (including good physical health), affection, respect, friendship, sociability, information, and entertainment unless other people make this possible. Part II therefore includes some suggestions to individuals about ways in which knowledge about social organization can be put to work in dealing with personal problems and aspirations.

Finally, the analysis that follows may help identify a variety of inquiries that would be rewarding to pursue. For example, it is clear that some traditional patterns of family organization do not harmonize well with the demands of complex societies. Frictions in this area contribute to the failure of a large proportion of marriages. The resulting frequency of divorce is related also to the fact that people in industrialized societies have so few children that essential functional groups cannot be staffed adequately. In more traditional communities, on the other hand, parents tend to have so many children that functional groups in these societies cannot be expanded rapidly enough to satisfy even the basic needs of the population. At the same time, extended families make it difficult for other essential functional groups to provide expected benefits. How can families and economies be organized so that, together, they will serve human needs and aspirations more adequately?

Similar questions arise with regard to religions. Individual believers everywhere are increasingly demanding the satisfactions offered by both traditional religions and by modern complex societies. Yet, some belief systems harmonize with the increased importance of highly specialized functional groups better than others. Can the benefits of both traditional religions and specialized functional groups be realized at the same time? Might more people lead happier lives and contribute more to society as a whole if they had greater freedom to choose the religion they found to be most suitable for themselves as individuals? The strength of religious beliefs and the power of religious bodies in many areas of the world testify to the enormous benefits that people feel they derive from religion, but exactly what these benefits are and how they affect the operation of functional groups remains an important area for further investigation. In particular, it would be desirable to find better ways of assessing the impact of religious beliefs on the society in which the believer lives. It is possible that some belief systems give people peace of mind, security, and affection, but at the same time make cooperation among different individuals more difficult. The aim of research in this field might be to find ways to reconcile the personal rewards of religion with the benefits that various belief systems can bring to a society, and to maximize both.

A related field for inquiry, which has been little cultivated (except by anthropologists who are concerned mainly with simpler societies), is the comparative study of unwritten rules that people observe in their every day behavior. Some of these rules derive from religious belief; many more from tradition. Each society has its own behavioral codes that govern human relations, and various communities within societies have differing ways of satisfying needs and desires. Children start learning these rules and behavior patterns shortly after birth, and the learning process continues throughout life. How does one show respect? Whom should one trust? What behavior is considered polite and honest, and when is an action or statement dishonest or impolite? Which values are most important? Is it better to obey the law or to feed your family well; to accumulate wealth or to prepare for life after death? In what ways should one behave when dealing with the opposite sex? Differences among these rules of behavior are increasingly troublesome as we become more and more dependent on functional groups that include people from many different communities and cultures. Further study could help not only in avoiding misunderstandings but also in gradually developing rules that are widely accepted, or at least understood, in many communities and societies.

Most of the hypotheses and assumptions on which the following discussion is based would benefit from additional research. What characteristics are shared by functional groups of all kinds and sizes? Is it correct that, even when confronted by powerful authoritarian rulers, most people will not give up their tastes for what they regard as more comfortable lives? Are current forms of democracy the best ways of assuring freedom of communication, increased creativity, and the fullest use of human capabilities, or are there other systems of governance that might do just as well or better? How can the growth (or decay) of a world society be measured most reliably? Is improved cooperation among human beings indeed the most efficient way of achieving a society that makes a good life possible for the most people, or might there be other avenues that would provide realistic alternative routes to the values people want?

A list of such questions could be continued almost indefinitely. Instead of speculating further, however, I would prefer to repeat a wish expressed earlier in this introduction, namely, that readers will be motivated to find ways of enriching and enlarging the discussion—by consulting their own experience as well as by further reading and investigation. When it comes to improving the conditions under which succeeding generations will live, there is much that we can do now.

2
Functional Groups Enable People to Exist

The numbers and categories of other individuals on whom people depend for the satisfaction of their wants and needs have been steadily increasing ever since the emergence of humankind.

Many of the small bands of humanoids that took shape hundreds of thousands, or even millions, of years ago became independent societies, in that each had to be able to supply the necessities of life to its members. These basic needs were taken care of by the adult members of the little societies, who cooperated with each other in providing food and security for everyone, and in caring for and training the children. Most men had about the same skills as other men; there were almost no specialists, and the same was true of women. Consequently, each adult usually played several roles—if a woman, as a parent and a food gatherer, for example; and if a man, as a warrior and a hunter.

Social organization gradually became more complicated. As populations increased, large and small groups of people with specialized skills developed within each society. Individuals no longer had to depend on the nuclear family for the satisfaction of nearly all their needs. There might also be farmers who raised particular crops, skilled weavers, carpenters and tool makers, as well as experts in herbal medicine, magic and religion. Members of the various skill groups often cooperated with each other in doing their jobs and in developing their skills still further. Everybody in the band or tribe became dependent, directly or indirectly, on other people in various specialized groups, as well as on their own families. The gradual development of additional specialties—such as boat building and animal husbandry, for example—tended to increase expectations and to encourage the growth of still more skill groups, such as deep-sea fishermen, traders, and carters, to satisfy these expectations. The extent of interdependence within societies grew at the same time that social complexity, specialization, expectations, and populations grew.

When the time of recorded history arrived, there were thriving civilizations in many parts of the planet. Each of these was composed of populations organized in such a way that the basic needs of most members of the society could be satisfied, as well as many additional desires and aspirations of the fortunate (and more powerful) few. The degree of social complexity in various societies—the numbers and skills of specialists and specialized groups—increased or decreased from time to time, but the secular trend was always upward. As the author of an overview of human civilization observed a few years ago: "archeologists can't help but notice that, as a rule, the deeper you dig, the simpler the society whose remains you find. Plainly, change in the structure of societies tends to happen sooner or later, and is more likely to raise complexity than to lower it." (Wright, 2000, p. 16)

What has been happening within industrialized societies in recent years is suggested by the number and character of entries in compendia that list specialized associations and periodicals concerned with a wide variety of human interests and desires. In the United States, the *Encyclopedia of Associations* (Gale Research Company) lists 13,589 nonprofit American membership organizations in its 1979 edition. Ten years later, the number is approximately 21,500—more than a 50 percent increase. The rapid addition of new organizations has continued and, as of 2003, the *Encyclopedia* editors note that the names of more than 500 associations have been added to the most recent annual edition (the 39th) of this publication. Many of the very specialized associations listed were founded toward the end of the 20th century. For example, the International Trade Commission Trial Lawyers Association shows a founding date of 1984; the National Association of Retail Collection Attorneys was organized in 1993.

Similarly, the *Standard Periodicals Directory* (Oxbridge Publishing Company) shows a very rapidly growing number of specialized journals, especially in the fields of medicine and law. In the 1980-1990 decade, the number of legal periodicals published in the United States and Canada grew from 1120 to 1700. (Numbers are approximate, the totals being based on a column count rather than an item count.) As of 2003, the 137th edition of the *Gale Directory of Publications and Broadcast Media*—a successor to the former *Ayer Directory of Publications*—included over 850 new listings of media outlets in the United States and Canada. In contrast, it listed only some 180 U.S. and Canadian media enterprises that had ceased to appear since its previous edition.

The way journals provide indications of the formation of new and specialized functional groups, as well as of the ability of established groups to provide new services, is illustrated by listings of publications concerning Acquired Immune Deficiency Syndrome (AIDS). In 1978, the *Standard Periodicals Directory* mentioned no journals specializing in this subject, but a decade later there were eighteen such entries. Most of these were medical journals, but one was *AIDS Policy and Law,* suggesting that major new developments in almost any field can lead to new areas of specialization for attorneys. Especially in litigious societies such as the United States subjects given attention in law journals over the years can often stimulate insights about social change.

There are many other indications that the numbers and categories of specialized functional groups, and the capabilities of some existing groups, are rapidly increasing in modern societies. Classified telephone directories usually show a steady growth in the variety of goods and services advertised over the years, whether or not the number of telephone subscribers increases. People want more things and more services.

Even the fact that people are living longer stimulates the organization of new or revised functional groups that can satisfy their wants and needs. In 1776, average life expectancy in the North American colonies that subsequently became the United States was 35 years, according to an article by Dr. Robert N. Butler in the *World Almanac* for 2003. By 1900, life expectancy for Americans was 47 years, and by the year 2000 it was 77. Increases in longevity during the 20th century followed the same pattern in many areas of the world. According to Dr. Butler, these recent increases in life expectancy are greater than those that occurred during the preceding 5,000 years of human history.

New scientific research organizations, medicines, and treatment facilities are partly responsible for the fact that people are living longer. Additional knowledge about good health, and a variety of new services delivered by families, government agencies, and businesses also contribute to the trend. But many desires and needs related to longevity are still to be taken care of, and these unsatisfied wants may presage the organization of still more kinds of functional groups and the reorganization of existing ones. Dr. Butler notes that, in the United States, only a few medical schools currently have departments of geriatrics, long-term care facilities are insufficient, and additional employment opportunities for the elderly would be desirable.

Today, modern, complex societies consist of thousands of large and small groups of people, each of which helps to satisfy the particular needs and desires of multiple individuals, both members and non-members of the social groups that serve them. The quality of life in these societies depends on the extent to which specialized groups can provide people with what they want, how efficiently these groups operate, and how well the activity of each group fits in with the activities of all the others. So let us look more closely at the structure and characteristics of these ubiquitous human groupings that make civilization possible.

How People Cooperate. Individuals help to satisfy each other's needs and desires by coordinating their behavior in "functional groups" or "social organisms" of many types—families, businesses, churches, governments, military forces, voluntary associations, criminal gangs, casual gatherings of friends, and countless others. These groups are highly diverse, but they all share certain common characteristics. They consist of two or more people who (1) expect to get something they want as a result of belonging to the group, even if what they want is only to avoid punishment for non-cooperation; (2) are organized according to a particular pattern or structure, which often calls for several categories of personnel, certain material resources, various lines of authority, and particular channels of communication; and (3) play prescribed or agreed roles in accordance with identifiable rules.

But why do we have to use such awkward expressions? "Functional group!" "Social organism!"—that's jargon. Why not explain what we mean in terms that are in general circulation?

The reason for the jargon is that, strangely enough, there is no generally accepted term that refers to groups that are of all sizes and that satisfy the three conditions in which we are interested here—namely, that these groups serve certain human needs and desires, have definable structures or shapes, and have rules that their members usually observe. The word "institution" sometimes meets these requirements, but not always. When we speak of "legal institutions," for example, we may be referring to rules about the ways in which lawyers do things, rather than to specific groups of people who practice law. "Organization" is too narrow a term, usually implying that there is a formal structure, that there are records, and that someone is in charge. "Association" almost does it but is unduly vague, in that people may be associated without having a purpose or sharing rules. "Group," by itself, could be taken to include many kinds of aggregations in which we are not interested here. So it is hoped that the reader will put up with this modicum of technical language.

The common characteristics of all functional groups can be seen clearly in the social organism that is most basic to human survival—the family. People establish households to satisfy a variety of wants and needs. Some individuals are interested in giving and receiving affection, and probably hope for the sense of well-being that comes from having a congenial partner for social and sexual activities. In traditional societies, youthful marriage partners may follow the orders of senior family members because they fear punishment if they disobey. Stereotypically, in past centuries, men have wanted a woman who can sew and cook, and women have wanted a man to provide food and security. Both may want children. Many people expect that acquisition of a spouse will yield economic benefits, a higher status, and greater security in old age. There is frequently the conviction that forming a family is a step in life decreed by higher powers. It is the right thing to do. Parents and ancestors, living and dead, will be pleased, and the tribe or nation will be strengthened when there are children. Once children are born, satisfaction of their needs usually becomes a principal preoccupation of the family.

As for structure, nuclear families have traditionally been diagrammed in such a way as to show the male at the top of the chart, joined by a wife, or several wives, just below and often in parentheses. Children occupied the space farther down on the page, with lines connecting them to their parents. In contemporary family diagrams, the partners are likely to be shown on the same level (usually without parentheses), with lines connecting them with children, if any. Portrayals of extended families require more complicated diagrams, and sometimes provide information not only about the numbers of individuals in different generations but also about lines of authority within the group. Certain types of shelter and equipment are associated with families in most cultures—a house or hut, cooking implements, and a hearth. Indeed, in some civilizations, the presence of a hearth, or some other cooking facility, is equated with the existence of a family. This was true, for example, in parts of France during the Middle Ages. (Ladurie, 1978)

Then there are the rules and roles of family life. Adult partners, whether or not formally married, usually have to agree to do and not do many things, and to behave in defined ways. Otherwise, they may be punished by their friends and neighbors, or by the government. Or the partnership may break up. Some of the rules that govern family members, and the roles they perform, are predetermined and are generally accepted in the society; others are worked out by the partners. Traditionally, the male member of a household was expected to support the family financially, while the female was to take care of the household and the children while also satisfying the sexual demands of the male. Affection often didn't matter much. In modern, complex societies both partners are usually expected to behave affectionately or at least civilly toward each other, and to love their children. Adult partners often modify traditional patterns and gender roles by making their own agreements about household administration, jobs, child care, and sex.

There are rules governing the children, too. They are expected to play defined roles at home and at school. As in the case of adults, some rules are generally accepted in the society, and are enforced by laws and social pressures. Other rules are worked out by each individual family.

Organizations that employ one or more people are nearly as omnipresent (if not as numerous) as families in complex societies. These, too, are functional groups that satisfy many human needs and desires, are structured in a particular way, and impose certain rules and roles on individuals who work in them. Jobs serve multiple human needs. A job usually provides an income, and in addition may be fun, make a person more respected, result in friendships, and give the job holder an opportunity to display his or her expertise in certain areas. As in the case of families, most organizations that employ people can be represented on charts that indicate the categories of people involved and the relationship of each job-holder to others in the working group—'e.g., whether he or she is a superior or a subordinate. Sometimes organization charts also show the principal channels through which information flows. Members of functional groups that provide employment must ordinarily consent to certain financial arrangements, play prescribed roles, and observe rules that may be unwritten or may be spelled out in detail.

Belonging to a family group and a working group satisfies some of our wants and needs, but far from all of them. Other desires and aspirations, most of them non-material, may be served by participation in sporting clubs, churches, neighborhood communities, or informal friendship groups. The huge number and variety of these functional groups testifies to the large proportion of human requirements that can be supplied only if two or more people collaborate in some way—whether they wish to collaborate or not. All human beings must have input from other people, directly or indirectly, if they are to have not only food, clothing, and shelter, but also affection, security, power, information, good physical and mental health, entertainment, and other non-material benefits.

Large functional groups are usually made up of several smaller ones. Thus, a basketball team may consist of five or more people who behave according to the rules of the game and are rewarded in that they have a good time, acquire prestige, and sometimes get scholarships or money. But such a team is likely to be part of one or more larger organizations—perhaps an athletic department which, in turn, is part of a university, which is part of an educational system. In addition to serving various needs of its members, and of the larger functional groups of which it is a part, the team may provide entertainment to spectators, employment for coaches, and business for sporting-goods manufacturers. Similarly, governments and large corporations are composed of smaller social organisms—departments, divisions, branches, stores, bureaus and so on.

The kinds of groups that exist within a society, and how well they satisfy the wants and needs of the population, help to determine the quality of life for all society members. In some societies, the way people are organized means that a few enjoy wealth and power, while the rest are hungry and miserable. The king and his court live in splendor, while the masses of peasants are restricted to bare necessities. In other societies, functional groups are of such a nature that the good things of life are distributed more widely. But the bottom line is that, collectively, functional groups of one kind or another must provide sufficient food, shelter, security, and other material and non-material necessities to most people. Otherwise, the whole society, even if it includes many satisfied members, is likely to disappear.

The extent to which any particular functional group is seen as contributing to the quality of life in a society often depends on whom you ask. The opinions of rank-and-file members may differ from the views of group leaders or managers, and outside observers may make still other judgments. Workers in a unionized shop may be well satisfied, while management is unhappy and economists predict that the enterprise will be unable to compete with low-cost producers in other countries. The owner of a profitable business that uses sweat shop labor would be likely to say that the enterprise not only benefits him but also has a positive effect on the quality of life of his employees, since they would not take the jobs unless they wanted them. The workers themselves, however, might say they were miserable. Government officials might conclude that this business was beneficial to the nation because much of what it produced was exported, thus providing the country with needed foreign exchange. A few functional groups are judged harshly by most of their leaders and members, while outside observers might rank them positively. For example, some educational institutions are seen as contributing to the welfare of a society despite dissatisfied students and poorly paid teachers.

In a perfect society, all functional groups would be seen as having positive effects on everybody's quality of life, whether you asked the members, the managers and owners, or outside observers. These are the most "efficient" functional groups. Even in the imperfect societies of the real world, there are quite a few social organisms that pass this three-fold test. For example, there are happy families that are well liked by those who know them. There are profitable businesses with enthusiastic employees that provide society members with just what they want at reasonable prices. And there are neighborhoods that are regarded as good places to live by both residents and outsiders and are seen by local governments as excellent sources of tax revenues.

Diverse Groups must be Compatible. A society is more likely to survive and prosper if the activities of its various functional groups are complementary, or at least do not conflict. But two kinds of tension inevitably arise. In one variety, two or more groups make simultaneous claims on the time, attention, and behavior of the same person, thus pulling him or her in different directions at once. The other variety of friction appears when various groups interfere directly with each others' operations.

Most of us are aware of conflicts that fall into the first category. Many people experience difficulties in satisfying the demands of both their families and their jobs, or they may be distressed because their country's laws and regulations prescribe one kind of behavior, while the demands of their religion pull them in a different direction. Wars have been lost because soldiers had stronger ties to their farms and families than to king and country. Young people often experience tensions caused by competing demands of peer groups, on the one hand, and families and educational systems, on the other.

Tensions in the second category are less likely to be directly experienced by individuals, but are equally disruptive to a society. The most obvious case is the conflict between organizations that have been classified as criminal and those that are regarded as legitimate. Criminal groups prey on businesses, violent gangs terrorize neighborhoods, houses of prostitution are condemned for undermining family life, and merchants of addictive drugs enable people to destroy their own capability to participate in almost any worthwhile functional group. However, there may be serious conflicts among functional groups that are recognized by many people as desirable. Religious wars have resulted in enormous death and destruction, labor-management conflicts are frequent and, as tragically demonstrated in Somalia and some other areas, the power of extended families or clans (on which most individuals in traditional societies are heavily dependent) can make it difficult for a viable central government to exist.

Those societies that have survived and prospered have found ways to control both kinds of tensions. The separation of church and state in many countries has clarified areas of civil and religious authority. Legislation and changes in public opinion have frequently reduced the power of both governments and religious bodies to interfere in the affairs of private organizations and individuals. Regulatory agencies sometimes make it possible for families and neighborhoods to contest what they consider to be excessive demands on the part of big business. Dissonance has not been completely eliminated by any of these strategies, but it has often been reduced to tolerable levels.

But the major way surviving societies have been able to lessen the damage done by dissonance among desirable functional groups has been to develop systems for conflict resolution. Disputes among farmers and herders may be handled, if not solved, by compromises made in legislative bodies. Collective bargaining often facilitates the settlement of labor-management disputes without strikes. Courts of law and various arbitration mechanisms may make it possible for disagreements among functional groups to be resolved in an orderly way, even if some members of the groups involved do not like the solutions. In traditional and authoritarian societies, especially, one or more elders or officials often are empowered to make binding decisions in arguments between functional groups. Societies that lack effective systems for dealing with intergroup disputes are likely to suffer from family feuds, strikes and boycotts, armed conflict, or other forms of disruptive behavior.

Regulation of dissonance among desirable functional groups is frequently preferable to its elimination. Dissonance can lead not only to conflict that is costly in lives or money but also to constructive competition that benefits the society. If two or more groups compete to see which can satisfy a human need better, the result is likely to be that both groups become more efficient and that at least some people lead more satisfying lives. Competition between modern medicine and traditional medicine, for example, has added to the resources of both. Tensions among educational institutions have led to the development of improved educational methods. Commercial rivalry is generally recognized as favorable to the improvement of consumer goods and services. A substantial body of research suggests that rivalry among religious groups can increase the responsiveness of these groups to the needs and desires of their constituents.

The problem for all societies has been to determine, first, which dissonances are potentially constructive and which are destructive and, second, what regulatory systems work best. No completely reliable way of making these determinations has been found. Some functional groups, which are classified by majorities as criminal, immoral, or undesirable, serve needs or desires that substantial minorities regard as legitimate. The use of certain categories of addictive drugs is supported or accepted by large numbers of people in many societies—e.g., for pain relief. Minority religions, which have often been classified as criminal, or at least undesirable, since they compete with established churches or are thought to undermine individual morality, are still supported by enthusiastic adherents. Eliminating youth gangs, which generally are regarded as criminal or undesirable, often proves impossible unless some other way can be found to satisfy the needs these gangs serve. Public opinion may give one verdict about the desirability of a particular functional group, while civic, religious, or scientific authorities differ among themselves. With regard to gambling, for example, some churches and governments are opposed on moral grounds, while the majority public often favors betting at race tracks and casinos. In other situations, governments and some religious bodies may see gambling as a useful source of revenue, while majority public opinion condemns it. In authoritarian societies, certain groups may be classified as criminal or undesirable by governments that are out of touch with the views of major segments of the public.

Even when there is fairly general agreement that a group is undesirable, it may later turn out to be essential to a society's welfare. A nonconformist political or religious group, members of which have endured discrimination and have risked punishment by a country's rulers, has sometimes become the wave of the future. Feminist organizations, whose leaders were ridiculed and often arrested, provide one example. Extralegal political machines have been cited as another example by some American political scientists, who have concluded that 19th century corrupt politicians, especially in large cities, facilitated urban development and helped to provide work for millions of immigrants by cutting through red tape.

The complexity of regulating frictions among social organisms classified as desirable, and the difficulty of determining which are "bad" and which are "good" groups, emphasize how difficult it is to devise and operate functional groups that serve human needs and aspirations and at the same time fit together in a society. In the foreseeable future, all societies are likely to suffer from continued unresolved conflicts and ideological disagreements when it comes to deciding which groups have a net effect that is positive or negative. No society has yet found a system of social organization that can guarantee all members adequate opportunities to develop their abilities and enjoy a comfortable life. A realistic goal is not to completely eliminate frictions among desirable functional groups but to reduce them to the lowest possible level.

The bottom line is that *all* surviving societies must be doing something right, in that they have found ways to provide for at least the minimum needs of most of their members. We tend to give a lot of attention to deficiencies in functional groups, and to conflicts among them, because these can be identified fairly easily, while the substantial number of human needs and aspirations being served are often ignored.

Major social organisms in all societies are the result of enormous amounts of past thought and experience. Whether we classify them as "good" or "bad," they deserve respect. The belief, often shared by street demonstrators and members of radical groups, that the human condition can be improved simply by clearing away existing corrupt institutions and putting honest ones in their place is usually an oversimplification. The complex interrelationships of functional groups with each other, as well as human tendencies to persist in past patterns of behavior, makes the revision of social organisms extremely difficult. Every society faces and will continue to face the necessity of designing and operating functional groups that do a better job of serving everyone's wants and needs, but this will require increasing time, effort, and resources as modern societies become ever more complex.

Successful Groups as Works of Art. A principal purpose of the above discussion is to emphasize the value of functional groups that work, even if imperfectly. Better ones can often be devised, but it may take years or even generations to do so. Finding organizational patterns and rules of behavior that enable major economic, governmental, and cultural bodies that serve the needs of a society's members and also harmonize well with each other often requires a lot of trial and error, individual effort, and sacrifice. To create a school system that serves a society well requires work by dedicated teachers and administrators, parents, students, and often volunteers, over long periods of time. Even such a small group as a nuclear family, if it satisfies the needs of parents and children well, fits comfortably into the community, and harmonizes with the families of both parents, is often difficult to organize. Especially in rapidly changing modern societies, where traditional patterns of men's work, women's work, and children's behavior are often seen as impractical or inappropriate, it may take years for a family to find a viable structure that more or less satisfies each of its members—or such a structure may never be found.

Difficulties in creating and operating efficient functional groups are compounded by the necessity of updating them frequently. In an era when the social and physical environment is changing rapidly, many organizations and institutions have to be constantly revised if they are to serve a population's needs well. Changing conditions—for example, the rapid disappearance of the family farm—often make it inappropriate for the members of contemporary families to behave according to rules that prevailed in the families of their grandparents. The advent of e-mail makes it necessary to reorganize postal services. Discoveries by medical researchers have forced nearly all organizations that provide health care to revise their procedures. It's not enough for a functional group to be tried and true; it must also be in tune with the times. An observation about jobs made by an official of the United States Federal Reserve system suggests what happens to roles in all kinds of functional groups: "Large-scale upheaval in jobs is part of the economy; the impetus for it comes from technology, changing trading patterns and shifting consumer demand." (*New York Times,* November 7, 2003)

In view of the enormous efforts necessary to organize and update functional groups that serve our needs and desires well, it is alarming that most of us simply take them for granted. We assume that the family, the school, the post office, the hospital and the government will be there when we want them. It is understandable that a small child treats its family as a convenience that will always be present and can absorb any amount of abuse. Nor is it surprising that less-educated employees often fail to realize that their jobs exist only because of the thought, money and time of those who helped build and administer the organizations in which they work. And it is routine for most people to travel without giving thought to the numerous government and private agencies that are continuously monitoring the safety of roads, rails, and aircraft.

But it is shocking when public authorities fail to give adequate support to a well-functioning school system that makes it possible for almost all complex functional groups to find qualified personnel. It is equally alarming when successful executives convince their boards of directors that a company's profits are due exclusively to their own abilities and fail to give credit to the labor force, to those who helped to design the organization's structure and rules, and to the many other functional groups (some of them government agencies) on which the business must rely. Similarly, a neighborhood may deteriorate simply because residents do not take the trouble to get to know people who live next door or to support local community organizations. Indeed, when there is a deteriorating quality of life in a society, lack of awareness of the extent to which the population benefits from existing functional groups may be one of the major reasons.

Even some who must be aware that their own welfare depends on the good health of a particular functional group often seem to assume that it can be abused with impunity. This is true of many employees who steal from their employers and students who cheat in examinations. Some wealthy corporations utilize tax loopholes to avoid paying for public services without which they could not exist, including security, education, and communication facilities. The ordinary taxpayer, likewise, is unlikely to worry that government services on which he depends will be cut if he falsifies his tax return. The professional bank robber assumes that there will always be banks—indeed, he sometimes stashes his loot in one—and the pirate on the high seas is unlikely to worry that his activities will stifle international trade.

Examples of the ease with which people ignore their dependence on supporting functional groups can frequently be found in news stories. One such account concerns an immigrant from a developing country who made a substantial amount of money in the United States and then returned to the land of his birth. He was quoted as saying that if he could succeed in the United States—where the language and customs were different—he could certainly do even better back home. He seemed unaware of the many functional groups that played a part in his business success in the United States: well-developed transportation systems, public communication channels that enabled him to sell his products, honest and competent government agencies, and the schools that educated his employees and his own children

In short, functional groups that serve human needs and desires efficiently, and that harmonize well with each other, often fail to receive the support they deserve. There is insufficient realization in all societies that functional groups are often difficult to develop and can be among a society's most precious possessions. Because of their critical importance in satisfying almost all human wants and needs, they should be valued highly and defended as stubbornly as a nation defends its territory. Every society should be prepared to invest generously in their maintenance, modernization, and improvement. Ideally, consideration of all major actions, whether by individuals, governments, or other organizations, should include an estimation of their probable effects on the social organisms that, together, enable societies to exist and sometimes to prosper. That is a lot to ask, but at least we could probably do a bit better than is now the case.

The above paragraphs, originally written several years ago, restate an idea that has been expressed on many occasions both before and since then. It is especially well put in a column by Thomas Friedman (*New York Times* March 7, 2004), which discusses the outsourcing of jobs from the United States to India. Americans should be worried, writes Friedman, not about the loss of these jobs but about preserving and strengthening the groups that made the jobs possible in the first place—legal institutions, regulated financial markets, efficient bureaucracies, and good schools and universities. These social organisms "are our real crown jewels that must be protected—not the one percent of jobs that might be outsourced. But it is precisely these crown jewels that can be squandered if we become lazy, or engage in mindless protectionism, or persist in radical tax cutting that can only erode the strength and quality of our government and educational institutions."

Some thoughts about various ways in which societies can encourage the development and efficiency of functional groups of all kinds are the basis of the following three chapters.

3

The Process of Group Formation

The definition of a functional group suggests how it comes to be formed. Certain people become conscious of a need or desire. They then agree, or sometimes compel others, to coordinate their behaviors in such a way as to satisfy the need or desire. This means that the various group members assume a particular relationship in time and space as superiors, inferiors, or equals, and that they follow certain rules. It also means that they can communicate with each other—by words, pictures, gestures, or blows. Those who are compelled or persuaded to join the group serve some of their own interests by participating. They may want to avoid punishment or to earn money, or they may expect to be rewarded by affection, respect, or some other value.

A few functional groups are formed as a result of trial and error. This was probably especially true in the very early years of human experience. Some groups of hunters may have formed this way. Very young children, also, sometimes form play groups as a result of propinquity rather than planning. They feel a need for association with other children, and as a result a structure, along with the rules and roles that govern the behavior of the small participants in the play group, gradually takes shape.

Most social organisms, however, do not coalesce and become active unless three conditions are satisfied in advance. There must be people who have ideas about how the group might be organized and where essential money or materials can be found. Necessary communication channels must also exist. And qualified personnel must be available. The need for these three prerequisites can usually be seen when substantial numbers of previously unacquainted individuals, suddenly cut off from the outside world, have to form functional groups to take care of their own immediate needs. One of many fictional representations of this process has been given in William Golding's *Lord of the Flies (1954)* and in the movie with the same name. In this story, children being evacuated from England during World War II become isolated on an uninhabited island as a result of an airplane accident. The children discuss with each other what should be done, they set up a government of sorts, and they also form smaller groups (mostly informal) to take over various tasks, such as providing friendship and information. They turn themselves into a society—that is, a collectivity that attempts to take care of most of the basic needs of its members—although in this fictional case they do not succeed very well.

In the real world, similar processes can be observed when crowds consisting of strangers have suddenly been isolated by bad weather. This happens from time to time on the New York State Thruway, which cuts across a long stretch of fairly open country south of Lake Ontario. During heavy winter snow storms, substantial numbers of previously unacquainted individuals take refuge in one or more of the highway's service areas. Some motorists, realizing that the road will soon become impassible, pull their cars into the service area's parking lot. Others, stopped on the highway by deep snow drifts, abandon their vehicles and walk to a service area. A few more are brought in by police or by rescue crews. The result is that large numbers of previously unacquainted individuals find themselves together in small spaces, and sometimes have to stay there for many hours, or even overnight.

In the course of such incidents, new functional groups have almost always been formed to satisfy the immediate needs of these refugees from the storm. Some of those present have ideas about what has to be done and persuade others who are around them to cooperate in various kinds of specialized activities. A common language and opportunities for discussion (the most important requirements for communication) make it possible for agreement to be reached on various courses of action. Qualified people are usually available to perform the necessary roles. The functional groups that are eventually formed may include some that take care of small children, some that offer emergency medical care, and some—like card playing clubs—that provide recreation.

In spite of the obvious desirability of these activities, there are nearly always individuals who do not take part in them. These people may point out that it is someone else's responsibility to provide the necessary services, or they may be in poor mental or physical health, or they may be too young to understand the situation. Perhaps they don't share a common language with others around them, or cannot communicate for other reasons. If there are too many such individuals, the needed functional groups do not form.

A Case History from World War II. The story of a large number of people, most of them strangers to each other, who were suddenly thrown together in an internment camp in China during the second world war, provides an opportunity to look in more detail at the three principal requirements for the formation and operation of functional groups—namely, ideas, communication channels, and qualified people. This account is taken from a book entitled *Shantung Compound—The Story of Men and Women Under Pressure,* written by one of the internees, Langdon Gilkey and published by Harper & Row in 1966. The author, who was 24 years old and teaching English at Yenching University in Peking when he was interned, conscientiously maintained a journal of both major and minor daily happenings in the camp during his more than two years of internment. He later became a professor at the University of Chicago.

In February, 1943, Gilkey and many other foreign residents in North China received an official letter from the Japanese, who at that time occupied a large portion of Chinese territory, announcing that citizens of anti-Axis powers would be transported immediately to a

"Civilian Internment Center" near Weihsien, about two hundred miles south of Peking. The center turned out to be a former Presbyterian mission compound—an area of about 150 by 200 yards that included several school buildings, small rooms for resident students, and other institutional facilities, all of which were surrounded by high walls on which Japanese guards were stationed. This space had to accommodate between 1,500 and 2,000 people. The exact numbers varied from time to time during the following two and one-half years.

Internees were highly diverse. British citizens constituted a majority but several hundred Americans were there also. Smaller numbers of other nationalities came from Russia, Cuba, Belgium, The Netherlands, and a few other nations. Many of the British and some Americans were executives or employees of international corporations. Other internees had been proprietors or employees of small businesses in China, and there were substantial numbers of teachers and Christian missionaries, both Protestant and Catholic, from several countries. There were others who were members of a jazz band and some whose former occupations and sources of income were obscure. All age groups were represented; there were about equal numbers of males and females, and quite a few families with children were in the camp. Nearly everyone had some relatives, friends, or acquaintances there, but most people had never previously met or even heard of most of the other internees. Members of the Catholic clergy constituted a partial exception, in that many of them had been associated with each other for some time, and were members of a preexisting social structure.

The conduct of Japanese personnel in charge of the camp could be described as "correct." A few officers and guards behaved in a hostile and unpleasant manner and a few were kind and friendly, but there were "no extreme hardships of limb, stomach or spirit." (p. ix) The internees experienced many discomforts, but were given everything necessary for survival. The Japanese authorities did, however, expect the camp to be self-administering. Starting almost from the moment of arrival at the camp, most problems of daily life had to be solved by the internees themselves.

These problems were severe. "In our internment camp," the author writes, "we were secure and comfortable enough to accomplish in large part the creation and maintenance of a small civilization; but our life was sufficiently close to the margin of survival to reveal the vast difficulties of that task." (p.ix) The Presbyterian mission compound had been looted—probably many times—since the onset of war in Asia. Pipes had been torn out, furniture had been broken or stolen, and piles of debris were everywhere. The internees from Peking slept the first night on straw mats in the wet basement of a school building. There were several big kitchens, but few of the internees had experience cooking for large numbers of people or using institutional cooking equipment. There were four latrines with five or six toilets each for around 2,000 people. The hospital was totally inoperative. Beds, boiler, pipes, and even the operating table and dental chair had been ripped from their places and discarded inside or outside the building.

Longer-term problems included dividing the available living space among both families and unmarried people, training cooks, creating schools for the children, reconnecting or installing water pipes, removing debris and keeping the area clean, repairing broken equipment of all kinds, and finding ways to relieve the inevitable boredom caused by living in the small compound. Most of these problems were obvious, but who was to do what? How could the efforts of this huge crowd of strangers be coordinated? Nobody knew what skills were available, or—until much later—exactly how many people were there. Even the Japanese authorities had only approximate numbers.

Two emergencies had to be dealt with immediately. There were sick people among the internees, but there were no medical services. In addition, the toilets—already small in number—were not connected with water pipes. They quickly became filled to overflowing, and became so disgusting that some who tried to use them ended by vomiting instead.

Doctors and nurses among the internees recognized the medical problem right away. They started to get the hospital back into serviceable shape, assisted by several volunteers. (The health professionals had the necessary ideas; they knew what to do.) By dint of furious work, the hospital was within a few days able to feed and accommodate patients. In a little over a week, operations were being performed and babies were being delivered. Unfortunately, a member of the jazz band from Tientsin developed acute appendicitis before minimum repairs had been made. He died while being transported to a hospital six hours away.

A solution to the toilet problem was less obvious. Nobody felt responsible for dealing with it. Finally, a group of volunteers composed of Catholic clergy, Protestant missionaries, and a few nuns put on crude face masks, managed to locate boots and mops, and waded in to clean up the mess. They kept at it until a self-constituted group of engineers, some from the Massachusetts Institute of Technology and the Royal College of Engineers, after canvassing various more complex alternatives, devised a way to hand-flush the toilets with a small amount of water after each use. Another example of specialists who knew what to do.

Japanese camp authorities initially provided some help. For the first few days they brought bread in from a nearby city and they also assigned temporary quarters to the internees. After his first night in the school basement, Gilkey reports, he and ten other bachelors were shown to three tiny rooms "comfortable for only four or five people," and "dirty beyond description." (p. 12) Otherwise, internees were on their own.

As far as food was concerned, a few individuals, including a restaurant proprietor, a former marine cook, and two aged owners of a Persian bakeshop, assisted by volunteers, were able to see that everyone was more or less fed. The internees had been informed that the bread supply from outside would stop almost immediately; and bread was the only solid food available in the camp. The Persian bakers therefore spent forty-eight hours training green recruits to mix, knead, and bake the four hundred daily loaves that were required to feed everyone. Other pressing needs during the first few days were handled in much the same way. Jobs that had to be done were initially taken in hand by experienced people who understood the problems and had some ideas about how to solve them.

But there was a great deal of other work for which nobody seemed to be especially qualified, much of it of a manual nature, and which had to be done to sustain orderly life in the camp. This included cleaning and janitorial work, carrying in supplies, making repairs, and so on. How could available human resources be used so as to ensure that everyone's basic needs were met? There was no existing social organization in the camp (except for families, small groups of friends and the Catholic clergy). As a result, there was no recognized leadership to allocate jobs and responsibilities. Nevertheless, it was clear that everyone would have to take on one or more assignments if decent living conditions were to be maintained over a period of time.

This organizational problem was initially addressed by a self-selected group of leaders who had previously occupied important positions, mainly in the business world, in various areas of North China from which the internees had come. Most of these men were known, at least by reputation, by other internees who came from the same region, and thus already had some legitimacy as leaders. (There were apparently no women in the group—which probably was not surprising in the year 1943.) These volunteer leaders met constantly during the first days of camp life to discuss what should be done. They were probably motivated in part by a sense of responsibility and partly by a desire not to be left out of any emerging power structure. Their frequent meetings testified to the fact that organization could not take place unless there was intensive communication among those who had ideas about what kinds of functional groups would be needed.

But before an administrative system could take shape, and jobs assigned to various people and groups, a Japanese official appeared at one of the meetings and directed that nine committees, which would represent all internees and would deal with the Japanese authorities, should be organized within forty-eight hours. The committees were labeled: General Affairs, Discipline, Labor, Education, Supplies, Quarters, Medicine, Engineering, and Finance.

After discussing how to comply with this order, the informal leadership group of internees decided that an election would be meaningless, especially since the time to organize it was so short. Even if candidates could be chosen in some rational way, few voters would be familiar with their qualifications. Instead, they decided, one member for each committee should be appointed by each of four categories of the temporary leaders. Three of these categories consisted of people who had been resident in or around Peking, Tientsin and Tsingtao, respectively. The fourth consisted of members of the Catholic clergy. Then the nine four-person committees would meet and each would choose a chairman.

Even this simplified selection process involved considerable discussion and jockeying for position. It appeared to some members of the informal leadership group that the General Affairs Committee would most likely be the one to deal with policy questions, and that the chairman of this committee would, in effect, be leader and spokesman for the whole camp population Several men who had occupied positions of power before being interned seemed to be interested in the chairmanship. The former head of a large mining company finally maneuvered himself into the position, but it soon turned out that an intercultural misunderstanding was involved. The committee title—"General Affairs"—had been mistranslated from Japanese to English. What the military authorities wanted was a *Miscellaneous Affairs* Committee, which would be in charge of such things as sports events, the barber shop, and the library. When this was explained, the mining executive withdrew gracefully.

As time went on, leadership responsibilities were more widely shared. Some members of the group, who helped to guide the initial organization process, were past middle age and found they lacked sufficient physical energy. Further, it turned out that executive responsibilities had many frustrations but few rewards, such as prestige and special privileges, and this led to further withdrawals.

After formation of the nine committees, it was possible to inventory systematically what had to be done and to assign individuals to particular jobs. "Thus, bank clerks, professors, salesmen, missionaries, importers, and executives became bakers, stokers, cooks, carpenters, masons and hospital orderlies." (p. 15) A great deal of heavy, unskilled work that at first had been done largely by volunteers was soon assigned to particular individuals. In a short time everyone had a set job. "The first rude form of our camp's civilization started to appear." (*Ibid.*)

Most people had to do at least some work for which they had not been qualified by training or experience. Whether or not they performed well in these unfamiliar capacities had little relationship to their previous rank or education. "A man's excellence was revealed by his willingness to work, his skill at his job, his fundamental cheerfulness." (p. 24) Gilkey notes that the three most valuable people in the kitchen where he was assigned at one point were two former British sailors and a tobacco expert from a North Carolina farm. The laziest member of the cooking shift was a well born and highly educated executive from a shipping company who "was neither cooperative nor charming and so of little use to anyone." (p. 24)

Of equal or greater importance were the ethical principles observed by each individual. Indeed, the survival of the camp society depended heavily on the honesty of the food workers, since the Japanese authorities provided barely enough meat, vegetables and flour to satisfy the minimum food requirements of the internees. For example, 150 pounds of raw meat, including skin, fat, and innards, was the three-day ration for the 800 people fed by one kitchen. This meant that less than one ounce of edible meat per person could be incorporated in the daily bowl of soup. If personnel working in the kitchen stole meat, vegetables and flour, as happened increasingly as time went on, others in the camp would eventually starve. Theft of coal was also common.

Stealing scarce supplies was especially difficult to control for several reasons. First, it was easy to steal because those handling scarce supplies were often alone in the kitchens. The result was that "the mechanics of prevention were difficult…[while] the mechanics of stealing were easy." (p. 142.) Also, the camp leaders had no police power. They tried to shame flagrant offenders by posting their names on bulletin boards, but this had little effect. People who stole the most were also those who were least sensitive to public disapproval.

Another reason enforcement was difficult was that some workers in the kitchens and heating plant were parents of small children. It required enormous strength of character for these people to resist the temptation to steal when they saw their families suffering from cold and hunger day after day. Gilkey observes: "I was struck by the strange way in which the natural—and in most respects noble—loyalty of a man to his family can, unless tempered by some wider loyalty, become the springboard for dangerous social chaos." (p. 143) This same devotion to the family, combined with the absence of other strong ties, probably played an important part in stimulating the widespread looting that occurred in Iraq after the elimination of the Hussein government nearly 60 years later.

One of Gilkey's related observations was that a person's previous job or profession was a poor predictor of such qualities as honesty, public spirit, or a sense of responsibility. The categories of internees who came from professional, business, religious, or blue collar backgrounds all seemed to include about the same proportions of saints and sinners. Fortunately, enough internees had moral fiber that was sufficiently tough to prevent disaster—although it is uncertain what would have happened if protracted war had prolonged the existence of the camp.

Other personal characteristics, including tolerance and empathy, also affected morale and interpersonal relations among people who were forced to share extremely crowded rooms and dormitories. Families were housed in small rooms, nine by twelve feet each, with parents and several children often sharing the space. "In some of the dorms, men were jammed so closely together that they could hardly turn around.... every one of us in a dorm had only 18 inches between his bed and those on either side, and three feet at the end of the bed to keep all that he owned." (p. 17) It occasionally happened that dormitory dwellers would move their beds an inch or two at night when others were asleep in order to gain more room. The Quarters (housing) Committee received frequent (and sometimes completely justified) complaints from people who felt they had been allocated too little space, but committee members found that those who occupied more than their fair share of space would almost never agree to reallocation, and sometimes threatened to resist violently if their allotment was changed.

In addition to the functional groups formed in areas where immediate needs were obvious, informal social organisms of many kinds gradually took shape. Some of these were recreational or educational, and included card playing clubs, a vaudeville group, evening lecture programs on a wide variety of subjects, and a baseball league—the Peking Panthers vs. the Tientsin Tigers. Others were economic or political. One creation was an informal banking system that sometimes could extend credit to internees who wanted to purchase the few necessities available at the Japanese-run canteen, or to patronize a black market that existed from time to time, or perhaps to bribe a guard to do them a favor. Another social organism was an "underground" group of internees that had found ways to communicate with Chinese guerrillas who operated in the vicinity of the camp. Members of this group were able to receive some information about what was happening in the outside world and also to send out a message occasionally. Otherwise, internees were completely deprived of news about the progress of the war.

A thriving black market in eggs existed for a few months in 1943, thus providing a valuable supplement to the otherwise meager rations.

One of the most active participants in this traffic was a Trappist monk, who had somehow made contact with Chinese farmers outside the camp, and received supplies of eggs through a small hole he had managed to make in the compound wall. His activities at the wall were screened by clerical colleagues, who also served as lookouts and warned him when Japanese guards approached. When this happened, he was able to conceal large numbers of eggs under his capacious robes.

In spite of these precautions, Father Darby was eventually caught by a guard. The camp's military commandant was furious, and decided to punish this infraction severely. The Trappist monk was sentenced to six weeks solitary confinement. Obviously, the Japanese authorities had not known that solitary confinement was one of the things Trappist monks did best, and they were baffled when the internees greeted announcement of the sentence with howls of delight. The internees were less pleased when the possibility of smuggling eggs through the wall was cut off by construction of a deep trench and high fence around the camp. However, another black market developed when some of the guards agreed to take watches, jewelry or other valuables and trade them to Chinese merchants for various kinds of supplies.

In the late summer of 1945, the secretive group that was in touch with Chinese guerrillas was the source of news for which the internees had been waiting impatiently for so long. The war was over. The camp's informal leadership tried initially to restrict this news to a small and trusted group of internees. They feared that knowledge of the war's end might inspire hotheads to attack Japanese personnel, who then would respond with violence of their own. Gilkey was informed of this development (and was also pledged to absolute secrecy) by the Congregational missionary who had been a key figure in maintaining contact with the Chinese guerrillas.

Despite these strenuous efforts to keep news of the war's end secret, it turned out that almost all internees had heard about it fairly promptly—and that each had promised not to tell anyone else. Very efficient person-to-person communication networks had developed during the period of the camp's existence. It was no longer a collection of strangers but had become a tight society in which multiple information channels connected everyone, directly or indirectly, with the leadership and other internees. Fortunately, no violent disorders resulted.

Within a short time, American paratroopers dropped from the skies and took control of the camp—although the Japanese military personnel were requested to stay on in an administrative capacity and as protection from marauders—but it was several more months before arrangements could be made for the internees to be transported to their homelands or other destinations.

The Role of Ideas in Group Formation. What happened in the Shantung internment camp illustrates various ways in which ideas, communication channels, and qualified personnel play a part in the formation of specialized functional groups and the emergence of a society. Let us look first at the role of ideas.

Nearly always, before any functional group can be formed, someone has an idea, or several people, have ideas—a conception of what needs or desires the new group might serve, what has to be done, what the group would look like, where it would obtain resources, and how it would operate. This is true whether the group in question is a creation of powerful individuals or agencies, who force unwilling participants to play certain roles within the group, or whether the new social organism arises from the felt needs of its constituents. Someone nearly always has to envisage the structure, rules, and requirements. In the Shantung camp, many of the necessary ideas were provided by cooks, doctors, engineers, and others who had previous experience in groups that served basic human needs. Other ideas developed after the camp leadership and members of the various working groups had experience and time to think.

After a functional group is organized, it nearly always needs a steady supply of additional ideas, some of them new and some dredged up from the past. Changes in the group's environment, which may be political, economic, social, demographic, climatic, or of other kinds, can require it to find new ways of doing things if it is to prosper, or even to survive. When fashions in children's clothing change, manufacturers, retailers, and parents all have to adjust their behavior to the new situation. An enterprise—or a family—that insists on continuing exactly as it did before the environmental change is likely to be in trouble. Conversely, groups that encourage thought, experimentation, and discussion about ways in which their purposes can be achieved as conditions change are more likely to adjust successfully.

This is true of nearly all large and small organizations in a society. Some of these groups prosper because their leaders and often other members as well are alert to new ways of utilizing personnel, taking advantage of available technologies and materials, modifying operating rules, and providing better training. Who is to do what? How many people will it take to perform a particular function? How can necessary resources—whether material or other—be obtained and used? Will the activities of the new or revised institution conflict with those of existing institutions? That businesses should be continually concerned with such questions is usually taken for granted, but many other functional groups, whether families, social clubs, or neighborhood communities often behave as though they were immune to change. Nevertheless, they too are likely to serve the needs of their members more satisfactorily if they are open to new ideas.

The range of ideas that can be useful, directly or indirectly, in the formation and operation of functional groups is very broad. Indeed, it is difficult to think of any ideas that are not in some way relevant to group activities. Creative musings of a poet may be incorporated in a school's curriculum; and scientific inventions often lead to the formation of business enterprises. Almost any observation about human behavior, whether made by a professional psychologist, a theologian, or a thoughtful observer from some other field, is likely to have implications for the way people in social organisms coordinate their activities to achieve the purposes of the group. Accumulated historical knowledge and daily news items, also, often provide information that affects what functional groups do and how they do it.

Ideas needed by a particular group may be generated by a single person, but more commonly they are contributed by many people over a period of time. For example, a number of young people may gather to satisfy needs for companionship and amusement by talking and playing games, but then ideas for additional activities are suggested from inside or outside the group—perhaps stealing cars, or perhaps organizing a neighborhood soup kitchen. Ideas such as these are rarely completely original. They come from models that already exist within a society, or are based on information about what has been done in the past, whether in the society where the group exists or elsewhere.

The role of ideas in the design and operation of social organisms can be appreciated most easily if one thinks about relatively small groups close to home, perhaps the family or the school. A married couple, for example, in consultation with each other, and with one or more relatives, may decide to reorganize their home life in such a way that the family will better serve the emotional and material needs of its members and will conflict less with the professional careers of both partners. They have small children and jobs they like, but they cannot afford to buy a house and at the same time pay for the children's day care. So Aunt Lucy, who lost her husband years ago and now finds it difficult to live alone, agrees to make the down payment on a house with an extra room and bath. She moves in, and takes care of the children while their parents are at work. Will this arrangement be successful in providing for the needs of the parents, their children, and Aunt Lucy? Perhaps not, in which case more thought will be necessary, and a new pattern of family structure or of professional activities will have to be worked out. Also frequently encountered in current complex societies are the problems of the "sandwich generation"—people who are trying to bring up children and take care of elderly parents at the same time. They often have to experiment with several patterns of household organization.

As the above examples suggest, all of us design functional groups that help satisfy our wants and needs. The better ideas we have, the more we are satisfied, and sometimes at lower cost. If you decide to have lunch with the same two or three friends every month, you may be setting up a mechanism to help satisfy your desire for companionship, or information, or perhaps professional advancement. But how will this new activity be organized? Will you meet in a restaurant, or will all group members bring brown-bag lunches to a public park? Numerous possibilities may be considered, and your solution may show great creativity—or you may borrow an idea from someone else.

The role of new ideas in keeping industrial and governmental institutions up to date is even more obvious. Indeed, specialists—often called consultants—frequently assist in drawing up plans for new structures and operating patterns in large industrial or governmental institutions. Drawing up such plans is a difficult task, which can involve hundreds of new and old ideas. Some big organizations that are redesigned have large numbers of component parts, all of which must be able to function together harmoniously. Further complications are introduced by the necessity that the redesigned functional groups be compatible with each other and with other social organisms. Large corporations pay millions to those who can come up with viable designs and rules of behavior that will satisfy their requirements. Even then, the new organization may not work, and the corporation must try again or suffer financially.

Governments, especially in democracies, are likely to have more difficulty than private bodies in organizing and reorganizing structures and work rules for major components. They usually cannot reward professional innovators with the huge fees that corporations can afford. And each change must be approved, or at least not opposed, by numerous politicians, bureaucracies, and public constituencies. Requirements of compatibility among component functional groups are particularly stringent for government agencies. They must at least seem to be working together smoothly. Because of such requirements, official bodies tend to adapt to changed conditions and new needs more slowly than even the largest non-governmental organizations. Nevertheless, the fact that innovation in government is difficult makes it no less necessary. How to keep a large government structure responsive to individual and social needs is a challenge that calls for increasing creativity as agencies become more and more complex.

When it comes to educational institutions, the demand for new ideas at all levels is insatiable. Different designs and rules of behavior are being tried all the time. A new teacher arrives in the classroom and changes the size and composition of the reading groups. She is also stricter than the old teacher. Meanwhile, the news media are full of stories about charter schools, colleges, and adult education services that are experimenting with different organizational patterns and new educational philosophies. Various ways of teaching mathematics and other subjects are tried out: Some are accepted and some rejected after experimentation. These innovations also illustrate the problem of assuring harmony among different functional groups. For example, parents are unlikely to understand new teaching methods and therefore find it more difficult to help their children with school work.

Experimentation in educational institutions not only tests new ideas about education, but may also be designed to stimulate creativity and criticism on the part of the students—thereby benefiting many other categories of functional groups with which the students may later be involved.. One innovative teacher and administrator writes that she had five questions posted on classroom walls in her school: (Meier, 1995, p. 156)

- How do you know what you know?

- What's your evidence?

- How and where does what you know 'fit in?'

- Could things have been otherwise?

- Who cares? What difference does it make?

An assignment given by the same teacher to her students was: "Make up three sentences beginning with the words 'I have a theory that...'" (*Ibid.*, p.155) Many of those who attended school during the 1920's and 1930's, including this writer, would have been shocked if they had been faced with such an assignment. Knowledge taught in schools was not supposed to be questioned, and the job of the student was to absorb ideas, not to create them.

Even relatively small changes in prevailing conceptions about the structure and operation of a functional group, whether the group has few or many members, can have a significant impact on the extent to which it achieves its purposes. Some businesses have found that productivity increases when they encourage personnel at all levels to make suggestions about the way their work is organized. Urban neighborhoods sometimes become more secure, and also neater, when the residents are urged to get acquainted and to greet each other when they meet on the street or in apartment house lobbies. (Davison, 1987)

An example of creative vision that had a strong emotional component, and contained ideas about the structure and operation of both large and small social mechanisms, is Dr. Martin Luther King's "I have a dream" speech, delivered at the Lincoln Memorial in Washington in 1963. King painted a picture of social institutions that would be inclusive rather than exclusive, whose operations would be governed by new rules for behavior, and which would better serve the needs of all Americans. The ideas in the speech were not new to most of those who heard them expressed that day, but contrasted starkly with conceptions that had enjoyed acceptance by large portions of the United States population for many years. Carried by the mass media to all corners of the country, they encouraged discussions of race relations in thousands of public and private functional groups and hastened important changes in American society.

While both new and old ideas are often vital to the successful operation of functional groups, it is also true that most of the ideas (both new and old) that are advanced do not work well. Every social organism is faced with the necessity of sorting out good and workable ideas from bad and unworkable ones. Critical judgment and often experimentation are necessary to protect functional groups from ideas that, no matter how well intentioned, would make the performance of the group worse rather than better. Educational institutions that are under pressure to improve performance, especially, may adopt new structures and rules that have not been criticized and tested adequately.

One reason critical appraisal is especially necessary when it comes to trying out new ideas in education is that most society members expect schools to serve a large number of different goals, which often conflict with each other. Educational bodies are called upon to inculcate essential information, teach basic skills and ethics, develop leaders and innovators, serve as parental surrogates (and as baby sitters in the early grades), preserve cultural heritages, encourage patriotism, keep students interested, and so on almost ad infinitum.

Whether criticisms and evaluations come from inside or outside the group to which a particular idea may apply, the sorting out process is likely to be more effective if there is a communication network that makes full discussion among all interested parties possible. If communication channels are inadequate, wise decisions about new ideas are more difficult to reach. For example, social scientists who have tried to help developing societies create modern institutions have noted that these societies frequently suffer because of the isolation of intellectuals from each other and from the political and military figures who make decisions about alternative ways of doing things. And both groups, the intellectuals and the decision makers, may be isolated from the public as a whole. If, as sometimes happens, the educated elite and the mass of the population within a single country speak different dialects, it becomes even more difficult to find workable national policies. A common language, shared by members of all interested parties in a society is important, and communication channels of many kinds and at many levels are essential if new ideas are to be adequately critiqued. These channels include formal and informal meetings and discussions, small magazines and newsletters, computer hookups, and the mass media.

But a communication network has many utilities in addition to helping ensure that new ideas that may affect the organization and operation of functional groups are subject to penetrating criticism. As we have seen from the experience of snowbound motorists on the New York Thruway and interned foreigners in China, functional groups cannot take shape and operate at all unless people are able to exchange ideas and emotions with each other. And it is difficult for these groups to become parts of a society if the groups cannot communicate with each other. A more systematic discussion of the nature of communication systems and the part they play in the formation and operation of functional groups is therefore relevant at this point.

Communication Channels: Another Basic Requirement. Language (including mathematics), pictorial representations, and gesture are the basic tools that enable individuals to coordinate their behavior with each other so as to satisfy their own needs, and often those of fellow human beings as well. Devices that extend the reach of these basic tools make it possible for huge organizations to exist, and for people to coordinate their behavior with that of others almost anywhere on the earth. Available devices for communicating ideas to large numbers of people include drums, postal services and person-to-person networks, as well as the mass media, telephones, and computers.

Most communications flow through networks, which may be short or long, temporary or enduring, and may link a few individuals or millions. Relatively stable person-to-person networks, which connect family members, neighbors, and people who come in frequent contact with each other through their work, are present in even the most primitive societies. In more complex cultures, person-to-person networks may link people who belong to many varieties of groups, such as those who attended the same school, who share a hobby or interest, or who belong to the same political or religious bodies. The potential size and reach of person-to-person networks have been greatly increased by the growth of cities and the development of postal services, telephone and wireless facilities, photocopy machines, and computers.

Communication networks often consist of several channels. To evaluate the reach of a television program, for example, one should know not only how many people viewed the program, and the extent to which it was commented on in printed media, but also how many and what kinds of people talked about it to others. A printed message that first appears in a newspaper, magazine, or book, and is seen by relatively few readers, may ultimately reach millions if it is copied and enclosed in mass mailings, or if it is repeated in a broadcast or motion picture. The interdependence of media channels makes it difficult to evaluate the effects of any one channel by itself.

Facilities for storing and retrieving information are an essential part of a communication system. These facilities may consist of libraries and archives of printed or electronic materials, or of individuals with very good memories. Such facilities make it possible for functional groups to draw on ideas developed throughout the course of human history, and to apply these ideas to current problems as needed.

Historians, both amateur and professional, contribute heavily to major communication systems, although their contribution is often overlooked. They are largely responsible not only for assuring that libraries, archives, and data banks—as well as the memories of individuals—are well stocked with potentially useful information, but also for making the ideas in these collections available to those who can use them. Societies and functional groups that lack historians, or hamper their work, serve human needs and aspirations less well than those whose members have better access to the records of the past. How can we learn from experience if we don't know what that experience was?

These communication tools, networks, and channels—from neighborhood gossips to historical tomes—perform five vital tasks that enable societies and their component functional groups to take shape and operate. The accounts of unacquainted individuals who suddenly had to take care of their own needs, which were given at the beginning of this chapter, illustrate these five ways in which communication makes social organization possible. Both the stranded motorists in snow-covered service areas on the New York Thruway and the internees in the Chinese rural countryside would have suffered extreme hardship if they had been unable to communicate with each other. Although the communication systems in these two isolated communities were dominated by word-of-mouth, much more complex systems, including mass media, postal services, telephones, and computers, provide the same five services to societies with millions of members.

What are the five basic services? First, communication channels that are available to large numbers of individuals make it possible for society members with particular interests or needs or skills to identify each other and to get together. This leads to the establishment of functional groups, such as those composed of people who wish to play cards, are willing to work in a kitchen, or are qualified to provide specialized services. Second, internal communication channels within each group make it possible for these functional groups to organize and conduct their business—e.g., to decide who will be the leader and what roles each person should perform. Third, channels linking functional groups with members of the public enable existing groups to disseminate ideas, recruit additional personnel, sell products, and engage in other activities. Some of these channels also allow people to ask existing social organisms for information or assistance—and to make complaints. Fourth, various functional groups have to communicate with each other constantly, whether directly or indirectly. Schools have to know about family requirements and vice versa; businesses have to keep an eye on their competitors, or they may want to discuss methods of cooperating with these competitors to achieve shared goals. Fifth, every society has to develop communication channels that link everyone, directly or indirectly, with government and with decision makers in particular functional groups. In the Shantung internment camp, for example, rudimentary two-way channels developed that connected nearly everyone in the little society with members of the committees that took care of food, housing, and other basic necessities. Similarly, isolated travelers on the New York Thruway sometimes had to find ways of rationing scarce supplies or space. Neither society had a formal government, but some governmental-type decisions had to be made. Eventually, some way would have had to be found to enforce these decisions more rigorously, or serious hunger and conflict could have resulted.

It is striking that *all* information channels can enter into *all* five linkages—a reminder that one cannot make judgments about the adequacy of a society's communication network unless this network is viewed as a whole. For example, in an authoritarian state where the mass media are heavily censored, a rumor network or a network consisting of "small media" such as leaflets and disks may provide information about political matters that in democracies would be carried by newspapers, radio, and television. Similarly, in those developing countries where illiteracy is common, radio, television, and motion pictures can make a relatively well informed citizenry possible. Each of the five linkages that are identified in the two cases described above can be found in a wide range of situations and can affect functional groups of many varieties.

#1. The first linkage, which helps people find others with similar needs and interests, plays a major part in the formation of new families, and in the formation of voluntary associations of all kinds. A man who feels the lack of female companionship may talk with his more sophisticated friends to get the name of a woman who might be interested in a date, and also to get advice about what he might do to make a good impression. If the date goes well, this may lead to the establishment of a household and eventually to children. The importance of communication links in the establishment of families is illustrated by the frequently-asked question: "How did you meet your spouse?" This question is usually answered by referring to a friendship network, or to person-to-person communication channels in a neighborhood, at college, or on the job.

A similar service, which enables new groups of almost any kind (including households) to be organized, is provided by the mass media. Classified advertisements and announcements of meetings and demonstrations bring together people with similar interests. Specialized newsletters and magazines often help individuals join both informal and formal associations. A would-be Appalachian Trail hiker advertises in the *Appalachian Trail News* for hiking companions, a financial newsletter announces a seminar for investors to be held in a local hotel, or model airplane builders get in touch with each other through the letters section of a hobbyists' magazine. Some of the new groups that are formed are initially composed of two people, but soon expand. Computer chat rooms and other facilities of the internet facilitate the formation of functional groups composed of individuals who have never even seen each other.

The early history of the Nazi Party in Germany, as described in Adolf Hitler's biographical polemic, *Mein Kampf,* includes a dramatic illustration of the role of communication in the organization of a new group. Founded in 1919, the Nazi party had seven members for the first few months of its existence. These men tried to attract other people to the party's "public" meetings by appealing to their friends and neighbors, but failed. Nobody was interested—only the same seven individuals showed up each time. It is tempting to assume that their friends and neighbors knew these men well enough to realize that their judgment on political matters could not be trusted. Then the seven members began distributing machine-duplicated notices in a wider area, and the attendance at successive meetings grew from 7 to 11, then 13, then 17, then 23, and finally to 34. This five-fold increase in attendees enabled the party to collect enough money to place a small notice of its next meeting in one of the Munich newspapers. To the amazement of the original members, 111 people showed up. A mass movement was born, and the most destructive war in the world's history ultimately resulted.

#2. Once a new functional group is formed, it requires internal channels—the second category of communication linkage. In relatively small groups, including families, informal neighborhood groups and small businesses, the most important channel is likely to consist of face-to-face conversations and telephone calls, which usually continue to dominate even after the group has existed for many years. In the case of social organisms that keep growing, the use of fax services, e-mail, and larger meetings becomes more common as time goes on. Photocopy machines and postal services also help to keep members in touch with each other, and to provide information necessary for day-to-day operations. When is the next meeting? Who is performing which functions? What should members do to advance the purposes of the organization?

If a functional group continues to expand, it is likely to develop its own internal mass media, including its own periodical publications and a site on the World Wide Web. These information channels, regardless of their extent, usually include announcements, instructions, morale-building communications, and information about developments that affect the organization.

In the case of very large social organisms, the internal communication system may duplicate channels available in the society as a whole. Big companies and governmental bodies, and sometimes religious organizations, ethnic groups, or political movements, often have their own broadcasting facilities, telephone systems, mail services, and computer networks, and may publish their own magazines and newspapers. These media may announce a schedule of meetings, training sessions, recreational activities and other face-to-face communication opportunities. In some societies, the technical quality of internal communication systems that are available to members, adherents, employees, or other affiliated persons, greatly exceeds the quality of facilities available to the general public. In the former Soviet Union, for example, the

Communist Party communication network was faster and more efficient than the one available to ordinary citizens or to non-communist associations. Large organizations are likely, in addition, to maintain specialized information-gathering, storage, and retrieval systems, such as libraries and clipping services.

Whether or not they have an elaborate internal communication network, nearly all large functional groups make use of the public media in keeping their members informed. Members of professions, and those who lead or aspire to lead in almost any organization, usually find it advisable to pay attention to printed and broadcast news that informs them about opportunities, threats and changes that might affect the organizations in which they are involved. Many business and professional people, and government officials, consider monitoring the public media to be part of their day's work. They also are likely to use newspapers, radio, and television to communicate with people within their own organizations. One amusing example of a government official who occasionally sent official messages through the mass media is provided by a former American ambassador to India, Kenneth Galbraith, who has said that when he had an important message for his boss—the President of the United States—it was sometimes preferable to call a news conference rather than try to reach the President through the clogged bureaucratic network.

Mass media are likely to cooperate in such efforts. In order to attract attention and build circulation, the public media usually make strenuous efforts to include information that will be useful to social organisms of many types. Newspapers, radio, and sometimes television are often happy to carry announcements of meetings and other organizational events, and to provide a forum for functional group leaders to express their views. General circulation magazines frequently publish information that is of primary interest to certain categories of people: for example, people who administer households and bring up children, hobbyists, or members of particular professions. Sometimes, specialized magazines provide a functional group with what is in effect a substitute for a private internal communication system.

A functional group's efficiency is often dependent on the quality of its internal communication linkages, regardless how these are provided. This is emphasized by the fact that large government and private agencies, and many corporations, often bring in consultants to advise them on ways to ensure that necessary information is available to all segments of the organization. Are instructions and morale-building communications reaching members and employees, and does management have an accurate picture of what is going on below? Ironically, some of the most difficult internal communication problems are to be found within very small social units, where opportunities for the exchange of ideas are numerous. Thus, husbands and wives, or children and parents, frequently suffer from serious misunderstandings due to inhibitions that block the flow of information within the family.

#3. A third way that communication channels make it possible for functional groups to serve human needs and desires is by providing two-way links between each group and outside individuals. Some channels, consisting largely of mass media, direct mail, and web sites, enable functional groups to reach members of the public with appeals to join, buy, support, contribute, or cooperate—and with instructions or rules that should be obeyed. These and other channels also allow members of the public to communicate with the organizations in question by voting, buying, writing letters to an editor or a complaint department, signing petitions, and participating in radio talk shows or sending messages via the computer.

Ordinarily, communication networks do a better job of conveying information *from* functional groups *to* outside individuals than the other way around. This is to be expected, in that an organization can nearly always speak with a louder voice than an individual. Designated staff members who are specialists in communication disseminate information to the public, and large organizations usually have advertising or public relations departments. In contrast, not many individuals can find time plus motivation to write more than a few letters and e-mails or to make more than a handful of personal visits or phone calls to businesses, government agencies, or interest groups, whether their purpose is to protest something they dislike or to compliment an organization on doing a good job. Most of us confine ourselves to ignoring products or organizations of which we disapprove, or else we complain to our friends about them. But the fact that we ignore something, or complain about it privately, does not provide the organization concerned with enough information to allow it to correct its ways—assuming that it would want to do so.

This presents a problem in complex industrial societies. To obtain necessary information about public reactions, many large functional groups have to rely on special information-gathering systems to find out what the public thinks about them and their various activities. Commercial enterprises frequently turn to market research firms, or they send questionnaires to their customers themselves. Public opinion polls sponsored by news media, commercial bodies, and non-profit organizations increasingly serve as channels through which various publics can communicate with functional groups that are important to them. In addition, public attitudes can sometimes be inferred from reports and expressions of opinion in the mass media. Rulers of authoritarian societies, where opinion polls often do not work well because of fear, and where media are often controlled by the government, sometimes rely on the secret police or political party organizations to supply information about public attitudes toward events and institutions. The information these governments receive is often insufficient or unreliable, inasmuch as neither the police nor party officials are necessarily skilled in monitoring public attitudes, and both may be afraid to report bad news to their superiors.

How to build better communication channels from the public to major functional groups is a problem that will become more important and also more resistant to solution as societies become increasingly complex. This is likely to be true whether societies are predominantly authoritarian or democratic. Even now it is frequently difficult for a member of a complex society to find out which business or government agency should be addressed with a complaint, suggestion, or inquiry.

#4. A fourth major service provided by information channels is to enable functional groups within the society to communicate among themselves. This helps insure that the activities of different social organisms are harmonious—that is, either complementary or compatible. Of course, harmony is not always achieved if organizations talk with each other, but without communication channels linking different groups it would be even more difficult for them to coexist. Intergroup communication is particularly important in modern industrial societies, where the number of functional groups is enormous and where new groups are constantly being organized and old ones are disappearing.

The public print and broadcast media and the World Wide Web, which in theory are accessible to everyone, play a major part in this intergroup communication. As has already been noted, most high officials in large organizations try to pay close personal attention to the important news channels, and they are especially interested in the behavior of other social organisms that might affect their own group's activities. Major governmental and private bodies are also likely to subscribe to reports that summarize television and radio broadcasts of possible interest. Some maintain their own monitoring facilities and prepare their own summaries. In addition, periodicals and newsletters that cover developments in an enormous number of fields—commercial, sporting, political, cultural, religious, scientific, and other—help many types of social organisms keep track of what other groups with similar interests are doing.

Important linkages among a society's major functional groups are provided also by person-to-person communication channels in formal and informal organizations whose members come from many walks of life. Churches, schools, social clubs and neighborhood organizations, for example, are likely to include people who play large or small roles in a variety of functional groups, and who exchange information with each other about what these groups are doing. Large businesses frequently encourage their employees to take an active part in local welfare and recreation groups in order to cultivate good relations with the community. In addition, associations such as Rotary Clubs, college alumni and alumnae associations, and community discussion groups draw together individuals, many of whom are influential, from different occupations. Government bodies at many levels sometimes serve as forums where representatives of many different organizations are able to exchange information—although often in an atmosphere of contention. In democracies, such forums are provided by national and state legislatures, and their various committees, and often by local governments as well. There are also many associations that bring together people who are affiliated with different organizations but share interests in a particular specialty *within* such areas of activity as teaching, business, politics, or cultural affairs. Thus, professional associations consisting of persons interested in a particular science are likely to have members from government agencies, businesses, and educational institutions.

All such information channels, whether provided by mass media, schools, governments, churches, neighborhoods, or associations of many kinds, provide valuable links among a variety of functional groups, but their coverage is necessarily spotty. No modern society has developed mechanisms for ensuring that all major social organisms serving widely varying human needs and desires are informed of each other's activities. The mass media come closest to doing this, but even in highly developed societies the resources of the mass media are too limited to provide complete coverage. Furthermore, developments involving important functional groups are not always newsworthy. And even when this information is newsworthy, and is reported, it frequently is overlooked by members of the media audiences who have limited time and have to focus their attention on selected items of interest.

Partly as a result of the limitations of information channels linking various kinds of functional groups, industrialized nations of today are characterized by difficulties in ensuring that the activities of different kinds of groups harmonize with each other, and that members of these groups understand each other. For example, it often turns out that there are jobs where there are few affordable homes, and there are attractive places to live where there are no jobs. Similarly, educational institutions have difficulty in qualifying the right number of personnel for different specialties. One year, there is a shortage of chemical engineers and a glut of specialists in certain branches of medicine, while the year after that qualified automobile repair personnel are difficult to hire, but teachers in the liberal arts have trouble finding jobs..

A further complication is that members of different functional groups sometimes cannot understand each other easily. Part of this problem is that many occupations and professions develop their own specialized terminologies, so that sailors, financiers, rap singers, lawyers, academicians, and doctors frequently use expressions that are incomprehensible to those who are outside their respective fields. Even families sometimes have their own private languages that mystify members of other families—and conversation between two teenagers may be quite incomprehensible to an octogenarian.

It would be too much to expect that conflict and misunderstandings among functional groups would vanish if there were better communication links among them. Many other factors are involved—chief among them being the competing needs and desires of different people and organizations. But, given the fact that the exchange of information among many of the diverse functional groups in complex societies is manifestly limited, one could reasonably expect improvements in cooperation and compatibility if these communication links could be strengthened.

#5. A fifth major job of communication channels is to link government with all other groups and individuals in a political unit. The channels that provide these links are in most cases identical with those that connect organizations with individuals and different social mechanisms with each other. But government-to-people and people-to-government channels should, in theory, be inclusive. For a society to achieve its fullest potential, government should be in touch with every adult individual and functional group, and every individual and functional group should be able to reach responsible government authorities.

The necessity of this two-way linkage is obvious in democracies where (again in theory) people and functional groups inform government of their wants and needs, and government then tries to find some way for these desires to be satisfied. Two-way channels are essential in authoritarian states also, although they serve somewhat different purposes. Dictatorships require channels that reach as many individuals as possible, directly or indirectly, primarily to convey orders, instructions, and propaganda. In the former Soviet Union, for example, people who refused to pay attention to the mass media were often regarded as enemies of the state. Authoritarian governments also need information *about* masses of groups and individuals primarily to maintain control of the population through police activity and propaganda output. George Orwell's description in his classic novel, *1984,* of a society where government controlled all but the most private information channels, and monitored even these, is a powerful reminder that two-way linkage can be used as an instrument of oppression as well as a tool of democracy.

The size of government, usually the central functional group in a society that is coterminous with a nation, depends in part on how two-way communication with all elements of the population is maintained. If officials gather and disseminate a large proportion of the information that flows between government and the public and try to control other information, as often is the case in dictatorships, then very large bureaucracies are required to staff secret police and propaganda agencies. But if governments interpret their responsibility as that of seeing only that two-way channels are available, then most of the gathering and disseminating of information can be done by private organizations.

In democracies, a large number of these non-official functional groups, including the major mass media—television, radio, newspapers, and news magazines—ordinarily provide the most important two-way linkages, bringing news about government to the public and information about activities throughout the society to the government. Specialized publications, serving both government agencies and private organizations with information about particular areas in which both have an interest, such as agriculture, banking, and manufactures, also help official and nonofficial groups keep in touch.

Additional messages from government to the public reach many individuals and groups through official and sometimes semiofficial publications, speeches by major government figures, newsletters from members of the legislature, and routine contacts of official personnel with the public. More and more government agencies are making use of sites on the World Wide Web to provide information for those who seek it.

Communication from citizens to their governments takes place in part through political channels consisting of legislatures and political parties. How well these channels succeed in linking citizens with government officials depends on the degree to which democratic principles are observed in any given country. In the case of authoritarian governments, legislatures and political parties are likely to provide a biased version of what private individuals are thinking and what private organizations are doing. Parties and legislatures in democracies usually do a better job of expressing the will of the people, but often give undue weight to the views of powerful interest groups that can employ lobbyists and public relations specialists.

In addition to the mass media and political institutions, channels that serve primarily to bring information to government from the population at large include forms and questionnaires that deal with such matters as taxation, population, and economic statistics; the lobbies that inform government officials about the needs and sentiments of various interest groups; and public opinion polls. Channels available to individuals who want to tell the government something have recently been augmented by facilities for reaching official agencies by e-mail.

Despite the many ways in which people can communicate with government, there are widespread feelings in most countries (whether or not they are democracies) that citizen access is inadequate and that communications from private individuals and organizations, even when received, are usually disregarded. Only very wealthy individuals, big corporations, and powerful interest groups are listened to, according to such views. Government investigations and questionnaires, while widely recognized as necessary, often arouse resentment because they are seen as time consuming, unnecessarily complicated, and intrusive. At the same time, governments are frequently regarded as secretive and unwilling to keep society members fully informed. Even in democracies, governments are often referred to as "they." Those who believe government should be not only a creation and instrument of the citizenry, but should also be seen as such, are still looking for ways to improve two-way communication.

◆ ◆ ◆

The five linkages provided by communication channels help to make possible the mobilization and effective utilization of human resources. Whole societies, as well as the functional groups within them, are more likely to prosper if they constantly try to assure that communication channels do the best possible job connecting their members with each other, and providing information people need to play their roles. Many businesses recognize this and try constantly to improve the flow of information among all their departments and between management and the labor force. Medical researchers have been impressed by the importance of two-way doctor/patient communication in assuring the best possible outcomes of many therapies. Political scientists frequently point out that well informed voters are vital to the successful operation of a democracy. And parents are constantly being told that they should know what their children are thinking and doing—at the same time that the children are being encouraged to consult their parents about the business of life.

A society's communication channels should, ideally, allow all functional groups to communicate with each other if their members want to do so, and should give every person and group access to ideas and information from the past that are stored in memories, libraries, and archives. Two-way communication between government and citizens should be possible, and internal channels should link all members of a functional group with each other and with the group leadership. Of course, such comprehensive links have never existed in any society. They are a goal to shoot for, and the capabilities of the computer make them seem almost attainable. The next goal—improving the quality of what is communicated—will doubtless be more difficult to reach.

Personnel: Education and Training. The third basic requirement for the formation and operation of functional groups is qualified personnel. People have to be trained to lead and staff the social organisms on which a society's welfare depends, and these individuals should then be helped to find roles for which they are well suited.

People are a perishable resource, in contrast to both ideas and communication channels. Ideas, once conceived and expressed, can achieve an existence independent of any one individual. In written or pictorial form, they may languish for thousands of years before they are rediscovered and become a powerful force. Similarly, communication tools—whether languages, stone tablets, printing presses, news organizations, computers, or relay satellites—are available to generations that come after those who first developed and used these devices. Two of the major requisites for social organisms can, therefore, be stockpiled or stored, at least to some degree, and are available to those who want to organize a new functional group, or perhaps to change the structure or rules governing behavior in an existing one. When it comes to personnel, however, each generation is responsible for ensuring that individuals receive necessary training and find appropriate roles.

Societies that make good use of the human capabilities at their disposal try to ensure that as many people as possible: (1) receive a basic education, (2) have opportunities to develop their unique talents, and (3) are able to find roles that are consistent with their special abilities. Appropriate qualifications are important not only for people in income-producing jobs, but also for those who assume roles in families, voluntary organizations, neighborhood communities, and other functional groups. The society as a whole benefits substantially when noneconomic roles, as well as paying jobs, are filled by people whose talents, training and motivation make them especially well suited to do what they are called upon to do.

At the most basic level, everyone should be taught skills, information, and values that will enable him or her to get along with and cooperate with other people in the same society—language, customs, "common knowledge," and a feeling for what is "done" and "not done."

The ability to communicate is particularly important. Even in the most primitive cultures it is desirable that as many people as possible should be able to express ideas in words that will transmit meaning to those around them, and should also be able to understand when spoken to. In complex societies, a common language in which all are fluent is especially important to assure efficient coordination and cooperation among much larger numbers of individuals and functional groups. This does not mean that everyone should be forced to use a single tongue and that deviant dialects should be stamped out, as has been attempted in some national states, but rather that all members of the society should be able to communicate with each other easily by one means or another. Most countries have designated a single language in which (ideally) all citizens should be fluent; several countries have more than one official language. When members of a single society cannot communicate with each other, interpreters and translators sometimes can help, but this requires time, and often money, and restricts functional group formation, thus tending to reduce the society's cost effectiveness.

Misunderstandings caused by lack of a common language are usually minor, but can also be serious, as when a doctor and patient can't communicate with each other. Even small misunderstandings, such as those caused by the inability of a taxi driver and passenger to communicate, are significant when cumulated. It is unlikely that any modern society will ever reach the point where all adults will be able to understand each other easily, but that is an ideal condition worth working toward.

In modern industrial societies, adult members are expected to have many additional communication skills besides the ability to speak a common language. They should be able to read and write, use a telephone and, increasingly, operate a computer. Skill in comprehension—the ability to understand what someone else is trying to say and to interpret instructions correctly—is becoming more and more important in the many specialized groups of complex societies.

As well as being able to communicate easily, it is desirable that everyone in a society share a stock of common knowledge and skills. This includes information about how to behave when interacting with other members of the same society. Each person has to become familiar with the society's customs, value systems, and behavioral codes (embodied in its folkways, mores, and religions), be able to cooperate with strangers in simple tasks, know how to address people of all ranks, and be familiar with units used to measure amounts of money and such dimensions as time and space, weight and volume. Table manners and knowing how to be polite are also important when it comes to getting along with others in a society. A shared value system is particularly important, in that it tells each person what is right or wrong, what is or is not desirable, and "what a chap must never, never do."

Acquisition of basic skills in communication and in getting along with other people, a fund of widely shared knowledge, and awareness of common values enable each person to enter into everyday relationships with nearly all other members of the same society. Those without this basic training will be unable to assume roles in most functional groups. No matter how intelligent, they are likely to be unemployable, and probably will have difficulty in establishing social relationships. They will be foreigners in their own country.

Additionally, most people also have to learn how to participate in a number of specialized groups. Members of primitive societies expected nearly all females to be proficient in cooking, housekeeping, child rearing, and other skills associated with family life. Nearly all males had to learn to find food for their families, perhaps by farming or hunting, and to serve as warriors when needed. Counselors, priests, medicine men, and politico-military leaders were sometimes trained also, but in small numbers. Most roles were learned in the family, in the community, or in apprenticeships, and few individuals had control over the roles to which they were assigned.

In modern complex societies, which try to meet the increasingly diverse needs and desires of their members, much larger proportions of the populations have to be qualified for very specialized roles in functional groups of many kinds. This is most obvious in the job market, but there are also many new roles in voluntary associations, religious bodies, communities, and other social organisms—even families. Some of the training for these roles can be given the way it was in simpler societies, as when a child follows in the profession or trade of a parent, but most of the required knowledge and skill for participation in specialized groups comes from advanced education, on-the-job training, and other sources outside the home. The growth of specialization in medicine, law, and science in general has been especially dramatic, as suggested by the sudden increase in the number of periodicals and Internet sources serving those who work in these new fields.

At the same time that the numbers of specialized groups in modern societies have been growing, opportunities for lifelong education—and therefore for becoming qualified for new roles as one gets older—have been increasing. This is due not only to the proliferation of formal adult education and continuing education programs. In addition, employers are providing help to employees who want to upgrade their skills. The mass media, as well as the Internet, enable almost everyone to continue learning at any age. Participation in a functional group is in itself usually a learning experience, and often a most important one. It follows that the emergence of new categories and kinds of social organisms provides additional opportunities for individuals to expand their horizons.

These expanded educational opportunities are especially significant in that people are living longer than before Almost all of us change jobs during our lifetimes, and sometimes enter new fields. As the years pass we are thrust into new roles in the family or community. Skills and information needed in these jobs and roles sometimes have to be acquired quickly. (Consider the woman who becomes pregnant for the first time after the age of 45, or even 50! She now can be encountered fairly frequently, but was almost unknown to previous generations.) And there are some individuals who don't find the work, hobbies, family relationships, or recreational activities they like best until after they have retired. Lifelong learning has become a hallmark of modern societies.

Increased educational opportunities help qualify more people for specialized roles, but in order to benefit from these opportunities each person must answer a difficult question. How can I discover which specialized roles are best for me? This problem is widely recognized when it comes to finding the right job, but in addition each individual has to decide in which other functional groups to participate, and which roles within these groups are most appropriate. Some of us make better spouses and parents than others. Different people fit into different kinds of communities; social, religious, or professional associations that one person finds satisfying may be of no interest to the next.

Despite widespread recognition that it is important, surprisingly little is done by modern societies to help people find the roles to which they are best suited. Even when it comes to gainful employment, most people have to find their own way. Some useful aptitude tests are available, but are sporadically applied. Job counselors in schools are few and overwhelmed. Young people are often given the opportunity to "look around," and a great deal of information about various kinds of employment is available to those who seek it in the mass media and libraries. Nevertheless, most people choose jobs without considering a wide range of possibilities. A large number follow in the footsteps of a parent or other relative, as has been the practice in human societies for countless generations. A great many people simply accept whatever jobs happen to come along.

The problem of choosing among the thousands of nonpaying roles that are available in complex, modern societies—in families, churches, neighborhoods, and voluntary associations of all kinds—receives even less attention. Most people are guided by chance or by advice of friends and relatives, and remain unaware of many possibilities and opportunities. It is a safe assumption that no modern society is benefiting fully from the range of abilities available to it. And most of us are not enjoying the friendships, knowledge, respect, and feelings of accomplishment that would be ours if we could find just the right roles, both in the world of employment and outside of it.

Placement: Ensuring that Necessary Roles are Filled. In the ideal society's commercial and non-commercial spheres, all adults would occupy roles that they enjoyed and for which they were well qualified. The constraints of reality, however, condemn many people to perform at least some roles that they would rather avoid. For societies to survive, they must find ways to ensure that unpleasant and/or dangerous roles in essential functional groups are filled. How can qualified people be persuaded to cooperate, or at least to serve, when they would rather not?

One frequently used method is to compel individuals to participate by threatening severe deprivation or punishment if they do not comply. A second possibility is that people can be designated at the time of their birth to engage in these necessary but uninspiring activities, and then never are given an opportunity even to consider not performing them. A third way of securing compliance is to offer rewards that are sufficient to make such roles attractive for at least some individuals.

All three techniques have been used throughout history to ensure that unpleasant roles, whether major or minor, are performed. For example, many societies solved the problem of disposing of smelly garbage and trash by forcing slaves to handle it. Other societies relied on tradition, assigning this and other unpleasant jobs to certain castes or to people of a certain age or sex. Still other civilizations found ways to persuade qualified personnel to apply for such jobs. In New York City, and probably many other municipalities, public employees who collect the garbage are well paid civil servants. As a result, New York usually has more applicants for jobs in its Sanitation Department than there are openings.

Analogous solutions for trash disposal can be seen within the family. The children may be forced to take it out, whether they like it or not. One or the other spouse may do it because he or she was brought up to believe that this was, for him or for her, an inescapable household task. Or the family member who takes out the garbage may be rewarded with smiles, chocolate bars, kisses, or perhaps a small allowance.

All kinds of societies use these three methods, but in different proportions, to fill difficult or unpleasant roles in their functional groups. Authoritarian governance often employs compulsion; in societies or groups where traditional governance prevails, things tend to be done the way they always have been done; and in democracies people are more likely to be attracted to the more disagreeable jobs by rewards—fame, love, money, or some other satisfaction.

Exceptions to the above generalizations are important. Even democratic nations use some form of compulsion to staff certain roles. They draft people for the armed forces, and exert strong pressure on mothers to take care of their children, whether they want to or not. Tradition, too, is still important in job placement within democracies, as when a son or daughter is compelled to follow in a parent's footsteps, or feels constrained by a long-established family commitment. Exceptions are also common within dictatorships, which sometimes use democratic or traditional means to assign individuals to certain roles; while societies that are usually classified as traditional may include some social organisms of an authoritarian or democratic character.

The secular trend in all societies has been for more people to seek roles that they like, or find sufficiently rewarding, and many individuals are successful in doing so. One reason for this is that, as societies become complex, there are increasing numbers of specialized roles that are performed better by people who are motivated rather than forced or fated to cooperate. A slave who helps build a pyramid or a palace may do as good a job as a laborer, but who would trust a brain surgeon who served unwillingly? Even dictatorships in Nazi Germany and the Soviet Union, which had ample means to compel almost anyone to do almost anything, found it expedient to reward some scientists, engineers, and artists more generously than many of their counterparts were rewarded in democracies.

Indeed, it is probable that some very ancient roles that many people were formerly forced to occupy are performed better in societies that offer more choice. For example, women who love children are likely to do a better job of nurturing them than women who are compelled to have babies; and people who enjoy farming, mining, or military service—even when they like the money or life style more than the activity itself—can be expected to be more productive than those who play these roles to avoid punishment or do so because they have no alternative. There must be many exceptions to these generalizations, but in the absence of systematic surveys it is difficult to determine how frequently they occur.

Whether or not volunteers perform their roles better than draftees, businesses, civilian government agencies, and other functional groups in complex societies are usually able to offer rewards, whether material or nonmaterial, that are sufficient to attract personnel. In addition, many functional groups—especially voluntary associations—are successful in finding people who feel rewarded by playing roles that have few obvious inducements but satisfy the incumbent's desire to perform a social service, help achieve peace and justice, or implement religious principles.

But there are some significant roles that complex societies have had increasing difficulty in filling. In most such societies, especially in Western Europe and Japan, there are not sufficient numbers of parents who are interested in having and bringing up enough children to staff essential functional groups. Those parents who want children often prefer to have one or two; and large numbers of adults prefer none at all, thus leading to a declining population curve. Industrialization has eliminated the roles formerly available to children on the family farm, and has provided new job opportunities to adult women. Economic incentives to have a large number of babies thus have been greatly reduced. Most complex societies have also reduced authoritarian and traditional pressures that favored big families, and at the same time have failed to make parenthood rewarding enough to compete with other roles, especially in the case of women. As a result these societies face a congeries of social and political problems, some of which will be discussed below.

Until recently, all peoples who survived and prospered on this earth had to ensure that as many babies as possible were born and cared for. This was believed to be necessary for the survival of the tribe or country—and it probably was. The infant mortality rate was very high. Some scholars estimate that as recently as 50,000 years ago, the earth's total human population was around six million, and many areas of the earth were unpopulated or populated very thinly. (Massey 2002, p. 5) It is not surprising that many tribes and bands had to struggle to maintain numbers large enough to ensure their own continuity. Even today, in some communities and societies, the only important function of the nuclear family is seen as that of producing and rearing children. Whether families provide affection, security, and creature comforts to either children or marriage partners is secondary.

Throughout history, tradition—often combined with pressure from religious or political authorities and some inducements, such as being sure of care in old age—ensured that most women and men married and had several children. Men who did not marry and support their families, except for those few who played a celibate religious role, were ridiculed and criticized. Conversely, those men who fathered large numbers of children were praised and honored.

Far stronger pressures were used to make sure that women would follow traditional female roles. These pressures on women were probably necessary to assure an adequate supply of children because, during most of human history, giving birth was a dangerous as well as painful experience. And even when a woman survived the rigors of childbearing she often died at an early age, crushed by physical abuse, an impossible load of household duties, and sometimes work in the fields as well. Large numbers of men, in spite of the fact that their life expectancy in past centuries was not very long, outlived several wives. It would be interesting to have numbers to document these generalizations about life in the distant past, but even the fragmentary historical records that are available provide substantial evidence that they are valid. In many old graveyards one can find multiple headstones that identify a man and two or three successive wives, one or more of whom died in childbirth.

In addition to conditioning women to perform female roles from the time of birth onward, nearly all societies in ages past made it difficult for women to exist in an unmarried state or to avoid bearing children. They were ordinarily excluded from most forms of gainful employment—prostitution was one of the few ways in which a single woman could earn a living—and they risked violent assault if they lacked protection from male family members. Once married, they were subject to the authority of their husbands in nearly all respects and could not refuse his sexual demands. The carrot, a small one in comparison with the stick, was that women who succeeded in bearing and bringing up many children, especially sons, were likely to be honored and given authority over less senior women in the family.

This pattern of behavior was probably important in assuring the survival of many tribes, and in enabling some of them to expand. There must have been societies in which women were treated more kindly than in others, but data to show the extent to which kind treatment affected the birth or survival rate are difficult to find. It is known, however, that availability of food was often important in determining population size, so women in areas where food was scarce may have had somewhat better lives. What is fairly certain is that most tribes must have tried to increase their numbers by whatever means were available, because a tribe that fell behind was likely to be "replaced." The fate of the Hottentots and Bushmen in large parts of South Africa suggests what was happening in many areas of the world. "They [Hottentots and Bushmen] became outnumbered and were replaced...[by] farmers." (Diamond, Jared, 1997, p. 187)

Whether or not low birthrates will eventually doom complex industrial societies, and what these societies will look like in the future if they survive, will depend in part on the proportions of their adult men and women who become interested in forming larger families or households. It will also depend on the qualifications these adults have for performing increasingly demanding roles as parents.

Many other functional groups, in addition to families, have disappeared or changed in character because few people were interested in assuming traditional roles. The necessary ideas and communication networks may still exist, but there are no longer either rewards or pressures sufficient to attract people to these activities. Other groups may do a better job of satisfying needs previously served, or the needs themselves may no longer be experienced by people in the society. Thriving religious communities have faded away when they no longer could find a sufficient number of young people to replace older members as they died off. Blacksmith shops and medicine shows no longer provide enough income to attract personnel. Quilting parties are rare; they can't compete with other groups that provide sociability, and there are now many ways of acquiring quilts.

But it is not always true that formerly popular institutions have become redundant. It may be that a need still exists, even though the old forms of organization have lost their original economic base. More and more, modern societies are recreating old villages, family farms, and centers for lost arts and handicrafts, which are supported by tourists and subsidies rather than by local residents. Indeed, canvassing the past for functional groups that might serve present interests is a fascinating pursuit.

◆   ◆   ◆

This chapter on how functional groups usually come into being started by citing a number of cases where previously unacquainted individuals, temporarily isolated from the larger society, attempted to set up social organisms that would serve their immediate needs. In each case, three preconditions could be noted. There had to be ideas about what should be done and how to do it, communication channels that enabled people to coordinate their efforts with other people were necessary, and qualified personnel who were motivated or could be persuaded to staff the various functional groups were needed.

How well each of these requirements for the establishment and operation of a functional group is satisfied affects the performance of any social organism. Societies which lack an infrastructure that encourages creativity, communication, and education have great difficulty in forming and operating specialized functional groups. For example, Muslim scholars have pointed out, often with bitterness, that some predominantly Muslim societies have had difficulty developing modern institutions because their governments persecute scholars, discourage public communication, and fail to emphasize education. One distinguished social scientist has complained that "...in the contemporary Muslim world scholars are silenced, humiliated, or chased out of their homes." He also quotes the President of the International Institute of Islamic Thought as saying that the scholar may be faced with the choice of going to hell or going to jail, and notes that the educational achievements in Muslim countries are among the lowest in the world. (Ahmed, 2003, pp. 91-92) The United Nations Development Program's *Arab Human Development Report* for 2003 advances similar criticisms, noting that Arab countries have failed to sustain their own rich cultural traditions, engage in harsh censorship of communications, and are among the most backward nations of the world when it comes to the availability of publications for their populations. (*Economist,* October 25, 2003)

The relationship between all three factors (ideas, communication, and personnel) and quality of output is often highlighted when a functional group, whether a government agency, commercial company, or voluntary association, is under attack. If, for instance, there are credible accusations that a police department is engaging in racial profiling, suggestions about improving the department's performance are likely to include the following: (1) The department should be reorganized, perhaps with a civilian review board as part of its structure. That is, some of the ideas and conceptions behind the functional group should be revised or augmented. (2) Communication channels should be improved. The department has misunderstood the mayor's policies, or the chief has failed to inform his subordinates properly. (3) The department needs more highly qualified personnel. Perhaps a new chief with a record of past achievements should be appointed, or perhaps department members should be given further sensitivity training. And, of course, pay should be increased in order to persuade more skilled officers to join the department.

Nevertheless, even when the police department is organized according to the best available theories about public safety, has a good communication network, and is staffed by skilled officers, who are also well paid, it may still be unable to achieve the results expected of it. The following chapter will explore some reasons why functional groups that meet these three basic requirements, and therefore are able to exist, often fail to satisfy the needs and desires they are supposed to serve.

4

Why Good Organizations May Perform Badly

The hypothetical police department mentioned at the end of Chapter III may not succeed in doing its job because of unfavorable conditions both inside and outside the organization. In spite of good training and good pay, the officers may not be sufficiently motivated to enforce the law. Or their performance may be inadequate because they have been brought up in a society where prevailing rules of conduct fail to discourage people from engaging in internal bickering or from behaving in a condescending manner toward those they believe to be of lower status. Or there may be powerful groups in the society—some well meaning and others criminal—that make it impossible for the department to assure law and order. In addition, the police may be hampered by an uncooperative public. People may be reluctant to report crimes or to assist in their solution because tradition or current public opinion holds that individuals who help the authorities are betraying their neighbors.

To say much the same thing in more general terms, a functional group that is based on good ideas, has adequate communication channels, and is staffed by personnel who are able to perform the necessary roles, may still do a poor job. The extent to which it succeeds in satisfying the purposes it is supposed to serve depends heavily on four additional factors: (1) the morale of its personnel; (2) whether the commonly shared behavioral codes in that society make it easy or difficult for people to perform their roles in that particular group; (3)

whether activities of other functional groups in the society support or at least are compatible with the activities of the group in question; and (4) whether public opinion regarding the group is favorable or unfavorable toward what the group is trying to do.

These four criteria can be applied to purposeful collectivities of all sizes, from families to nations. The degree to which each factor affects the efficiency of any particular functional group depends in part on how power is distributed in the society as a whole and in the group itself. Within a totalitarian state or authoritarian organization, the will to work together toward a shared goal (morale) may be created largely by the threat of harsh punishment for noncompliance; and public opinion may scarcely exist. But the other two factors—harmonization of the activities of various functional groups and the prevalence of behaviors that advance or inhibit cooperation (e.g., industriousness or sloth, civility or boorishness) in the society—continue to play a significant role even in a harsh dictatorship. In democracies, morale and public opinion may be especially significant. All factors can be seen at work in all kinds of societies, although the importance of each varies from one political and cultural setting to the next.

Motivation and Morale. When we willingly participate in a functional group whose purposes we share, and which we believe is reasonably well administered, our morale is likely to be good. If most of those in the group feel the same way, the group is well motivated and group members are happy to coordinate their actions with each other to achieve the desired results. A good example is a sporting club, whether formally organized or just a group of friends who meet to play football. The members participate voluntarily and usually observe the rules of the game without complaining. The same is true of happy families and friendship groups of all kinds. In these social organisms, good morale is rarely a problem; the participants cooperate willingly in order to satisfy both their own wants and needs and also the desires of others with whom they are sympathetic. Morale within a group may be good even if some members don't enjoy their roles but are sufficiently rewarded. One frequently hears statements such as "I don't like the work but the pay is excellent." Or, "I don't really enjoy it but it makes my wife (or husband) happy."

In contrast, every society includes many people who belong to essential functional groups and who cooperate (more or less) with other group members without getting much pleasure from this. Some such individuals are trapped in unhappy families. Others participate with little enthusiasm in religious bodies, neighborhood activities, and schools because they are expected to do so. In the hypothetical police department mentioned above, there may be poor morale because some personnel don't really like their work and joined the department under pressure from a parent who was a policeman or policewoman. Others may have joined because they were unable to get more highly paid jobs. The lack of enthusiasm of these officers is likely to make the department a less pleasant place for other members to work, and group morale suffers.

Other things being equal, one can expect that morale will be higher in functional groups where people are doing what they want and where rewards are substantial. But there are many exceptions, where motivation to perform unattractive jobs well comes from within. Military forces consisting mostly of men who were drafted and then paid little or nothing sometimes develop high esprit. Members of such units may be inspired by a determination not to let down their comrades, as well as by patriotism or religious commitment. Similarly, in societies or communities where arranged marriages are customary, and where women are forced to accept the dictates of a husband whom they dislike, there are still happy families. In such societies, some wives may be sustained by love for their children and (eventually) for their husbands, feelings of national or ethnic pride, the strength of tradition, and promises of rewards in heaven.

In families, armies, and many other functional groups, whether or not roles are pleasant or freely chosen, quality of leadership and style of governance affects morale. It is usually assumed, for example, that an army in which higher ranks listen to suggestions and complaints from lower ranks will have better morale than a force where nearly all communications are from the top down. And in families with children, parental skill is a major factor in determining household morale. This is suggested by the reply of a resourceful mother to a questioner who asked why her small children seemed to be so happy, at the same time that they were more restrained and helpful than most members of their age group. She said: "I *make* them do it; and I *make* them do it *willingly.*" One suspects that she used similar techniques in managing her spouse.

The kinds of leadership and governance that contribute to good morale vary from one functional group to the next and from one time to another. Some religious bodies and businesses thrive when most decisions are made at the top; others do better if decision making is decentralized. And the three patterns of group formation and operation—voluntary cooperation, observance of tradition, and forced participation—have different implications under varying conditions. In a time of national crisis, personnel drafted into the armed services may be motivated just as highly as professional soldiers, sailors, or air force personnel. The problem is to find the right mixture for each functional group in each situation. There is no algorithm for determining the kind of leadership that is most likely to promote good morale in all functional groups, but awareness of the various possibilities helps in arriving at viable solutions in each individual case. Classroom teachers, for example, often consider several styles of teaching and discipline before they decide which ones are most likely to motivate a particular group of students.

Rules and Principles Governing Interpersonal Behavior. The efficiency of a functional group in any society—how well it achieves its purposes—often depends heavily on the way people in that society have learned to treat other people and how much weight they give to different values.

Sometimes the differences in rules governing how people act in various societies are very small, but they add up. Tourists who cross a national or ethnic boundary frequently find that they get a different feeling when they enter hotels, restaurants and stores. Customs inspectors, taxi drivers, and policemen seem to behave in a distinctive manner, too. In one country, people impress the visitor as relaxed and unhurried, but a little dishonest. In another they tend to be punctilious and brisk. In country B, eating places are likely to be characterized by neatness and promptness; in Country A, the waiters are more often sloppy and slow, but the food is wonderful. Perceived differences of this nature may be small; nevertheless, their cumulative impact often determines whether or not the tourist has a pleasant experience.

Perceptions of different behavioral styles often lead to the emergence of stereotypes about people of different nationalities. These are often expressed in concise generalizations, which may or may not be justified, such as: "When three Germans meet, they will form an association." "The business of the United States is business." "In Poland, everyone wants to be in the opposition." "The Japanese like to work themselves to death."

Rules governing how members of a community or society interact with other people usually develop in the course of centuries or millennia of human experience. They affect all interpersonal relations. We learn how and when to be polite and honest, what one should do when wronged by someone else, what is to be sought after and what is undesirable, what is important and what is of less moment, what is moral and what is immoral, as well as innumerable other specific rules and behavioral guidelines.

These codes that govern interpersonal behavior have a powerful influence on the establishment and operation of functional groups of all kinds. Rules about proper conduct and worthwhile goals affect the numbers and types of social organisms that are formed and how well these groups do the jobs they are supposed to do. In societies where a high value is placed on hard work, honesty, punctuality, education, and teamwork, efficient enterprises of many types, whether profit making or nonprofit, can be expected to flourish. Some behavioral codes facilitate achievements in art and music, while inhibiting scientific investigation. Others favor the establishment and operation of businesses, while making it more difficult for strong families to develop. As a political sociologist points out, rules of conduct based on civility, or a concern for the common good, make it possible for people in some societies to cooperate with each other even though they differ strongly with each other on important issues. (Shils, 1997, pp. 70-71) He also questions whether some newly democratic countries will be able to engender enough civility to "resolve some of the very difficult problems of creating a productive market economy and a pluralistic but consensual system of political parties." (*Ibid.*, p. 354) And, to return again to our hypothetical police department, it may function poorly because in that society bribery of officials is common and accepted. Or the department may be inefficient because government employees tend to believe that their primary job is to satisfy political leaders and that service to the public is of secondary importance.

Religions have contributed heavily to the various behavioral codes that exist in the world of today. An example of important rules that were formulated in early recorded history, and have had a positive influence on most functional groups that were exposed to them, is provided by the Ten Commandments. These behavioral injunctions are especially helpful in strengthening families, but they are also relevant to social organisms of many kinds and sizes, whether tribes, governments, communities, football teams, or businesses. In societies where they are widely obeyed, the Commandments tend to reduce both intergroup and intragroup conflict and, at the same time, help to discourage the formation of organizations that make use of murder, larceny, or fraud in achieving their purposes.

Whether these Commandments were intended to have such effects on functional groups, and thereby to strengthen whole societies, cannot be determined. Perhaps they were originally seen as rules of behavior that should be followed to please heavenly powers—and just happened to grease the wheels of human cooperation. Or perhaps the Ten Commandments grew out of a combination of experience and inspiration, and then were incorporated into religions. It is tempting to imagine a council of tribal elders meeting on a mountain top several thousand years ago. The discussion might have gone something like this.

"We have a problem," says the chairman. "People don't cooperate with each other the way they are supposed to, and a lot of work just doesn't get done. Families are feuding, people don't support their old parents as they should, the number of law suits is increasing, and I hear more and more malicious gossip—mostly lies—around the camp. Why is this?"

"Well," replies another elder. "One reason is that too many people think it's smart to steal whatever they happen to want. They not only steal clothing and weapons, but they will lure away another guy's wife or his favorite servant. So you have a lot of fights, and people get killed."

"There's more to it than that," chimes in a third elder. "Everybody's short tempered because they're exhausted from working all the time. They need at least one day off each week. Also, we will have to find ways of reducing the extent to which people aggravate each other. How can we stop them from accusing each other falsely?"

Finally, the oldest member of the council speaks. "I agree with my colleagues," he says, "but we ought to think more about underlying causes. Most of this strife and unpleasantness is because people don't agree about what's right and what's wrong. Perhaps you could ask God to write down a set of basic principles. And explain to the people that there's only one God, who is the top authority, so they can't say that some other god told them it would be all right to behave differently.

We're never going to get along together unless we all share the same values."

The chairman gravely nods his assent. "You have a good idea. I'll ask God to put a short list of basic principles on some stone tablets. That will really impress the folks down in the valley."

Although it's unlikely that conversations of this sort ever did take place, it is clear that the rules of behavior prescribed in the Ten Commandments, when observed, have enormous effects on secular organizations—regardless of the religious preferences of organization members. Even the initial Commandments about monotheism can be regarded as secular if one is willing to assume that Israelite leaders included these commandments because they had learned by experience that sufficient unanimity could not be achieved as long as people believed in several gods who might differ with each other. The theory that such behavioral guidelines had a secular origin is somewhat strengthened by the fact that students of ancient history have found very similar injunctions in Egyptian writings that predated the Biblical Ten Commandments by over a thousand years. (Breasted, 1933, especially pp. xi-xii)

This interpretation, incidentally, would make it possible for an edited version of the Ten Commandments to be posted in public schools of the United States and other countries where the principle of separation of church and state is observed. The only necessary change would be to replace the initial religious commandments with some such language as: "Experience has shown that the world will be a better place in which to live if all of us observe the following rules."

Behavioral injunctions which, when observed, facilitate cooperation in at least some functional groups, can be found in all major religions. For example, the teachings of Jesus as recorded in the Christian Gospels and also in some of the earliest surviving Christian documents—the letters of Paul, "Apostle to the Gentiles"—embody behavioral rules that are likely to improve the performance of many types of social organisms. These rules were not presented in a neat package, as was the case with the Ten Commandments, but are emphasized again and again in parables, admonitions, and other contexts throughout the New Testament. In contrast to the Ten Commandments, most of these injunctions are positive rather than negative—"do this!" rather than "don't do that!" Jesus seems to have selected from the huge and rich Jewish tradition a more limited set of principles that should govern human relations, leaving out some that did not harmonize with his teachings. Nearly all—indeed, perhaps all—of the behavioral injunctions emphasized by Jesus thus belong to both Jewish and Christian traditions. A few examples of rules from other traditions that also tend to support cooperative behavior will also be noted below.

As in the case of the Ten Commandments, one can speculate that behavioral codes set out in the New Testament were deduced from practical experience over time but, even if this could be proved, their selection and formulation required intelligence of a high order. The Christian Gospels portray Jesus as a keen observer of people and society who knew a great deal about human psychology. He may well have concluded that everyone would be much happier and more prosperous if people simply treated each other better, and therefore prescribed conduct that would help bring this about.

Whether or not such an interpretation is reasonable, the patterns of behavior recommended by Jesus and his disciples, when followed, tend to facilitate cooperative human relationships and thus to increase the efficiency of a great many kinds of functional groups. For example, one of the fairly brief letters of Paul (Thessalonians I), contains 20 or more behavioral injunctions relevant to the way people live and work, individually and together. (The exact number of injunctions depends on how specific one wants to be in distinguishing among similar but different behaviors.)

Here are some illustrative excerpts from Paul's letter, arranged in the order in which they appear in the original: "We call to mind…how your faith has shown itself in action, your love in labor, and your hope...in fortitude/...may the Lord make your love mount and overflow towards one another and towards all. May he make your hearts firm.../About love for our brotherhood you need no words of mine, for you are in fact practicing this rule of love towards all your fellow Christians throughout Macedonia. Yet we appeal to you, brothers, to do better still. Let it be your ambition to keep calm and look after your own business, and to work with your hands...so that you may command the respect of those outside your own number, and at the same time may never be in want./We want you not to remain in ignorance, brothers, about those who sleep in death; you should not grieve like the rest of men, who have no hope./...we must not sleep like the rest, but keep awake and sober...we, who belong to daylight, must keep sober, armed with faith and love for breastplate, and the hope of salvation for helmet./Therefore, hearten one another, fortify one another—as indeed you do./We beg you, brothers, to acknowledge those who are working so hard among you...your leaders and counselors. Hold them in the highest possible esteem and affection for the work they do./You must live at peace among yourselves...admonish the careless, encourage the faint-hearted, support the weak...be very patient with them all./See to it that no one pays back wrong for wrong, but always aim at doing the best you can for each other and for all men./Be always joyful; pray continually; give thanks whatever happens.../Do not stifle inspiration, and do not despise prophetic utterances, but bring them all to the test and then keep what is good in them and avoid the bad of whatever kind./...have this letter read to the whole brotherhood." (Quotations are from *The New English Bible—New Testament,* Oxford University Press and Cambridge University Press, 1961.)

With appropriate editing, such passages from Paul's letters could be made into a pep talk for a football coach, a memorandum on how to run a business, or a formula for keeping peace within the family: Love and encourage one another, work hard, do your best, look at the bright side, never give up hope, be nice to everybody—not only your own family or your own people. And don't automatically reject new ideas but check them out to see if they are any good. It should be emphasized once again, however, that the extent to which these injunctions help a functional group perform more efficiently depends on the extent to which they are actually observed—and they are not easy to follow.

The theme of forgiveness, which is implicit in Paul's letter to the Thessalonians, is spelled out repeatedly in the Christian Gospels. Ability to forgive is especially relevant to efficient organizational functioning, in that it helps to reduce conflict and often facilitates input by people who otherwise would be excluded. For example, in the parable of the prodigal son—who has left home and has wasted his inheritance on wine, women, and song—the father turns out to be a smart business man, as well as a kind and loving parent. By forgiving his errant but now penitent son, the father not only restores the unity of the family group but also helps ensure the survival and prosperity of the family farm. Having another son on the property will increase its productivity. Every member of the family, including the resentful son who had labored so long by himself, will benefit. And the society as a whole will be strengthened by the increase in its food supply. If the father had refused to forgive his prodigal son, both the family and the public in general would have been poorer. Was the parable intended to increase organizational efficiency? Whether intentionally or not, it may well have had that effect for the past 2000 years.

Similarly, the phrase—"blessed are the meek, for they shall inherit the earth," can be interpreted as meaning that people who learn how to work peacefully with others will do better than in the end than those who are on the alert for real or imagined insults. Perhaps the many generations of young Sunday School boys who have been mystified by this verse from the Sermon on the Mount—because they knew that ability to fight is essential if one is to defend one's rights and develop manly qualities—should have been informed about this possible interpretation. They might have been told: "You may have to fight sometimes, but you will get much farther ahead if you can avoid fights by trying to understand other people's points of view and treating them nicely."

That people who display the kinds of behavior recommended in Judeo-Christian traditions are sought by many employers is often suggested in announcements of job openings. I remember in particular a hand-written sign on the door of a shop in Ft. Myers, Florida. "HELP WANTED. Must be reliable, upbeat, and able to relate to customers and other staff members." Newspaper advertisements placed by organizations looking for personnel sometimes emphasize similar qualifications. And even when the ability to work together with others is not mentioned in print, it is usually uppermost in the minds of those who interview applicants for jobs.

Groups and organizations of all kinds—not only economic ones—prefer members who have the characteristics emphasized in these early Christian documents, as long as such personnel also have the necessary technical competence. People who are reliable, cheerful, tolerant, and not easily discouraged are more likely to be admitted into voluntary associations and welcomed wholeheartedly as neighbors. Similar characteristics play a role in the choice of a spouse, the durability of a marriage, and the morale of a family.

It should be emphasized that this discussion does not assume Judeo/Christian religious traditions to be the only ones that include behavioral injunctions favoring efficient functional groups. All major religions and philosophies that have endured for more than a few generations advance at least some rules of behavior (often very similar to the Judeo-Christian rules) that have beneficial effects on the efficiency of important social organisms. Otherwise, these religions and philosophies would probably not have survived. For example, admonitions similar to the "golden rule" of Confucius—don't do to others what you don't like others to do to you—can be found in several theological and philosophic traditions. The Jewish formulation of the rule, like that of Confucius, is in the negative—what you do not like yourself you shall not do to your neighbor. The usual Christian form, as given in the Gospel According to Luke, is positive—do unto others as you would have them do unto you. (Black and Rowley, 1985, p. 780) The Koran warns against starting interfamily feuds: "If a man is slain unjustly, his heir shall be entitled to satisfaction. But let him not carry his vengeance too far, for his victim will in turn be assisted and avenged." (Sura 17, Verse 33.)

This quotation and other quotations from the Koran in the following pages are taken from *The Koran: Translated with Notes by N.J. Dawood.* Revised Edition. London: Penguin, 1993. The Dawood translation is quoted here because it uses more colloquial English and is more easily understood than the widely accepted translation by Abdullah Yusuf Ali: *The Meaning of The Holy Qur'an.* Revised Translation, Commentary and Newly Compiled Comprehensive Index. Tenth Edition. Beltsville, MD: amana publications, 1999. The latter volume includes both Arabic and English texts, together with extensive notes and fascinating interpretive material.

While all major religions include precepts regarding the formation and operation of functional groups, it is a mistake to conclude that the precepts of different religions have substantially the same impact on the way people behave. Differences in behavioral codes prescribed by different religions, and in the interpretations given these codes, help to account for varying patterns of social organization: e.g., why families are more central to some societies than others, and why businesses are conducted differently in different parts of the world.

For example, the Koran contains a large number of instructions about how members of families should behave, and how the sexes should relate to each other. Many of these behavioral injunctions are far more detailed than guidelines provided in the early Christian literature. One can hypothesize that the rules have encouraged a high birthrate in predominantly Muslim societies, have increased the care with which children are nurtured, and have helped assure that family members behave in specified ways. In particular, rules about inheritance and divorce may have diminished both interfamily and intrafamily arguments. The Koran's injunction that prohibits burying unwanted babies alive—a practice that apparently was common among very poor families in some areas at the time of Mohammed—must also have led to population increases. The Koran says: "You shall not kill your children for fear of want. We will provide for them and for you. To kill them is a great sin." (Sura 17, Verse 31)

Here are a few examples of the Koran's injunctions about family matters. They are presented only to illustrate the high degree of attention to details of relationships in and among families; this writer is unqualified to speculate about how Muslim scholars would interpret these and other rules given in the Koran.

"Divorced women must wait, keeping themselves from men, three menstrual courses. It is unlawful for them, if they believe in God and the Last Day, to hide what God has created in their wombs: in which case their husbands would do well to take them back, should they desire reconciliation...." (Sura 2, Verse 228)

"Divorce may be pronounced twice, and then a woman must be retained in honor or allowed to go with kindness. It is unlawful for husbands to take from them anything they have given them, unless both fear that they may not be able to keep within the bounds set by God; in which case it shall be no offence for either of them if the wife ransoms herself." (Sura 2, Verse 229)

"Mothers shall give suck to their children for two whole years if the father wishes the sucking to be completed. They must be maintained and clothed in a reasonable manner by the child's father...The same duties devolve upon the father's heir.... Nor shall it be any offense for you if you prefer to have a nurse for your children, provided that you pay her what you promise, according to usage...."(Sura 2, Verse 233)

"If you fear a breach between a man and his wife, appoint an arbiter from his people and another from hers. If they wish to be reconciled God will bring them together again...." (Sura 4, Verse 35)

"If a woman fear ill treatment or desertion on the part of her husband, it shall be no offence for them to seek a mutual agreement, for agreement is best...." (Sura 4, Verse 128)

"Try as you may, you cannot treat all your wives impartially. Do not set yourself altogether against any of them, leaving her, as it were, in suspense.... If they separate, God will compensate both out of His own abundance..." (Sura 4, Verse 129)

"If a man die childless and he have a sister, she shall inherit the half of his estate. If a woman die childless, her brother shall be her sole heir. If a childless man have two sisters, they shall inherit two-thirds of his estate; but if he have both brothers and sisters, the share of each male shall be that of two females...." (Sura 4, Verse 176)

Not all the Koran's instructions regarding family matters are this specific. There are also important general guidelines. For example: "God enjoins justice, kindness and charity to one's kindred, and forbids indecency, wickedness and oppression...." (Sura 16, Verse 90) Or: ".... Women shall with justice have rights similar to those exercised against them, although men have a status above women...." (Sura 2, Verse 228)

There is no way to prove that the Koran's injunctions about the behavior of family members influenced particular historical developments, just as the effects of Judeo-Christian rules governing interpersonal behavior on social, political, and economic functional groups must remain hypothetical in many cases. Nonetheless, it is striking that the period when the power of Muslim states and the achievements of Islamic cultures were at their height overlaps extensively with the times when extended families were the basic political and economic functional groups in most nations. It seems reasonable to assume that by following rules in the Koran, as interpreted by religious leaders of the times, Muslim families became strong and stable building blocks for the states or tribes to which they belonged. These families were not only efficient administrative units, but were also successful in providing personnel who were courageous, dedicated, and obedient to higher authority. People with these characteristics were able to fill with distinction the political, economic, cultural, military, and other roles that were most important at that historical juncture. Rules prescribed by the Koran may have helped to reduce conflicts within and among extended families at a time when frequent intra- and interfamily conflicts bedeviled relationships among members of the political elite in remnants of the Roman Empire and in the nascent national states of Europe.

We can hypothesize further that, as world conditions changed during the following centuries, extended families became less important as pillars for national states. Indeed, extended families may have weakened national structures. More specialized functional groups, especially in commerce, industry, and education, began to dominate increasingly complex societies. Thus, some of the Koran's rules governing family behavior may have become dysfunctional for innovation, population mobility, and other prerequisites for the complex patterns of social organization that were gradually emerged in industrializing nations. And, it may be significant that extended families still provide the basis for the governments of several relatively underdeveloped and predominantly Moslem nations.

Islam, Christianity, Judaism, Buddhism, Hinduism, Confucianism, and other religions and philosophies may be important in shaping the generally accepted guidelines governing interpersonal relations even in societies without powerful organized religious bodies. Major portions of behavioral codes that were originally set forth in religions or philosophies have frequently been incorporated into traditions that are shared by most members of societies and communities, irrespective of their religious beliefs. To accept such codes, one does not have to belong to a religious body. Indeed, it is often true that, within a society or a community, members and nonmembers of religious organizations adhere to about the same patterns of conduct. This apparently was the case in the Shantung Compound, where religious affiliation and profession proved to be poor predictors of behavior under the rigorous conditions of internment. (Gilkey, 1966) Similar findings have been reported by public opinion research organizations over the years. For example, a recent survey funded by music publishers in the United States found that 77 percent of born-again teenagers in the United States engaged in illegal downloading of music from the internet, and that about the same proportion (81 percent) of all other teens also engaged in musical piracy. (*Washington Post,* May 1, 2004)

It is also frequently the case that within complex modern societies one can distinguish between civil codes—both written and unwritten—that govern behavior in some areas, and religious codes that apply in other areas. The former are observed by most society members, without regard to their faith, while the latter govern the behavior of people who identify with one or another religious body. In most cases, there are few direct conflicts between the two codes, in that the religious codes add rules about sex, diet, dress, charitable giving, and so on, which principally affect the way members of the religious group treat each other. There may, however, be serious conflicts, as when the religious code allows violence to be used in taking revenge, while the civil code does not; or when the civil code allows greedy, fraudulent, or cruel conduct that is forbidden by a religious code.

Tradition, public opinion, economic forces, and political pressures, along with theology and philosophy, help to shape behavioral codes. Business transactions, for example, may be affected not only by behavior advocated by the precepts of one or more religions—such as "do unto others as you would have them do unto you"—but also by secular ideas inherited from past generations that have been modified by public opinion and sometimes enshrined in law. For example, what one does when buying or selling a house differs from place to place, since the roles of buyer and seller are determined partly by what has always been done in that locality, partly on current economic conditions, and partly on legal requirements imposed by political bodies in the locality.

The importance of various influences on behavioral codes frequently varies from one type of activity to another, as it does from one society to another. Fashion is an area where current public opinion is the strongest influence on behavior in some countries, while in others religion and tradition are more important. At least a few laws governing how one dresses, or undresses, still survive in nearly all parts of the world. Tradition, sometimes based on religion, is the main influence on cooking in most societies. In modern complex societies, legal specifications that may have no antecedents in religion or tradition play a significant role, especially in financial transactions and when driving automobiles.

In general, very ancient elements of behavioral codes, including some that developed in the earliest days of human civilizations, are more difficult to adapt to modern conditions than those which emerged later. Many such admonitions became part of a religion and could not be questioned by believers even when the behavioral guidelines in question became inappropriate as social and physical environments changed. For example, rules specifying that the oldest male should exercise extensive powers as head of the family, and that the family should have as many children as possible, are still observed in many parts of the world, even though they frequently prove dysfunctional.

Whatever their origin, rules and principles governing behavior in a society help to determine how well functional groups serve the needs and desires of their members and managers, and also the needs of the society as a whole. In the case of our hypothetical police department, generally accepted traditions about the respect with which people of different social ranks should be treated may affect the department's ability to ensure public order. Both police officers and influential members of the public may feel that the son of an old and distinguished family should of course not go to jail if he commits a minor offence, but it's best to crack down hard on young punks who live in the wrong section of town if they do anything suspicious! Or, the department's members may be unenthusiastic about enforcing traffic laws in a region where people like to make their own decisions about what is a safe speed and where one should park a car. (A friend in Paris pointed this out to me when he left his car in a space where parking was, in theory, forbidden.) Some law enforcement personnel may share the belief of community members that certain law breakers provide a necessary service and should be tolerated. This was frequently the case in the United States when the Eighteen Amendment prohibited the sale and distribution of alcoholic beverages.

Generally accepted behavioral codes can have massive effects on the performance of nearly all organizations, large or small. The rules their members have learned about what is important and how to treat other people influence how they play their roles. Businesses that expand from one country into others are especially likely to become aware of the importance of locally accepted patterns of conduct. They may obey all the formal laws of the host country, but if they fail to observe also the prevailing unwritten rules about human relations they are sure to have trouble with both their employees and the public. Different standards about punctuality, for example, can cause problems for a business that expands from a country where participants in a noon meeting are expected to arrive by 12 o'clock to a country where noon is defined as lasting for an hour or more.

The same is frequently true of functional groups within a country. If their members do not observe the generally accepted patterns of interpersonal behavior, these groups are likely to find themselves out of tune with the organizations around them. That is, two social organisms—both of which enjoy access to good ideas, have excellent communication channels, and are staffed with well qualified people—may be in conflict with each other because their personnel have different standards of behavior. Families that live next to each other, or work groups that are supposed to cooperate, are likely to start feuding if they have different conceptions of what is desirable and what is undesirable conduct. The differences may involve definitions of polite behavior, the degree to which verbal agreements are considered binding, whether one should work on religious holidays, and many other aspects of day-to-day conduct. If it is impossible to find ways of reconciling the differing behavior codes, tensions or conflicts will probably result.

Whole societies can be disabled if members of major ethnic, religious or political communities observe conflicting patterns of preferred behavior. These patterns usually do not lead to actions that make coexistence with others in the society impossible, but when they do there is trouble. In some cases, nations are threatened with a split into two or more parts—as when Abraham Lincoln proclaimed that the United States could not exist half slave and half free, or when ethnic groups that dominate a particular geographical area, as in Chechnya or Kosovo, feel they cannot live according to their inherited behavioral codes as long as they belong to the larger political unit.

Intergroup Dependency and Patterns of Intergroup Conflict. A functional group that enjoys good morale and can operate efficiently without violating generally accepted standards of behavior may still not survive, or it may have to change its procedures and limit its activities. One reason for this may be that its activities are not supported, or are opposed, by other social organisms within the same society.

Nearly all functional groups in modern societies need support from a myriad of other groups that provide security, communication channels, materials, information, and trained personnel. Even a rural family that grows or hunts its own food, and creates its own clothing and shelter, is likely to require tools and other supplies from the outside world, as well as medical and police services. It follows that the failure of a functional group, no matter how well organized, may be caused by actions or by nonaction of other social organisms.

Problems caused by this interdependence can frequently be seen in developing countries. An efficient factory may be built, but it is bedeviled by poor training facilities for operating and maintenance personnel, lack of adequate channels of communication connecting the factory with suppliers and those who use its products, and difficulties in obtaining spare parts. This is one reason why so many factories built with foreign assistance in less developed parts of the world have been wholly or partially abandoned. Similarly, countries that have tried to shift from traditional or authoritarian patterns of government to some form of democracy have frequently suffered from the absence or weakness of organized groups representing the interests of important population categories—urban workers, large and small businesses, intellectuals, farmers, and professionals. If such groups exist in formerly traditional societies, they are likely to be small and poorly organized; and in addition they may fail to cut across ethnic and religious lines. Nascent political parties in developing countries, likewise, are more likely to represent tribal or religious interests than the needs and desires of citizens who are concerned with taxation, tariffs, education, and other issues of national interest.

States emerging from authoritarian rule sometimes have labor unions and professional and business associations, even token opposition political parties, but these organizations need time in order to learn how to administer themselves and to represent their constituents in the new environment. Democratic governments, no matter how honest and well-intentioned, cannot do a good job without input and cooperation from functional groups such as these. (Almond and Verba, 1963, pp. 486-87) Individuals, too, have to learn how to perform their roles in a democratic society, and much of this knowledge is gained through participation in voluntary associations and in the political system itself. (*Ibid.*, pp. 498-503*)*

Elections, even when well conducted, are less likely to result in able leadership when there are few institutions that have familiarized both voters and officials with the ways of democracy and when facilities for public discussion of the issues and the candidates are rudimentary. Both industrialization and democracy presuppose extensive networks of supporting functional groups.

New democracies frequently suffer especially from the lack of facilities for training leaders, lawyers, and administrative personnel who know how to make democracy work. Not only are formal educational institutions usually insufficient in new democracies; former traditional or authoritarian countries are also likely to suffer from the lack of private functional groups that are administered according to democratic principles. Members of such groups learn how to elect and frequently rotate their officers, keep minutes of meetings, maintain an honest treasury, and have orderly discussions. They serve as training grounds for democratic leadership.

One reason huge numbers of immigrants to the United States in the 19th and 20th centuries were able to participate so quickly in the political and economic life of their new country was that, immediately after arrival, they formed extensive networks of private groups in which those who did not come from democratic states learned democracy by doing it. These private collectivities included burial societies, small insurance companies, singing societies, political discussion groups, and athletic clubs. When African-Americans were finally enabled to participate more fully in the political life of their country during the 20th century, their leaders and spokespersons tended to be people who had learned about administration and leadership in black churches.

In formerly traditional societies, where such self-administering private groups are few or nonexistent, it is much more difficult to make either modern industries or democratic political institutions work. As one authority puts it: "…many countries have come to independence before they had sufficient nationals trained to take over the governments, schools, and businesses that had been established in these countries during the colonial era. A notorious case is the former Belgian Congo, which at independence had a sophisticated array of industries and a complex government, but only about a score of Congolese university graduates." (Sutton, 1968, p. 568)

Similar problems caused by institutional interdependence are experienced by much smaller functional groups also—not only by governments and large corporations. In all parts of the world, families that move into new neighborhoods often find that life is made difficult by the absence of accessible employment opportunities, stores, schools, and congenial religious institutions. In many areas of the United States, farmers have been forced off the land not by lack of markets but by the absence of local sources for fertilizer and other farm supplies, as well as by a dearth of facilities for repairing farm equipment.

Public Opinion. Whether or not conflict among functional groups is involved, or whether or not one group is supported adequately by others, the diffuse social organism we call public opinion frequently plays a major part in determining whether a particular functional group prospers, survives at a modest level, or atrophies. As reflected by elections, opinion polls, financial contributions, purchases, and expressions of other kinds, public opinion affects the nature of governments, the size and influence of political parties, the capabilities of political advocacy groups and the profits of businesses. Even governments that are able to remain in power because they are supported by the police and armed forces have trouble implementing their policies when public opinion in major sectors of the population is against them. It is not comfortable to sit on bayonets, as the 19th century French diplomat, Prince Talleyrand, is said to have remarked.

Political advocacy groups are especially sensitive to the rise and fall of public opinion. Such groups sometimes remain small or inconspicuous for many years after their initial organization, but changes in public opinion then turn these previously weak bodies into major players in the game of politics. For example, organizations advocating equal rights for women existed in many parts of the world for several generations during the 19th and early 20th centuries, but their members were usually seen as wild-eyed radicals. When feminism became a popular cause, however, feminist advocacy groups rapidly gained members and financial strength and in many countries led the way to the passage of laws designed to promote equal status for males and females.

Much the same course of events took place with functional groups advocating the abolition of slavery. Abolitionist organizations in Europe and America existed for generations before they became an important political force. In the North American British colonies, during the 18th century, the relatively small Society of Friends was the only significant religious body to take an unequivocal stand opposing involuntary servitude. In the following century, antislavery sentiment increased rapidly, permeating some of the largest religious denominations and turning abolitionist groups into major actors on the political stage.

Changes in public opinion can reduce the influence of advocacy groups with equal speed. The Women's Christian Temperance Union and the Anti-Saloon League, both of which built huge memberships and exercised impressive political power in the 19th and early 20th century United States, shrank in numbers and lost influence as public opinion turned against government control of alcoholic beverages following the First World War. Well before the middle of the 20th century, antiliquor organizations had ceased to be a significant political force nationally, although they retained considerable power in some sections of the country where public opinion still supported them. The Watch and Ward Society, and other organizations that saw themselves as guardians of public morals, suffered a similarly sharp decline in political influence at about the same time.

Business organizations are even more sensitive to public opinion. This can be seen most clearly in the world of fashion, where manufacturers and retailers make great efforts to determine popular preferences in styles of clothing, automobiles, housing, or other goods and services. Those who are out of step with public opinion in the population they are trying to serve are likely to be in trouble.

Indeed, few functional groups are not affected in one way or another by the generally held opinions of people with whom their members come in frequent contact. A family that is unhappy in one part of town, and feels unwelcome there, may move to another location that has a reputation as a friendly neighborhood. And both parents and pediatricians are heavily influenced by current opinions about the best way to bring up a child—although the former are likely to pay attention to what their friends think, while the latter are influenced by prevailing attitudes in the medical community. Similarly, fashions among educators often determine how the schools teach reading or enforce discipline.

To return (for the last time) to our hypothetical police department, community public opinion on one or more issues may make it difficult or impossible for officers to enforce the law. People may refuse to cooperate with the police because they distrust government in general, or perhaps because they feel that to assist the police is to betray others in the society. During the decades following World War II, for example, American college teachers were often reluctant to give information about their former students to FBI agents who were making background checks of applicants for sensitive government jobs. In many cases, this was because public opinion in the academic community regarded such background checks as a threat to academic freedom. Similar reluctance to cooperate with law enforcement personnel can sometimes be found in neighborhoods where drugs and drug dealers are widely accepted as part of the normal scene. Indeed, numerous studies have found that, at least in democracies, many laws cannot be enforced unless they have substantial public support.

◆ ◆ ◆

To summarize, this chapter has attempted to show that the efficiency of a functional group—the extent to which it succeeds in doing what its members, managers, or the public think it should do—depends not only on sound organization, adequate communication channels and qualified personnel, but also on good morale, patterns of behavior that are prevalent in the society, support or opposition of other functional groups, and public opinion on current issues. A group's morale can, to some extent, be controlled by its leadership, but the last three of these factors—behavioral codes, intergroup relations, and public opinion—are part of the social environment in which a group exists, and over which its members or management often can exercise little or no control. Other aspects of the environment, including a harsh or an inviting climate, the state of technology, and population size, also are likely to change over time—and sometimes do so very rapidly.

Many social organisms, such as business and political groups, do try to control various elements of their environments—and especially public opinion—through advertising and propaganda. In addition, governments, criminal organizations, and powerful associations, such as large corporations and labor unions, occasionally attempt to create more hospitable environments by eliminating or taking control of other functional groups that give them trouble. Large religious bodies have sometimes exerted significant environmental control by using a combination of persuasion and violence to suppress competing religious organizations, to gain political power, or to limit scientific investigation. Most functional groups, however, are unable to control their shifting environments, or can do so only very slightly, and must find ways to adapt. Functional groups that are unable to adapt usually disappear—in some cases taking their entire societies with them.

Indeed, environmental influences are so important in determining the existence and character of functional groups that the following chapter will be devoted to problems involved in adaptation.

5

Adaptation to Environmental Changes

When the social or physical environment in a society changes, new functional groups often emerge, while existing ones change their structures and operations or vanish altogether. Relationships among functional groups may also change. People have to find different ways of collaborating to satisfy their needs and desires when the old institutions no longer work or are unable to compete with new social organisms that satisfy needs and desires better. And if the new groups that can serve human requirements under the changed conditions are not organized, the whole society suffers.

Significant environmental changes can be large or small, gradual or sudden. A major and fairly sudden development, the Black Death, helped to demolish the feudal system and create a different social order in Europe during the 14th century. More gradual military and economic pressures, as well as mass migrations from modernizing national states in Europe, have hastened the destruction or reorganization of traditional societies in other parts of the world during the past five centuries. Scientific advances and inventions have led to major and minor alterations in the structures, procedures and personnel of countless business enterprises in many countries. The ebb and flow of fashion and public opinion has influenced the behavior of many organizations, great and small—as when a manufacturer who senses the trends of the times decides to discontinue producing straw hats or to give female employees maternity leave. When more people choose to live in gated communities and locked apartment houses, these new residential patterns influence the behavior of door-to-door sales companies and cause problems for evangelical religious sects that send their members to urban and suburban neighborhoods seeking converts.

Adaptation caused by environmental changes, whether gradual or not, often necessitates further adaptations in functional groups. A circular process becomes evident. In past centuries, increasing numbers of individuals found that some of their needs and desires could be satisfied better if they used products produced in other countries. Additional import/export businesses were then organized to meet the new demands. The international traders tended to congregate in places that were conveniently located for both shipping and overland transportation, often on oceans or rivers, thus stimulating the growth of new towns. As these urban centers gained population, new enterprises that provided a still wider range of goods and services to prosperous artisans and wealthy merchants grew up with them. Invention of the compass and improved techniques for ship construction encouraged fishermen, traders, and explorers to expand their activities and range farther afield. This hastened the formation of colonial settlements in many parts of the globe. Resulting changes in the balance of political power led to the organization of new political units and to revisions in the activities of old ones.

During most of human history, major environmental changes, both physical and social, were likely to be gradual. There were some cataclysms or disasters that occurred without warning, such as volcanic eruptions, enemy attacks, droughts, floods, or plagues, but ordinarily there was time for functional groups to adapt to slowly changing conditions, and for new groups to be formed, without serious social dislocations. Indeed, during long periods when populations were gradually increasing, agriculture was becoming more widely practiced, and increasingly seaworthy ships were being built, most members of the affected societies probably were unaware that their environments were changing and that new patterns of human behavior were developing.

When sudden environmental changes did occur, primitive societies sometimes were able to adapt to them by using existing functional groups, but if this was not possible the societies in question suffered serious damage or even disappeared. Thus, a tribe experiencing a food shortage due to drought conditions might send warriors to seize supplies from a more fortunate neighbor. An unexpected attack from a stronger or more warlike people might cause a tribe to disappear, as adult males were slaughtered and women and children were enslaved. When Europeans started migrating to the Americas, Native American peoples were overwhelmed before they could find ways of coping with the better-armed invaders, or with the diseases the colonists brought with them.

During the past five centuries, the pace of both physical and social change in the environment in all parts of the world has increased. Modern, complex societies are now faced with the necessity of organizing new functional groups and revising old ones more rapidly than ever before. Within a single generation the airplane made the world smaller, altering trade and travel patterns and forcing reorganizations in defense establishments of almost all countries. Radio and television affected patterns of behavior in families, politics, and business. Only a few decades later, widespread availability of computers made vast amounts of information more manageable. These developments led to new rules and roles in functional groups concerned with government, business, education, and crime control. It also affected the life style of many families, as e-mail provided a new channel for both entertainment and intergenerational communication. Discoveries about the human body have been followed within a few years by the organization of new medical specialties, and have led to changes in law firms, insurance companies, and other specialized organizations that deal with various implications of medical advances. The opening of most occupations and professions to women in industrialized societies during the 20th century was a major factor in the development of different kinds of family structures and new operating rules for family members.

Global warming and environmental pollution in general, even if proceeding more slowly, have within half a century stimulated the formation of new scientific, commercial, and political groups. These environmental factors have also affected the operation of countless government and business organizations and have influenced decisions of many individuals about where they want to live or work.

Today, most people in all societies are aware of massive changes in functional groups that have occurred during their own lifetimes—whether they happily welcome or strongly oppose such changes. Few businesses can be conducted the way they were in grandfather's time. Children are more likely to watch television or play computer games than to use jump ropes or play hopscotch. Developments in manufacturing, transportation, and communication make possible the formation of huge businesses that provide goods and services to people in all parts of the world, often squeezing out smaller enterprises. Augmented communication facilities make it easier for individuals to keep in touch with friends and relatives wherever they may be, and for like-minded people to form international organizations. This shrinkage of the globe, combined with scientific advances, has forced all nations to face the possibility that they may be subject to military attack and to institute or at least contemplate changes in their foreign policy organizations and defense establishments. In the modern world, the pressure for functional groups to adapt rapidly is continuous. How do today's societies manage this adaptation process?

Characteristics that Favor Adaptation. Adaptation is partial re-creation. The ability of a society or a social organism to cope with rapid change depends largely on the presence and vitality of the same factors that enable any functional group to take shape and operate successfully. There must be a capacity to develop, criticize, and experiment with new ideas. Some of the new ideas may be about ways to acquire and use needed money, power, or materials; other ideas may suggest new group structures, behavioral rules, and operating methods. Also needed are communication channels that link people together in new patterns and disseminate relevant information and ideas to increasingly large audiences as well as to highly specialized small audiences. The third requirement—personnel qualified to participate in the new or revised functional groups—makes it necessary for many people to acquire new knowledge and skills. Some individuals may go back to school or participate in adult education or mid-career education programs; more are likely to learn by doing, whether in an informal social group or on the job. Leaders at various levels, both in the groups directly affected and in higher management or government agencies, have to find new ways in which various functional groups or sub-groups can collaborate or at least avoid destructive conflict.

While the processes involved in adaptation have been substantially the same at all periods of history, the increasing rapidity of environmental change, together with the emergence of countless new desires and aspirations among human populations, has made adaptation a more difficult process than ever before. Today, the process is likely to simultaneously involve functional groups of many different varieties in all parts of a society and to require decisions by large numbers of individuals. Successful adaptation of the society as a whole is more likely if each component group, whether large or small, has the characteristics that facilitate adjustment—including hospitality to new ideas, a well developed communication system, and people who are qualified to make decisions. The behavior of decision makers in many different groups can determine whether or not a society as a whole suffers or prospers as a result of sudden environmental change.

Some of the problems that arise when a complex society must adapt to a major environmental change can be seen in time of war, or when a nation is involved in a severe financial crisis. Not only must national leaders and governmental agencies make decisions, but so must nearly all families and businesses, as well as voluntary associations of many kinds. They all have to determine new courses of action. In 2002, when Argentina devalued the peso, press reports described many of the ways in which that country's component functional groups sought to deal with this development. Some families organized "mom and pop" enterprises to support themselves, other families cut back on expenses in an effort to survive, and still others made arrangements to emigrate. Countless small businesses had to revise their structures and procedures in order to make the best of the situation. Street demonstrations occurred, some spontaneous and some carefully organized. Most workers decided to stay on the job, even though their pay was now worth much less. Numerous large companies increased their efforts to find foreign markets.

Even more rapid adjustments were necessary following the September 11, 2001, attack on New York's World Trade Center. Kathleen Tierney, a sociologist who specializes in disaster research, has noted that coping with the results of this event required a high degree of improvisation. There often wasn't time to wait for the usual authorities to make decisions; people at lower levels of many different organizations and some without organizational affiliations felt they had to take action immediately. Loss of life would have been even greater if the occupants in the doomed buildings had not found ways to help each other escape, and blood donors lined up at hospitals spontaneously. An air traffic controller, without waiting for orders from above, instructed all commercial flights to clear the skies. The sociologist is quoted as saying that "one of the strengths of our culture is that it empowers people in pivotal positions to make choices." (*New York Times,* September 7, 2004)

As the examples from both New York and Argentina suggest, very small as well as very large groups need ideas, communication networks, and skilled personnel if they are to adjust successfully. A family that lacks these resources and breaks apart in a crisis is likely to be one in which nobody knows what should be done, the members don't speak to each other, and children and parents lack skills and values that would enable them to adopt new roles. Similarly, a very large group, such as a national defense establishment, may be unable to counter an external threat because it has insufficient intelligence about the enemy, its internal communication networks are disrupted, and personnel at various levels are not well trained.

Functional groups that lack any one of the characteristics necessary for successful adaptation will adapt to both large and small environmental changes less well. If good ideas about how to satisfy the group's purposes are not available, an excellent communication system, capable personnel, and skillful leadership will not help. If there are promising ideas, but the communication system cannot disseminate these or enable group members to coordinate their actions, competent personnel and able leaders will be ineffective. If there are not enough well qualified group members who know how to work together, the presence of good ideas, able leaders, and adequate communication channels is unlikely to be sufficient. And if the group leadership cannot manage internal or external conflicts successfully, the availability of the other three characteristics may not be sufficient to avoid catastrophe.

Style of Governance and Adaptability. Which kinds of functional groups adapt most successfully to frequent and rapid environmental changes—those groups that are organized along democratic lines, those that are mainly authoritarian in character, or those that follow traditional practices? A simple answer is difficult, because many social organisms tend to have at least some characteristic of all three modes of governance. Furthermore, there is far from universal agreement as to exactly what any of the three terms mean. Nevertheless, most students would probably agree that a "pure" democratic society would be one in which not only government but also most other functional groups depended on voluntary cooperation to satisfy the needs and desires of population members. A "pure" dictatorship would be one in which all actions that were not expressly commanded were forbidden. The ideal traditional society would be one in which all actions were governed by generally recognized precedents.

In actuality, all societies and most functional groups use a mix of traditional, authoritarian, and democratic styles of cooperation to get things done. Nearly all human collectivities follow tradition in at least some respects, because "that is the way these things have always been done." Dictatorships or traditional polities may use democratic methods in certain situations, while in democracies some institutions behave in either an authoritarian or traditional manner—e.g., when the police make an arrest or a court follows an established precedent.

Private functional groups, too, may simultaneously use several styles of governance. A corporation where most decisions are made at the top may also allow some matters to be settled by discussions among employees. Families that follow tradition in some of their activities, and at the same time allow the children many opportunities to make their own decisions, may still have a strong-minded matriarch or patriarch who has the last word. Some voluntary associations look like democracies because they hold elections and encourage participation, while actually they are run by an oligarchy composed of a small number of dedicated and active members.

Nevertheless, despite the prevalence of mixed styles of governance, students, journalists, and other interested parties are usually able to decide whether a particular functional group should be labeled as predominantly democratic, authoritarian, or traditional. This is true whether they are referring to a nation, a business enterprise, a family, or some other form of association. Furthermore, within societies where most people share common standards of judgment there is likely to be substantial agreement as to which groups fall in which category. For example, in its annual surveys of the state of freedom throughout the world, New York's Freedom House is able to classify nations according to the degree of freedom they allow the press and the extent to which their governments are chosen in free elections. Similarly, political scientists frequently rank nations according to their stage of political and economic development. (Observers who use different standards of judgment—for instance, those who favor government by religious leaders or by a small political elite—would probably come up with very different rankings, but they would still be able to separate functional groups into various categories according to their mode of governance.)

The ability to differentiate among the various political styles is important, because what we are most interested in here is the extent to which functional groups in one or another of the three categories are likely to be most successful in adapting to rapidly changing environments.

Our conclusion is that none of the three methods of coordinating human efforts works best for all functional groups in all situations, but that democratic polities are likely to have substantial advantages in most cases. This is because democracies are more often best at producing, criticizing, and testing new ideas, maintaining communication systems that convey adequate and accurate information, educating and training members or participants to coordinate their efforts, and providing capable leadership.

To make such a sweeping determination as this may be considered presumptuous. Quantitative supporting data are unavailable, and one can easily compile a list of doubtful or clearly wrong decisions made by democratic organizations in both private and public spheres. But the conclusion may be more defensible if we emphasize that the superiority of democracies in adapting to changing environments is relative only, and that there are also circumstances in which authoritarian or traditional polities are more efficient.

As far as the development, presentation, and criticism of new ideas is concerned, democracies are usually more encouraging and accommodating than traditional or authoritarian societies. Furthermore, because they include relatively more independent private and voluntary functional groups, democracies make it possible for larger proportions of their populations to participate in discussing and criticizing new ideas. When a society has to adapt to major environmental changes, more brain power at many levels is likely to be at work in democracies than in dictatorships or traditional societies. There are also more opportunities to experiment with new ways of doing things, since various private organizations or lower level government agencies may try out an idea and thus serve as laboratories for the whole society. This is not to say that democracies do not offer barriers to the expression and testing of new ideas. Democratic governments, corporations, religious groups, and even scientific organizations may attempt to suppress new ideas they find disturbing. Nevertheless, these are exceptions rather than the rule. Opportunities for finding the best ways to deal with environmental changes remain relatively more numerous in democratic polities.

Similar observations can be made about communication systems. Here again, democracies have a substantial advantage when it comes to building and maintaining facilities that link people together and provide accurate information on a wide variety of subjects. At least some channels—whether consisting of large or small mass media, books, word of mouth, or computers—are available to almost anyone in a democratic polity who has something to say or who wants to be informed. These channels are also open to a wide variety of organizations, which can use them to make their viewpoints known, and to obtain relevant information about almost any issue. Although wealthy and powerful elements in democracies are sometimes successful in using mass media channels to overwhelm ideas with which they disagree, all democratic polities maintain communication systems that are sufficiently open to allow groups and individuals with varying orientations to compete in finding ways of satisfying human needs and desires. Freedom of information and expression cannot guarantee appropriate adjustments to environmental change, but they make such adjustments more likely.

It is relevant also that a society's ability to develop and criticize new ideas is closely linked to the efficiency of its communication systems in disseminating accurate information. People who try to think of better ways to satisfy human requirements are stimulated by each other, as well as by what has happened or been learned in the past. Ideas about how to cope with change can develop more quickly if these people are in touch with each other, and have reliable information about what has already been tried. Critics of new ideas and people who want to resist change, also, have access to communication channels and stimulate each other. As a result, new ideas are better tested.

In contrast, authoritarian or traditional governments and functional groups impose greater limitations on the development of new ideas and on freedom of communication. Expression of unorthodox views is discouraged, and the mass media are subject to a higher degree of control. Traditional and authoritarian polities also tend to emphasize the value of secrecy, restricting important information to an elite, thus making it difficult for competing groups to organize and function. Some primitive traditional societies lack mass media altogether, while most other channels are under the control of conservative religious authorities or a small group of political leaders.

As a result, when a new situation requires a change of policy in authoritarian or traditional polities, both innovators and critics have fewer opportunities to be heard. If the leadership approves a course of action that proves inappropriate, it is more difficult to reverse. An example is the disposal of nuclear waste. In countries where critics of government policies with respect to nuclear energy are silenced, lakes and streams are more likely to be poisoned. Similarly, one of the reasons industries in authoritarian states are frequently noncompetitive with those of more democratic polities is that management decisions are shielded from criticism by people from both inside and outside the enterprises concerned.

Whether democratic polities usually make more efficient use of available personnel than authoritarian organizations is more debatable. Dictatorships can ensure that people are assigned where the authorities want them, and that these people get appropriate education, and advanced training where necessary. Key personnel receive generous rewards—both financial and honorary. In some cases, authoritarian governments have shown skill in identifying individuals who have unusual talents, whether in sports or in science, and giving them special training. When East Germany was ruled by a Communist oligarchy, for example, its athletes were able for several years to win more Olympic gold medals than countries with over ten times its population. (It later turned out that these victories were due in part to extensive use of drugs, but as an Olympic Games official remarked, "Their system was successful if you count the medals.") Authoritarian governments can be more ruthless than democracies in stamping out crime also, although sometimes they simply take control of criminal organizations and operate them for the benefit of the ruling elite.

Democratic polities, where individuals have greater freedom to decide what they want to do, appear at least superficially to be more wasteful in their use of human resources. Talented young people are frequently denied opportunities for advanced training in important specialties. Sometimes they cannot even get a basic education because they lack money or belong to the "wrong" ethnic group. In the United States, there are frequent complaints that illiteracy is widespread, and that not enough students develop their capabilities in science and mathematics. At the same time, highly intelligent people are attracted by enormous salaries to occupations of doubtful social value—e.g., trafficking in entertainment materials that emphasize violence and cruelty, or finding ways for wealthy persons to avoid paying taxes. Individuals who wish to avoid difficult or unpleasant roles can often do so.

Authoritarian functional groups within democracies have many of the same advantages as dictatorial governments when it comes to making use of available personnel, in that the management of these social organisms—especially business corporations and some religious bodies—controls selection, assignments, rewards, and opportunities for advanced training. Talented personnel in such functional groups are likely to end up with major responsibilities, inasmuch as most of these business and religious bodies have vigorous competitors and therefore feel pressure to make assignments on the basis of ability.

Business and other organizations in authoritarian and traditional societies, however, usually have fewer competitors and can more easily base selection and assignments on such factors as political reliability or family relationships. Governmental and many business personnel in authoritarian or traditional societies are less likely than their opposite numbers in democracies to be rewarded for skills in dealing with their subordinates, or customers, or the public in general.

There are no quantitative data, as far as I know, to back up any of the above assertions, but they are supported by countless anecdotes. One of my favorite recollections in this connection is that of a police official in Nazi Germany who refused to accept my signature on a document because I signed it with my left hand. When I remonstrated that I was left handed and always signed this way, the officer replied gruffly: "Would you expect me to accept that document if you signed it with your foot?" (One result of this bureaucrat's decision that I had to sign with my right hand was, of course, that my signature was useless as a means of identification.) Some readers may object that bureaucrats all over the world behave in much the same ways, regardless of the society in which they are located. The answer to this, I think, is that rigid or corrupt bureaucrats can be encountered anywhere, but that democracies are fortunate in having fewer of them.

On balance, then, in spite of some advantages enjoyed by authoritarian groups, democratic polities appear to have an edge when it comes to utilizing human capabilities in the functional groups of a changing world. Allowing individuals a high degree of freedom to choose where and how hard they will work is wasteful, true, but the countervailing advantage is that morale tends to be fairly high in most workplaces. People usually do well those things they enjoy, and are likely to work harder at jobs for which they feel more generously rewarded. Self selection thus helps lead people to functional groups and roles for which they are well adapted, or reasonably well compensated, or both. At least one specialist in economic development sees a close relationship between job satisfaction and the quality of work:

"The economy will prosper again when more Americans can do the work they love." (Florida, 2001, p. 26) Reliance on the marketplace to determine the size of an individual's economic gains, while it results in many cases of unjustified wealth and undeserved poverty, also goes a long way to insure that quite a few occupations and roles in democratic polities are meeting widely felt needs.

Nonmaterial rewards supplement market forces more frequently in democracies than in countries or groups with other styles of governance. Many talented individuals who are less concerned with money are attracted by the satisfactions offered by roles in private groups concerned with educational, welfare, and cultural activities. Sometimes they work as volunteers. Such groups and roles are less frequently found in authoritarian or traditional societies.

Greater freedom of choice for individuals, whether relating to religion, political preference, marriage, life style, or occupation, is one reason democracies have benefited enormously from an influx of human talent from both traditional and authoritarian societies. The "brain drain" from the former and highly skilled refugees from the latter have, in turn, added even more to the ability of democratic societies to prosper in a changing world. One authority estimates that during the last two decades of the 20th century almost 30 percent of new businesses in California's Silicon Valley were started by foreign-born people. (*Ibid.*, p. 28)

Traditional societies and functional groups are in more trouble than either democracies or dictatorships when it comes to making the best use of human resources in rapidly changing environments. Where there is traditional governance, most individuals are tightly tied to predetermined roles, and members of functional groups are more likely to feel threatened by efforts to adapt to environmental change. Nor do traditional societies have in place the schools, universities, specialized government agencies, and other functional groups that can help the society find and equip people for new or revised roles.

One potential advantage in some traditional societies, however, is the solid adherence to a set of established values that help people work together while adapting to new conditions. Honesty; an ethic of hard work; trust in neighbors and co-workers; respect for family, religious, and political authorities—these values can sometimes help a traditional society adjust to the modern world. The ability of Japan and some other East Asian countries to adjust so rapidly to massive environmental changes was probably due in part to the continuing strength of traditional values that enabled these countries to mobilize and utilize their human resources. Similarly, although Germany was far from being a traditional society in the 1940's, the commitment of the typical German to traditional values—such as duty, diligence, and education—was a major factor contributing to the rapid economic recovery of Germany following the Second World War.

When it comes to good leadership—an additional consideration that affects the abilities of societies to deal with environmental change—it is even more difficult to generalize about the virtues and vices of various styles of governance. The best leader of each functional group is the one who can insure that the group does the best possible job in serving the needs of its members, or the purposes for which it was organized, depending on one's observational standpoint. The ideal leader of a tribe or state is able to see that necessary and desirable social organisms exist, or are quickly organized, and that these groups work smoothly and support each other, or at least do not become involved in internecine conflict. How can good leadership be assured? Traditional, authoritarian, and democratic styles of selecting leaders and of awarding powers to them all have positive and negative features.

In traditional societies and some authoritarian polities, there often are methods of leadership selection that help avoid violence or destructive controversy. In a well-functioning monarchy, or traditional family, the transition from one chief executive to another is usually accomplished quickly and smoothly according to a long-established formula, of which "the king is dead—long live the king" is one. Once installed, the legitimacy of the new leader is likely to be generally acknowledged. Similarly, authoritarian polities, whether dictatorships, some churches, military organizations, and some corporations, frequently have ways of choosing leaders who are accepted by the powerful elite and are installed without delay. Many dictators can designate their successors in advance, a board of directors can elect a new chairman promptly, and in most military organizations the next ranking officer automatically becomes the commander if the previous leader falls in battle. In traditional or authoritarian religious bodies, a previously designated small group of elders usually makes the selection. These "neat" methods of choosing a leader, while they do not guarantee that the most competent person is selected, have the virtue that the selection process is likely to be both orderly and rapid.

The other side of the coin is that authoritarian and traditional polities can have great difficulty in removing leaders when they prove to be incompetent, cruel, or dishonest—or when environmental conditions change. A dictator who is an outstanding leader in war may prove to be a poor administrator in peace time. And there are likely to be serious crises when there is no established formula for choosing a new leader, or when the customary procedure breaks down and there are competing candidates for the top position. Civil war may result.

Democracies, for their part, often use leadership selection methods that tend to be slow, cumbersome, and in some cases divisive. Nor do democratic methods offer assurance of a wise choice. Popularity is not necessarily associated with competence—although neither are the two qualities incompatible. On the other hand, bad leaders in democracies can usually be removed more easily than in traditional or authoritarian societies. The removal process may be lengthy and bitter in some cases, especially if there is no legally established term limit, but less often results in violence. Furthermore, elections or other selection processes used in choosing a new leader can stimulate thought and lead to the choice of a well qualified individual. The survival and in many cases the prosperity of predominantly democratic societies and functional groups suggests that their methods of leadership selection, if not ideal, may be the best methods available at the present time.

Several conclusions are suggested by this discussion of the degree to which various styles of governance facilitate adjustment to environmental change. One is that successful adaptation often requires that a functional group or nation find the right combination of democracy, authoritarianism, or tradition. No one style is likely to be best for every situation. In a family, as in a government, all three approaches may have to be used, and the skill with which they are balanced may determine success or failure. There are some things the children must be compelled to do, whether they like it or not; the course of action in other situations can best be decided by discussion; and there are some activities that are part of the family tradition. Similarly, a democratic government may behave much like an authoritarian executive when it intervenes peremptorily to uphold the law. And democracies resemble traditional polities in some areas where laws are unnecessary because enough people adhere to traditional patterns of behavior.

The challenge to functional groups in complex societies of the present era is to find the right mix. Those who are committed to democratic principles are well advised to look for ways to control and limit autocracy rather than to eliminate it altogether. Dictatorial capabilities to deal with some situations may be needed if a democratic functional group is to survive.

An authoritarian style of governance is likely to be dysfunctional, however, when a multitude of adjustments affecting many areas of society have to be made over a time period that is neither very short nor very long—in the course of decades rather than days or centuries. And in the present-day world, complex adjustments over an intermediate time period are frequently required. The benevolent philosopher king envisaged by Plato could probably have done a fairly good job in the relatively simple societies of his time, but the poor fellow would be overwhelmed by the thousands of decisions necessitated by changes in the social and physical environment that have to be made in today's complex societies. How could an all powerful executive formulate appropriate decrees prescribing how families, businesses, religious bodies, educational institutions, and other functional groups should adapt to changes in the role of women, or to rising demands for thousands of new consumer goods, or to increasing urbanization and the decline of agriculture?

Although it would be inappropriate to equate the Soviet Union's Lenin and Stalin with philosopher kings, it is striking that their emphasis on central planning was fairly successful in achieving some key objectives of their governments. They built an impressive military establishment, were able to orbit an earth satellite before any other country, almost abolished unemployment, and assured nearly all citizens of at least minimal education, housing, food, and medical care.

But their regimes also showed the limitations of an authoritarian style of governance. The Soviet Union never succeeded in eliminating long lines at grocery stores, in providing much choice in consumer goods, or in assuring a stable supply of minor conveniences such as paper clips and rubber bands. Institutions devoted to meeting consumer demands in general remained underdeveloped. The USSR also fell behind the industrialized democracies in nearly all branches of knowledge that were not selected for special emphasis, and its efforts to control literary and artistic activities proved counterproductive. It never was able to build a society where most society members could feel satisfied.

Another general observation is that peaceful competition among functional groups in almost all areas of society (a state of affairs that is characteristic of democracies) seems to favor successful adaptation to change. Adaptation involves effort, and a monopoly position reduces the pressure on a social organism to take the trouble of exploring new ideas, maintaining efficient communication channels, improving the quality of its personnel, and ensuring that morale is high. In politics, a one-party system tends to emphasize orthodoxy, secrecy, and the choice of personnel more on the basis of loyalty than ability. Similar observations can be made in the fields of business and commerce, education and religion, or art and literature.

Peaceful competition can be useful in the search for the best possible adaptations even when contending functional groups are themselves authoritarian or traditional. If competition leads to violence, this usually has a negative influence on the satisfaction of human needs, but as long as competition is peaceful it constitutes one of the most effective guarantees that human needs will not be ignored in the process of adjusting to environmental change. That competition can be good natured, as well as peaceful and orderly, is illustrated by the behavior of most universities, as well as of many religious and commercial groups. Such behavior shows that it is possible to compete vigorously when searching for ways to provide people with both material and nonmaterial benefits, and at the same time to maintain cordial relations between members of the contending groups.

A major advantage that democracies have when it comes to adapting to change is that they more often try to control the *results* of freedom to organize rather than to prevent new forms of organization from developing. That is, controls over functional groups deemed to be objectionable are more often imposed by democracies *after* these groups have been formed, rather than before. These after-the-fact controls frequently are exercised by individuals when they vote, or make purchases and contributions, thereby expressing approval or disapproval. Other *post hoc* controls are applied by functional groups such as police, regulatory agencies, religious bodies, and businesses. The controls may sometimes be stringent, but if they are imposed only following opportunities for observation, experimentation, and discussion, something valuable frequently will have been learned.

Democratic polities are thus able to offer more choice in almost all fields than is available under other forms of governance. In authoritarian and traditional societies or organizations, some thinkers are not permitted to express their ideas at all, and some groups are not allowed to be organized because they *might* engage in prohibited activities.

Democratic states and organizations usually provide more opportunities to experiment and to consider. Although many of the groups or subgroups that spring up at one time or another in democracies are ultimately rejected by the society as a whole, or even by their sponsoring organizations, those that survive often contribute substantially to the quality of life. Similarly, some ideas that initially meet condemnation are accepted later.

The freedom to experiment and debate has often allowed democratic societies to benefit from the activities of functional groups that were at first disapproved by governmental authorities, popular majorities, or both. Among such organizations that met initial rejection in many countries are private foundations that engage in welfare and research, women's sports groups, labor unions, businesses that lend money, and religious bodies of many kinds. In the realm of thought, numerous philosophical conclusions and research findings that initially were condemned by powerful authorities and public majorities, such as some ideas of Socrates, Galileo, and Darwin, have become widely recognized as both truthful and useful.

◆ ◆ ◆

The relative superiority of democracies in adjusting successfully to environmental change is suggested by the rapidly declining numbers of aristocracies and traditional societies in recent centuries, and the increasingly short lives of authoritarian regimes in general. As of the year 2002, the annual survey by New York's Freedom House found that 121 of the world's 192 independent countries had governments that, in theory at least, were freely elected. Prior to the First World War, at the beginning of the 20th century, only a handful of such governments could be found. One reason for the growing number of democratic or partially democratic states is presumably that these forms of government are more successful in giving more people what they want.

Whether or not it can be convincingly demonstrated that democracy is a major factor in the ability of a society to satisfy human wants and needs, people almost everywhere increasingly appear to think so. A review in 2003 of recent public opinion polling data from more than 50 countries in Europe, Asia, Africa, and Latin America found that majorities almost everywhere agreed that democracy is preferable to any other governing philosophy. The major exception was Russia, where only 29 percent of the respondents chose democracy and 34 percent said that "in certain situations an authoritarian government can be preferable." Perhaps more significant is that 37 percent of those queried in Russia chose the alternative: "It makes no difference to people like me." (Lagos, 2003, p. 475) When surveys were grouped by regions, the following figures emerged: In Northern, Western, and Southern Europe, 75 percent of respondents voiced support for democracy; in Africa the figure was 70 percent; in Eastern Europe 61 percent; in Asia 59 percent; and in Latin America 55 percent. (*Ibid.*, p. 474)

The author of the article in which these results were reported, who is founder and director of the MORI polling organization in Chile, cautions that percentages may vary considerably as a result of small differences in question wording, and that people in different parts of the world define democracy differently. For example: "In post-communist countries, the ideal type of democracy will more likely be associated with liberty, while in Latin America it could be associated more with equality." (*Ibid.*, p. 471) Translation of a questionnaire from one language to another introduces additional variables. Nevertheless, if one disregards fairly minor percentage differences, various polling organizations give similar pictures of attitudes throughout the world. For example, the World Values Survey, coordinated by the University of Michigan, found that 67 percent of Chinese respondents were "rather satisfied" with the way democracy was developing in their country, while the East Asia Barometer recorded 52 percent as being "fairly satisfied". *(Ibid.*, p. 484) Both polls tell us substantially the same thing: democracy is a relatively popular symbol in China.

But, as Lagos observes, a popular symbol may mean different things to different publics. Furthermore, when democracy is suddenly imposed on a society, this sometimes provides opportunities for majorities to persecute or to settle scores with unpopular ethnic minorities, as happened in Serbia, Croatia, and Rwanda. (Chua, 2003) Observers of the current situation in Iraq worry that some forms of democracy might allow the majority Shiites to use the machinery of government to take revenge on the Sunni minority, which provided Saddam Hussein with his principal source of support. Nor are all versions of democracy equal when it comes to promoting cooperation and making optimum use of the human potentialities that are available in a population.

Nevertheless, the increasing number and durability of states that can be classified as democracies, together with the popularity of democracy as a symbol, does give grounds for a degree of optimism. With all its limitations, and despite lack of agreement on precisely what democracy is, governmental systems that embody at least some characteristics of democracy are more likely than competing forms of governance to encourage creativity and free communication and to provide for the development of qualified personnel who can operate complicated functional groups in complex societies. One can hope that definitions of democracy that favor these three processes will ultimately be adopted everywhere. All societies will then be better able to adapt to rapid environmental change and to provide their members with greater opportunities to develop their capabilities and satisfy their aspirations.

Or perhaps we are unduly concerned with labels. If more efficient ways of organizing human beings to help each other get what they want and need, no matter what these forms of organization are called, what we now know as democracy may prove to have been only one stage on the road to a more satisfying life for the people of the world. Other forms of governance that are even more favorable to creativity, communication, and the development of qualified personnel may still be devised.

6

A Peaceful and Democratic World Society?

More and more indicators suggest that all humanity will eventually belong to a world society. What kind of society will this be? Will it be based primarily on institutions of democracy? Or will it rely more on authority and tradition to ensure that people of the world work together to satisfy at least the minimum requirements for human existence? Will the world society be a peaceful one, or will it suffer from violent internal conflicts? Are present national identities likely to fade away?

It is the conclusion of this essay that some form of democracy will win out in the long run, although this does not mean that a worldwide democratic order will necessarily be established soon. Authority and tradition may experience substantial but temporary, resurgences at any point. Wars, or violent conflicts of other kinds, tend to concentrate power in the hands of authoritarian governments, which may endure for many years. Powerful religious bodies that emphasize tradition as the most important organizing principle for functional groups of many kinds—not only for groups concerned primarily with worship—may gain influence temporarily. Failure to control greed and criminal behavior may undermine the trust necessary for the formation of democratic institutions and complex functional groups in general. If people come to expect that only relatives and a few close friends can be counted upon to speak the truth and to cooperate in functional groups, both authority and tradition may temporarily become more realistic organizing principles than democracy. Sudden population explosions or steep declines in birth rates may lead to conditions under which functional groups are no longer able to satisfy more than minimal human needs. These and contingencies of other kinds—perhaps natural disasters—may delay the emergence of a democratic world society for many generations, but will not stop it.

This world society will also be an increasingly peaceful one. Violence will not be eliminated, but will become less frequent. Nevertheless, the process of global integration will cause hardships for many individuals and also for powerful functional groups. As a result there will be continuing tensions and controversies, even though these will less often lead to warfare.

Confidence in the eventual success of democracy and in the increased use of nonviolent methods for resolving conflicts is based on two assumptions. First, no matter what happens, the great majority of human beings will continue to want and to strive for benefits that can be assured only by thousands of disparate functional groups, many of which are highly specialized. Second, these functional groups are most likely to develop and prosper in a world society that is based on democratic principles and is able to reduce violence to the lowest possible level. Thus, even though authoritarianism, traditionalism, extreme nationalism, and various combinations of the three may gain ground throughout the world from time to time, in the long run they will be unable to compete with the vision of a peaceful and democratic international social organization.

While ethnic and national identity will more rarely be among the causes of violence, they are unlikely to fade away. They will remain a source of pride for large numbers of people in many nations and will help to assure that each society retains unique characteristics—although not necessarily the same characteristics that are currently dominant.

Indicators of the Developing World Society. Following the dispersal of human beings throughout this planet they gradually became involved in a process of global integration that is likely to proceed, with ups and downs, for the foreseeable future. As this process continues, most of societies we know today (usually identical with nations) will become less and less self-sufficient. Few, if any, large groups of people will be able to live the way they want to live without increased attention to and interaction with people from other parts of the world. Much as the diverse functional groups in any one society have gradually become shaped so that they complement each other, or at least can coexist, all nations will have to find ways of adjusting to or cooperating with each other if they are to survive and prosper.

The trend toward a world society has been reinforced by the fact that all humanity is gradually acquiring the characteristics of a single huge functional group. The three requisites for group formation—ideas, communication networks, and qualified personnel—are more and more being satisfied on a global scale. Nearly all earth dwellers, whether they realize it or not, now have access to a variety of ideas about what a global society might be like. Also, a gigantic international communication network now exists. It consists of personal ties and transportation facilities, as well as of mass media, telephone, and the World Wide Web. Substantial proportions of the earth's population are now in touch with each other, directly or indirectly. During the past century, millions of people have become personally involved in international communication—this privilege is no longer limited to a small elite. Also, personnel qualified to work in the institutions of a global society are increasingly available. Millions of people are learning rules and roles appropriate in multiethnic and multinational functional groups, and are helping to develop more rules and roles that are appropriate for these groups. Such people can be found in business, national governments, international public and private agencies, religious bodies, and educational institutions.

A seemingly contradictory trend at the present time is the concurrent growth of nationalism among ethnic groups within established national states. At the same time that interdependence among societies that previously were fairly self-sufficient is increasing, numerous ethnic minorities within existing societies are demanding greater autonomy or even sovereignty. Thus there are, or have recently been, separatist movements in Great Britain, Canada, Spain, Russia, China, Turkey, and elsewhere. The former Soviet Union, Czechoslovakia, and Jugolavia have broken into smaller states, mostly based on nationality. The former colonial empires of European states turned into a large number of independent states after the Second World War.

However, demands for a more distinct political identity are not inconsistent with greater international interdependence. Indeed, more autonomy for minorities and the emergence of additional sovereign entities are often facilitated by trends toward a world society. One reason for this is that an independent nation or an autonomous region now requires a lower level of self-sufficiency than was previously the case. Military power and economic diversity, especially, are less important than they used to be. Many smaller nations rely on other countries and on the emerging international system not only for protection but also for food and other basic material requirements. If threatened, they are likely to seek help from the United Nations or other international bodies. Ethnic minorities seeking independence in Kosovo, Chechnya and elsewhere appeal to international public opinion for support. The number of independent nations may continue to increase, but their interdependence is likely to increase at the same time.

. International business ventures and multinational political ties are the most visible manifestations of global integration, although their extent and influence tend to fluctuate from decade to decade. Indeed, downward fluctuations can be very large, and have led some authorities to conclude that the trend toward globalization might be reversed. Two writers for *The Economist,* for example, have pointed out that the terrorist attack on New York's World Trade Center in September,

2001, could lead to events similar to those that followed World War I. Just prior to that war, the trend toward globalization seemed unstoppable, they point out. "Who could resist new technologies [of that time], like the telephone, the airplane, the car and electricity? Or the logic of free trade, guaranteed by the acknowledged hegemonic power, Britain?" (Micklethwait and Wooldridge, 2003) The two writers conclude, however, that in spite of these innovations, which seemed to promote closer international relations, the aftermath of the First World War saw a contraction in the world's economies and also the rise of Hitler, Mussolini, and Stalin, all of whom made efforts to increase national self-sufficiency. Might the War on Terrorism nearly one hundred years later also result in setbacks to globalization? New security checks have hampered the expansion of international trade, the United Nations has been weakened, and cordial relations among the Western powers have been damaged. A dissenting view about the effects of the "Great War" of 1914-1918 has, however, been expressed by some social scientists who concluded that this conflict brought major nations closer together, even though their increased interdependence was not necessarily based on friendly ties. (Lasswell, 1927)

Slowing globalization is possible in the short run, whatever one concludes about the effects of major wars. But if one looks at a longer sweep of history, it appears that setbacks of even several centuries have been followed by events leading to still greater interdependence. After each setback, the number and strength of ties binding nations to each other tend to resume their growth and to become even more significant. The few international business and political connections that originated thousands of years ago, when travel and communication facilities first made it possible for peoples living far apart to satisfy some of their needs and desires by drawing on the resources of other societies, have burgeoned into millions of relationships. In recent history, the scope and authority of United Nations agencies have far outstripped those of the former League of Nations.

Current criticisms of globalization, which have been stimulated especially by the movement of jobs from industrialized nations to low-wage countries, agricultural subsidies that make it difficult for farmers in developing countries to compete with those in richer societies, and worldwide marketing of consumer goods do not necessarily represent a slowing of the trend toward a world society. They are in themselves an important multicultural activity involving cooperation among demonstrators from many parts of the world. Indeed, members of the organizing committee for the anti-globalization protesters at the annual World Social Forum, held in Bombay in 2004, told reporters that about 80,000 people from more than 100 countries were taking part in the protests. (*New York Times, Jan. 20, 2004*) In the previous year, protesters at the Group of Eight summit conference in Switzerland had demonstrated their internationalism by spray-painting slogans in four languages on buildings, bus stops, and fences.

A cause of the rapidly increasing international cooperation is that more and more of humanity's problems can be addressed successfully only if many nations work together. This usually involves coordination of the activities of governments, and private international organizations also are frequently involved. The problems to be dealt with include control of crime and disease, regulation of fisheries and the oceans, reduction of atmospheric pollution, administration of the worldwide Internet (including the assignment of addresses and the fight against worms and viruses), and security in general. Not all efforts to deal with such questions through cooperative action are successful, but even the fact that an international attempt is made to find a solution for a particular problem often represents a new development. A senior political scientist observes that: "since no government can do everything by itself, interstate organisms have emerged. The result, which can be termed 'global society,' seeks to reduce the potentially destructive effects of national regulations on the forces of integration." (Hoffman, 2002, p. 110)

For example, the United Nations Convention against Corruption, signed in Merida, Mexico, during the last days of 2003, requires participating nations to assist in finding and recovering money that has been stolen or embezzled. In the following March, the U.N. Security Council also took action along these lines by voting unanimously to freeze the assets of former Liberian President Charles Taylor. Will the U.N. actually be able to help poor countries recover funds that corrupt officials have looted and attempted to launder in foreign banks? What happens in the case of Charles Taylor may provide an indication.

A number of developments not directly related to specific governmental actions or to international trade have also made different societies more dependent on each other. One such development is that more individuals than ever before now participate in functional groups that include people from several countries and ethnic groups. As has been noted in previous chapters, the number of formally organized international associations has doubled every few decades during the past century. Vast numbers of people from various societies are beginning to cooperate with each other, thus increasing the degree of international dependency.

One reason for the increasing interest in international associations may result from the vast population movements from one country to another. For example, dual citizenship has become more and more common. According to Washington's Center for Immigration Studies, 90 percent of the more than one million immigrants who enter the United States each year come from countries that allow some form of multiple citizenship. A political scientist at the City University of New York, Stanley Renshon, estimates that about 40 million Americans are eligible to claim citizenship in another country as well. (*Washington Post*, Jan. 19, 2003) Almost 100 countries, including Australia, Ireland, Israel, and Mexico, now allow some form of multiple citizenship, and as of 2003 India was reported to be planning to follow suit.

We don't know what proportion of the world's dual citizens take an active part in the political processes of more than one country, but the numbers are probably substantial. When there are elections in San Salvador, candidates from that country often campaign for votes in New York and other North American cities.

The family, also, is becoming more international in many parts of the world. According to a survey by the *Economist* (Nov. 2-8, 2002), foreign mothers account for one out of five births in Switzerland, and one in eight in Germany and in Britain. And at about the same time Japan's Ministry of Health, Labor, and Welfare reported that one in ten Japanese marriages involved a foreigner. (*New York Times, July 31, 2002*) In the United States, interethnic as well as international households have become much more common in recent decades. In 1960, there were about 51,000 black-white married couples in the country, and by 1998 the number was 330,000—more than a six-fold increase. (Kennedy, 2003, pp. 126-27) This is still a tiny proportion of the total 55 million married couples in the United States, but the rate of increase is impressive. The number of black-white households would presumably be substantially larger if one included unmarried couples who are living together.

Similar trends can be seen in other categories of functional groups. All major religious bodies have adherents in several parts of the globe. Soka Gakkai International, based on Buddhism, claims a membership of some 18 million people in 115 countries. (Lester, 2002) The Cao Dai, based in Vietnam and blending elements of several religions, has more than three million members in 50 countries. (*Ibid.*) Major Christian and Moslem denominations have adherents, and often missionaries, all over the world. Scientific, professional and artistic associations, large and small, tend to ignore national boundaries. Athletic and sporting events bring together citizens of many countries, both on the contending teams and among the spectators.

Despite terrorist activities and anti-terrorist measures, the number of students involved in international education remains impressive, and appears still to be rising. Fifty public universities in the United States, which responded to a survey, reported that they had a slightly larger number of undergraduate students from abroad in 2002 than in 2001, and that numbers of foreign graduate students had increased by over 7 percent. According to the Institute of International Education in New York, nearly 600,000 students from other countries were on American campuses in the academic year 2001-2002, and a record 154,000 American students had studied abroad during that year—more than double the number that had studied abroad ten years earlier. (*New York Times,* Nov. 18, 2002)

Not surprisingly, many fewer students from abroad filed applications to enter American colleges and universities in the fall of 2004, in part because of more troublesome visa and security measures. A survey by the Council of Graduate Schools found that applications from China had fallen by 76 percent and those from India by 58 percent. However, universities in Australia, Great Britain, France, and elsewhere appear to be enrolling substantially more students from other countries, so that international education may still be increasing. In Australia, for example, overall foreign student enrollment was up over 16 percent, and the number of students from China increased by 20 percent. (Gates, 2004)

Many activities involving people from different national and ethnic groups—whether business, professional, or educational—probably lead to an increase in international and interethnic friendships, although no estimates of the numbers of people involved are available. What is happening can be inferred, however, from studies of racial diversity in schools in the United States. For example, one recent study concluded that "a substantial increase in racial diversity in schools will lead to a notable increase in cross-race friendships, relative to present levels." (Quillian and Campbell, 2003, p. 561) Of course, instances can be found where international and interethnic activities have stimulated hostile feelings, too, but these appear to be exceptions to the usual course of events.

The formation and operation of multinational functional groups has been facilitated by greatly augmented international communication channels. These have developed as a result of new scientific and engineering capabilities combined with more public demand and the increasing numbers of people who can speak "world languages." Air travel, telephones, radio/television, and the World Wide Web have allowed masses of people—not only small elites—to maintain contacts with relatives and others who are members of distant communities. Schools in nearly every country require that students become familiar with one or more major languages. In previous centuries, small numbers of traders, scholars, and the well born could converse with members of other linguistic groups in French, Latin, Greek, Arabic or Mandarin Chinese. Now, nearly all young people who have had more than a few years of schooling, wherever they live, have at least some acquaintance with languages other than the one of the community into which they were born. With each passing decade, more and more people have jobs or social relationships that involve crossing national borders frequently—in some cases, almost daily.

Some effects of new communication technologies in modernizing societies are illustrated in India, where "e-choupals" (electronic market places) have been established in thousands of tiny villages. Computers in the e-choupals facilitate new contacts among functional groups in various parts of the world. For example, they enable soy bean farmers in India to check prices of commodity futures on the web site of the Chicago Board of Trade, thus helping the farmers determine when to sell their crops. The company behind this innovation, ITC Ltd., hopes eventually to use these new centers to sell many kinds of merchandise, including tractors. (*New York Times,* January 1, 1904)

The development of new international functional groups has raised interesting questions about their management and control. For example, how should the directors of the Internet Corporation for Assigned Names and Numbers (ICANN) be chosen? Should anyone in the world with an e-mail address be eligible to vote? According to an American foundation executive, an ICANN election in 2000 showed the impossibility of assuring global representation through direct elections, but also made it clear that some way of representing the international public interest would have to be found. (Baird, 2002)

While many such questions remain unanswered, a body of rules governing behavior when dealing with those from other cultures has gradually been growing. Diplomats and international business people, especially, have developed techniques for getting along with each other and working together with minimal friction. Tourists often consult handbooks that advise them on how to behave abroad. International law increasingly limits, or purports to limit, what sovereign states can do. Courts in one country more frequently claim jurisdiction over those who are accused of committing crimes in other countries.

One striking example of the way law more and more tries to leap national boundaries occurred in 2001, when a Spanish judge requested Great Britain to extradite a former dictator of Chile on the grounds that he had committed crimes against humanity while in office. (The request was ultimately refused, but the significant fact is that it was made and then taken under serious consideration. Two years later, the same judge succeeded in gaining approval for a former Argentine military officer accused of crimes against humanity to be extradited from Mexico to Spain.) A number of other countries, including Israel, Belgium, and the United States, have adopted laws that, in theory and sometimes in practice, enable their courts to reach beyond national borders. For example, in December, 2002, Australia's highest court authorized an Australian businessman to sue an American publisher for libel in Australia. This was said to be the first decision of its kind in any country. (*New York Times, December 11, 2002*) Development of international behavioral codes has been advanced also by bilateral and multilateral arrangements among national states—e.g., in regard to copyrights of books and other intellectual property.

New international judicial and regulatory bodies, some affiliated with the United Nations or other multinational bodies and some independent, continue to be organized. As of July, 2002, an independent International Criminal Court opened its doors in The Hague. Created by the Rome Treaty of 1998, it received the required ratification of 60 nations in less than four years, and was authorized to try cases concerning the abuse of human rights anywhere in the world. United Nations Secretary General, Kofi Annan, was quoted as saying: "We hope it will deter future war criminals and bring nearer the day when no ruler, no state, no junta and no army anywhere will be able to abuse human rights with impunity." (*New York Times, July 1, 2002*) Whether or not the new court will be successful in its efforts to defend human rights remains to be seen, especially in view of the resistance of the Bush administration in the United States. Nevertheless, it is one more significant indicator of the trend toward a world society. In April, 2004, an international court established by the North American Free Trade Agreement overruled a judgment of an American court, which had ordered a Canadian firm to pay damages for breach of contract to an American family in Mississippi. An American law professor, Peter Spiro, was quoted as saying that this pointed to "a fundamental reorientation of our constitutional system. You have an international tribunal essentially reviewing American court judgments." (*New York Times, April 18, 2004*)

The principle that people everywhere should enjoy certain inalienable rights is already widely accepted, and is gradually becoming embodied in law and exemplified in practice in more and more national states. When a government, in effect, makes war on its own citizens—as in Cambodia under the Khmer Rouge or in Iraq under Saddam Hussein—loud protests can be heard in many parts of the world, and sometimes sanctions are applied or other actions are taken. Rules are gradually emerging about things that national or regional governments must do or cannot do, even though these rules may not be formalized in laws or treaties. Developments that tend to reduce national sovereignty are reported in the press with increasing frequency. The above illustrations represent only a small sample. .

Such indicators of an emerging world society are significant not so much because any one of them suggests a sudden and massive change but because there are so many of them—all pointing in the same general direction. They also continue a well-established trend For example, earlier steps toward an international society, such as those linking states that formerly belonged to the British or French colonial empires, were also based in part on shared cultural, humanitarian and democratic principles. Some of these principles were embodied also in the North Atlantic Treaty Organization and the European Union. Nazi Germany and the Soviet Union, too, seemed to anticipate a world that would be increasingly unified under the leadership of their respective nations, although on the basis of very different principles. In one case, the unifying factor was to be the dominance of "racially superior" peoples and in the other the acceptance of socialism as practiced in the USSR.

Visions of the future increasingly incorporate assumptions about growing international interdependence. For example, a principle that, if widely accepted, would hasten development of a world society was outlined in a 2003 Task Force report of the (nongovernmental) Council on Foreign Relations in New York. The report concluded that, once the people of a state choose democracy as their preferred form of government, other democracies have the right and the duty to help these people maintain their democracy when it is threatened by either domestic or foreign aggressors. Statements of several administrations in Washington have suggested somewhat similar ideas to the effect that democratic nations may have an obligation to intervene in order to promote both peace and freedom in other parts of the world.

The trend toward a world of increasingly interdependent nations does not mean that a global government will be formed within the next few generations—unless aliens from outer space bring such a government about by launching an attack on humanity. People in different areas will continue to live under different conditions for the foreseeable future, and will cherish different inherited traditions. Separate national and regional governments will be able to serve most human needs and desires more efficiently than one global colossus. Instead of the emergence of a world government, it is likely that the machinery of cooperation among national governments and nonofficial social organisms of many kinds will continue to expand and improve. Such a course of development is suggested by the situation in Europe, where powerful multinational European institutions have already been established for some time. After reviewing public opinion survey data from 19 European countries, two Australian social scientists conclude that "there is no sign that national identity is weakening in Europe in favor of a unified European identity," and that "cross-national diversity is clearly present…" (Evans and Kelley, 2002, pp. 304 and 330.)

Nevertheless, some national differences will disappear, or at least will become less significant, in a world society. For example, if agreed basic human rights come to be observed in all nations, migrating from one country to another may increasingly be like moving from one province or community to another within a national state. And there will probably be fewer minorities struggling to create new mini-states. Since political conditions everywhere will be more similar, the benefits of formal independence will be smaller and may not be sufficient to justify the costs.

Emergence of an international society does not mean that there will be cultural uniformity throughout the world. Indeed, the opposite will be true. Most individuals will be able to choose among a greater variety of beliefs, functional groups, and life styles in the pursuit of happiness and the development of their capabilities. Already there are many large cities in which one can move from one cultural milieu to another by walking a short distance. Many societies now offer their members choices among various styles of literature, entertainment, music, cooking, clothing, art and architecture. There is less cultural uniformity within national states.

In the world of the future, traditional ways of doing things that once dominated are less likely to disappear than to compete with new modes of behavior. Just as the world society will be composed of a large number of smaller societies, and individual societies will become culturally less uniform, many smaller social units (e.g., families and schools) will offer their members a wider variety of choices. There will be new possibilities for choosing friends, subjects for study, jobs, marriage partners, and life styles.

The likelihood that individuals will have more choice does not mean that the various national societies will present their members with the same menu of possibilities. Different traditions, historical experiences, and environments in each area will ensure that the various societies and most nations retain a unique cultural mix. The fact that the United States, Canada, and Mexico include a growing number of people who profess Buddhism, Islam, or Hinduism, while India, China, and Pakistan are experiencing increases in the availability of fast-food outlets and rock-music recordings, does not eliminate differences between Asian and North American cultures. Rather, cultural importations increase the choices available to members of the various societies on both continents. Some North Americans find that they benefit from the teachings of previously unfamiliar religions, while some Asians appreciate the advantages of having a quick lunch and enjoy the stimulation of imported musical styles. It is not unlikely that many people will become more and more enthusiastic about the unique cultural mix provided by their own society (as indeed is already the case in the United States), and that in this sense diversity may strengthen rather than weaken national identity within the world society.

Prospects for Peace and Democracy. Just as pressures for the emergence of a world society will continue in the future, whether such a society develops quickly or over a longer time period, forces favoring a peaceful and democratic world will not go away. As with the world society, there probably will be temporary setbacks to peace and democracy, but the long-term prospects for a worldwide increase in both are good.

Some reasons for this relatively optimistic outlook have already been mentioned. Peaceful and democratic nations are more likely to survive over the long run than are authoritarian or traditional societies. Not only are the former able to adjust more easily to changing environments; they can make better use of the talents of their individual members to provide the things that nearly everyone wants. Democracies are thus spared some of the pressures that lead to violence and instability in other societies, where those who are deprived of the good things in life often see war against more prosperous nations and/or rebellion against their own rulers as the only ways to a more tolerable existence.

The growing popularity of democracy suggests that it is likely to play an increasingly important part in the world of the future. Even though popularity by itself is an unreliable predictor of events, it is often a relevant factor in shaping the future. The World Values Survey, based on data from more than 100,000 interviews conducted in several waves on six continents between 1981 and 2001, found democracy to be considered "the best form of government" almost everywhere. Somewhat surprisingly, respondents in Arab countries were even more enthusiastic about it than were those in West Europe, Latin America, or North America. (Inglehart, Basañez and Moreno, 1998; Norris, 1999; *Washington Post,* April 28, 2002) Subsequent surveys, especially in Latin America, found a decline in the popularity of democracy; many respondents indicated that it had not improved their living conditions and thought that an authoritarian alternative might do better. Fluctuations of this sort can be expected, and are unlikely to alter a gradual trend toward democracy over the longer term.

Such findings do not tell us how different people define "democracy," but they do indicate the general direction in which people hope their societies will move. Furthermore, the increasing numbers of states that became classified as democracies during the past few decades, especially in Latin America, Africa, and Asia, suggest that some of these hopes are being realized. A Freedom House 2003 survey, which has already been mentioned, found that 121 independent countries (out of 192 recognized states) had at that time more or less freely elected governments. Of these 121, only 89 were classified as "free countries." The other 32 were classified as "partly free." Nevertheless, the rapidly increasing acceptance of at least some of the ideas identified with democracy has been impressive, especially if one considers that only a handful of nations could be identified as democracies 100 years ago.

Along similar lines, a political scientist notes that the world became markedly more democratic during the second half of the 20th century: "This is true if democracy is considered a dichotomous property...[or] is taken to be a matter of degree. Most countries became more liberal in the final decades of the twentieth century, even if they did not all have fully liberal political systems." (Mandelbaum, 2002, pp. 251-52)

Nor is the popularity of democracy likely to suffer from the fact that democracies are usually seen as providing a better quality-of-life than states with other forms of government. For example, the 2003 Human Development Report of the United Nations ranked 175 nations of the world according to an index based on a combination of per capita income, education, health care, and life expectancy. Norway was at the top of the list, followed by Iceland, Sweden, Australia, the Netherlands, Belgium, the United States, and Canada. Most observers would find multiple reasons for the attractiveness of life in these countries, but the fact that they are all among the relatively old-established democracies is noticeable. (*New York Times,* July 9, 2003) Similarly, the Freedom House 2002 survey found that the world's 89 free countries controlled 89 percent of the world's total Gross Domestic Product. (*Washington Post,* December 25, 2002) A forecast that preferences for democracy will continue to exercise a strong influence on the world of tomorrow is not difficult to defend.

In this connection, the *Economist* makes an extraordinary statement to the effect that "no democratic country with a free press [one of the key characteristics of democracy], no matter how poor it may be, has ever suffered a famine. Unfettered reporters provide early warnings, and accountable governments know they have to respond to emergencies." (July 31, 2004, p. 69) Although diligent critics might find exceptions to this generalization, it is consistent with a widespread tendency to associate democracy with material sufficiency.

The idea that increasing democracy will diminish violent conflict within and among societies of the future is more controversial. Indeed, the 19th and 20th centuries, during which the number of democracies rapidly increased, also saw several of history's most destructive wars—in which many new and old democracies participated. Further, some students see democracy as sometimes "detonating" violence when it is suddenly introduced into societies such as the Philippines, where most citizens live in extreme poverty while a Chinese ethnic minority controls most of the nation's wealth. (Chua, 2003, p. 263,) This creates a situation that is "extremely unstable." (*Ibid.*, p. 269)

When free trade policies, which are also among the likely hallmarks of the world society, are combined with democracy the resulting mix can be even more volatile, especially in cases where societies that are already poor are further impoverished by their inability to compete economically with industrialized nations.

An emphasis on problems resulting from increasing globalization and democracy is not, however, the same thing as predicting a return to previous patterns of government and international relations. Rather, these problems are usually seen as difficulties that must be overcome if people in less developed parts of the world are to benefit from the emergence of a world society. For example, Chua suggests that more effort be devoted to finding ways to "level the playing field" both within developing countries and for trade between modernizing and complex industrial societies. (*Ibid.*, p. 264) She does not advocate a return to previous conditions.

Another seasoned international observer who is concerned about conflicts likely to be caused by the combination of globalization, democracy, and free trade suggests that, in new democracies, delegation of decision-making powers to organizations that are shielded from day-to-day pressures may be a partial solution. He notes that non-elected bodies, such as the Supreme Court and Federal Reserve in the

United States and the World Trade Organization and European Union on the international level, are likely to enjoy greater public confidence than do elected legislatures and executives, and that more use of such bodies might be made in developing countries that are not ready for full exposure to the contending forces in a democracy. (Zakaria, 2003) He comments, somewhat facetiously, I hope: "The world has made more economic progress in the last fifty years than in the previous five hundred. Do we really want to destroy the system that made this happen by making it function like the California legislature?" (*Ibid.*, p. 246)

When it comes to the question of whether the world of tomorrow will be more peaceful than the world of today, numerous students of international affairs share the viewpoint that violence is increasingly becoming outmoded. A political scientist sees peace, democracy, and free markets as likely to provide organizing principles for international relations in the current century. (Mandelbaum, 2002) An influential columnist argues in a recent volume that war is no longer an efficient instrument of policy, in part because the destructiveness of nuclear weapons would make great power conflicts so costly as to be unthinkable and in part because partisan or guerrilla warfare has diminished the usefulness of modern weapons. (Schell, 2003) Some researchers have concluded that human beings are not biologically driven to make war. (Angier, 2003) No consensus has been reached, but more and more observers of world politics are finding that cooperation now yields more benefits than conflict and that peaceful ways of reconciling differences are gradually becoming more efficient than violence.

Threats to Democracy and Peace. While there is reason to believe that interdependence among societies and nations of the world will continue to grow in decades and centuries to come, it will certainly not grow always at the same rate. And is it likely that there will be periods when the world becomes less rather than more peaceful and democratic. Indeed, there may be times when development of a democratic and peaceful world society slows or even goes into reverse. If, for example, there is widespread acceptance of the idea that simpler and less complex societies are preferable to those in the industrialized nations, and that humanity would be better off without so many specialized functional groups, it would then theoretically be possible to recreate a world where the behavior of people in one geographical area would be irrelevant to inhabitants of other areas. Such a situation would make war more profitable, and could continue indefinitely, again in theory. Nevertheless, while possible, this scenario is highly improbable unless basic human characteristics should change. Curiosity, and the desire for better food, good health, and more material conveniences, would be difficult to restrain indefinitely. It is more likely that the creation of additional specialized functional groups and the resulting gradual social integration of the world's inhabitants will be slowed from time to time.

Three developments that could inhibit or temporarily reverse development of a peaceful and democratic world society will be considered here: intense and widespread violence, whether resulting from guerrilla or conventional warfare; a steep decline in the extent to which human beings trust one another; and population imbalances that result from very high or very low birth rates.

. The most immediate threat to trends toward peace, democracy and a world society is the possibility of destructive and protracted wars. Such conflagrations could be ignited by minor wars or by assassinations, suicide bombings, and kidnappings conducted on a large scale. Nations that perceived themselves as being nibbled to death by small wars or terrorism would see no reason why they should not raise the level of violence. They would have nothing to lose. As the level of violence increased, other nations would be drawn in when they perceived their vital interests to be at stake. Nuclear, chemical, and biological weapons would almost certainly be used, in some cases by relatively small groups allegedly unaffiliated with any recognized government. Conventional military capabilities, even if very great, would by themselves be unable to contain widespread violence, sabotage, and stubborn non-cooperation in many parts of the world.

Under such conditions, functional groups not directly related to offense, defense, and bare survival would gradually be deprived of all but minimal human and material resources. Families would be severely disrupted. Educational institutions would be starved. Freedom to innovate and experiment would be limited. The quality of life everywhere would be reduced. Successive emergencies would drive many countries back to dictatorship or other authoritarian styles of government. There probably would be no victors in such wars of the future. Even if a stable peace could be reestablished, few if any nations would be in a condition to give other nations substantial help in rebuilding. Simpler lifestyles everywhere would diminish pressures toward international cooperation.

Increasing the probability that there will be periods of sustained and destructive warfare is the fact that emotion still plays a powerful part in human affairs. (Massey, 2002) Even though its role in social life seems to have decreased somewhat during the millennia that *homo sapiens* has existed on this earth, leaders who wish to use violence to achieve their goals often can appeal successfully to nationalism, ethnic prejudices, or religious bigotry.

A second course of events, which could undermine a world society and lead to deterioration in the quality of life for nearly everyone, would be ignited if dominant behavioral codes throughout the world should change in such a way as to cause more and more people to distrust those with whom they previously cooperated. An economist has pointed out that a tendency to mistrust strangers is strongly embedded in the human psyche, but that at the same time economic life in modern societies is dependent on mutual confidence among huge numbers of individuals, most of whom do not know each other and perform very specialized tasks. (Seabright, 2004) It is probable that an increase in suspicion of those outside the extended family, the community, or the nation would lead to decreases also in noneconomic values such as security, knowledge, and justice.

Loss of trust would be particularly disastrous for democracies, which rely more extensively than other forms of governance on voluntary coordination of efforts in the formation and operation of complex functional groups. The World Values Study of 1990 showed a strong positive correlation between interpersonal trust and the functioning of democratic institutions throughout the world. "In most stable democracies, at least 35 percent of the public express the opinion that 'most people can be trusted;' in almost all the nondemocratic societies, or those that have only recently started to democratize, interpersonal trust is below this level." (Inglehart, 1997, p. 173) Societies in which authority and tradition play a larger role would be less affected, and it might be necessary for some nations that previously had been democracies to return to these forms of government in order to survive.

Existing (but usually unwritten) behavioral codes of many varieties already contain injunctions that tend to restrict or undermine mutual trust. Children in some communities learn as they grow up that only extended family members should be relied upon, or that one should be suspicious of people who belong to other religions or ethnic groups. There are regions where residents use one set of standards in dealing with each other, and another set of standards in relations with outsiders. If, especially in industrialized societies, more and more people come to hold that any behavior not specifically prohibited by law is moral and that it is acceptable to defraud others if a legal loophole for fraudulent behavior can be found, willingness to invest and to take risks in general is threatened. The belief that cooperative efforts are unimportant in achieving individual goals—that winning is the most important goal and that success is due largely to the individual's intelligence, unscrupulousness, and toughness—is already widespread in many cultures, as evidenced by such aphorisms as "nice guys finish last." If attitudes such as these become the norm, the effects on cooperative behavior—and on civilization in general—would be disastrous.

Behavioral codes that stress otherworldliness can likewise be a threat to cooperative behavior. Functional groups providing more than the essentials for survival are difficult to sustain if enough people come to believe that, since life is short and worldly things unimportant, one should ignore other human beings insofar as possible and devote one's efforts to following religious routines or philosophical principles that are believed to assure admission to heaven.

Apathy and destructive suspicion are strengthened when there is a perception that almost everyone else is disobeying a society's behavioral codes that were formerly respected—when people come to believe that dishonesty is increasing or is endemic in business, government and other private and public bureaucracies. Individuals tend to conclude that there is no reason for them to behave in a moral fashion if nobody else does. Disillusionment with allegedly cynical politicians leads many people to stop voting and to avoid participation in public affairs. Contributions to charitable organizations dry up following news stories about waste or embezzlement by those directing these organizations. And stocks decline when managements of large corporations are found to be cheating their shareholders and employees. A degree of suspicion is normal in most societies, and can be beneficial, but when suspicion burgeons and affects more and more decisions of society members, the outlook for prosperity, democracy, or a world society becomes dim.

Some social scientists see a trend toward increasing fraud in American society, whether among automobile repair mechanics, professionals, or business people (Callahan, 2004), and several public opinion surveys indicate that more and more high school and college students accept cheating as behavior that cannot be avoided in modern life. One researcher found that, in the year 2000, 34 percent of the high school students he surveyed agreed with the statement: "A person has to lie or cheat sometimes in order to succeed." Two years later, 43 percent agreed. (*New York Times,* October 4, 2003) It seems quite possible that this decline in standards was stimulated especially by the accounting and other scandals in large corporations that received front page attention in the American press during the relatively brief time between the two polls. In 2004, the *Washington Post* reported that Internal Revenue Service polls "suggest that the share of Americans who think it is acceptable to cheat [by evading taxes] has risen from 11 percent in 1999 to 17 percent in 2003. At the same time, the IRS has been starved of the resources it needs to go after evaders."

Not surprisingly, a growing decline in mutual trust in the United States has also been documented. In the late 1990s, public opinion researchers found that about 80 percent of Americans born before 1933 said they agreed with the statement that "most people are honest," while—in contrast—about half of those born between 1946 and 1960 (one-third of the adult population) denied that most people were honest. (Putnam, 2000, pp. 140-41).

A loss of trust may be occurring in other democracies also. As of 2002, 44 percent of a sample of Germans over 60 told poll takers that "most people can be trusted," but only 35 percent of a sample drawn from those between 16 and 29 agreed. (Noelle-Neumann and Koecher, 2002, p. 87) A decline of confidence in the major institutions of West Germany was registered in slightly earlier surveys. Between 1991 and 2001, the numbers of respondents who said they trusted schools, legislatures, the administration (government's executive branch), unions, large businesses, and newspapers all declined by about 10 percent. (*Ibid.*, 619)

It is interesting that there were some similar declines in East Germany (which in 1991 had only recently emerged from rule by an authoritarian communist government), but also some major differences between the two sections of the country. Confidence in the police increased by more than 20 percent among East Germans, and there was a slight increase of confidence in the civil administration, while trust in the churches declined sharply. (*Ibid.*) These differences between the two parts of Germany may be explained, at least in part, if one assumes that, prior to reunification, many people in the east saw the police and civil administration as instruments of oppression and saw the churches as institutions that shared their opposition to the political regime. After reunification, the new police and administrative agencies looked good in contrast to their predecessors, while the churches were seen as having much less political significance.

Loss of confidence in fellow human beings has been accelerated also by domestic and international terrorism. Even when this level of violence does not escalate to the point of warfare, it makes people cautious about air travel, living or working in tall buildings, and associating with those who look foreign or act strangely. Suspicion of other people has been augmented especially by the use of suicide bombers to kill random civilians in hotels, busses, train stations, housing developments, and shopping centers.

Suicide bombing is a particularly disturbing escalation in the cycle of violence, in view of the fact that it has proved possible to recruit people who are willing to blow themselves up in many different countries and for a wide variety of causes. The World War II Japanese air force, Viet Cong assault troops, Tamil Tigers, Palestinian extremists, and militant advocates of various religions and languages have all been successful in finding substantial numbers of volunteers for suicide missions. In his classic book, *The True Believer: Thoughts on the Nature of Mass Movements,* Eric Hoffer (1951) pointed out half a century ago that enthusiasts willing to sacrifice themselves or to murder others could be found in the ranks of those advocating all sorts of causes—even causes many people would consider trivial. Hoffer's gloomy conclusions are supported by recent studies. Polls of Moslems in various countries from Algeria to Indonesia show increasing support for suicide bombers, and a United Nations report states that as soon as the United States began preparing for the Iraq invasion, al Qaeda recruitment "picked up in 30 to 40 countries. Recruiters for groups sponsoring terrorist acts tell researchers that volunteers are beating down the doors to join." (Atran, 2003) Recent studies have emphasized that suicide bombers are in most cases rational individuals who often have considerable education. They do not necessarily belong to groups suffering from deprivations. Some come from high status families. (*Ibid.*)

When attitudes and behaviors that support people's willingness to cooperate are weakened, no matter for what reasons, it becomes more and more likely that harsh methods will be used to assure at least the minimum coordination of individual efforts needed if a society is to survive. These methods include forcing people to assume roles in the economy and the armed forces and also restricting freedom of communication and persecuting those who advance unorthodox ideas. Such measures lead to a decline in the ability of many social organisms to satisfy needs and desires of society members. Institutions that remain reasonably efficient are likely to be those serving the interests of elites.

A third situation, which can both promote and inhibit development of a world society, depending on how it is handled, is created when nations lose the desirable balance between functional groups and population. That is, a society's birthrate should be high enough to ensure that there will be hands and brains to operate and possibly to gradually expand schools, businesses, sporting clubs, religious bodies, and other social organisms, but not so high as to overwhelm these institutions. At present, numerous countries in both industrialized and developing parts of the world have lost this desirable balance.

If current fertility rates should persist, according to a United Nations report entitled *World Population 2300,* there would be 134 trillion people on the earth by the year 2300—or one million individuals packed into each square kilometer. The report notes, however, that the earth could not sustain such a population, and that fertility rates are coming down. Nevertheless, the report also forecasts that the populations of the world's poorer countries will grow from 4.9 billion people to 7.7 billion during the next three hundred years and that the birth rate in most industrialized countries will continue to be below replacement level. (*Washington Post,* December 9, 2003) This forecast, while somewhat reassuring, suggests that population trends could still lead to wars and other major disasters and thus tend to undermine both peace and democracy in the emerging world society.

If families in a developing country are very large, it becomes difficult, even though not always impossible, to organize and expand functional groups fast enough to serve the needs of the rapidly growing population. Most parents who have large families are unable to prepare their children to learn skills and values that are necessary if the children are to move into the demanding and specialized roles of a modern society. Children from such families who are fortunate enough to attend schools therefore start learning at a lower level than is the case when parents are able to help give their children a head start. Societies in which the education of women is discouraged discriminate against children of both sexes. The widespread practice of keeping older children in large families at home to take care of the younger ones, rather than encouraging them to attend school, also makes it more difficult to train personnel to staff specialized functional groups.

Unduly low birthrates, too, threaten democracy and a peaceful world society. When there are too few qualified young people to fill entry positions in the work force, as well as unpaid roles in other sectors of society, a country's economy may contract. Or, there may be mass immigration into that country from areas where the birth rate is high and jobs are limited. Either way, new problems result. On the one hand, reduced numbers of young people make it difficult to maintain existing functional groups that provide necessary services, such as care for aging members of the population; on the other hand, sudden influxes of immigrants are likely to overtax institutions of the host society and lead to resentment on the part of native-born citizens and (only slightly later) to complaints by the new arrivals that they are being treated unfairly.

Even when "guest workers" can find jobs, the host society's schools, hospitals, religious institutions, recreational facilities, mass media, and other functional groups may be unable to take care of their nonmaterial wants and needs satisfactorily. Workers from abroad often come without their families, so that they lack this source of support also. When immigrants try to satisfy their needs by organizing their own political and economic functional groups, they are then likely to be seen as threatening the culture of the host society. This is especially the case if the immigrants are numerous and are given the right to vote. Under such conditions, numerous members of the host society will support authoritarian leaders who are willing to sacrifice some of the institutions of democracy in order to uphold existing cultural patterns. There will also be pressures to limit population movements, and leaders emphasizing radical nationalism are likely to emerge. Again, a spiral is started that could eventually lead to dictatorship and a more primitive social organization.

Of the two imbalances, the one that arises when population size increases too rapidly for functional groups to satisfy the needs of more than a small elite is a greater threat to peace and democracy. Where the birthrate is low, many of the resulting tensions can be lessened fairly rapidly by even a temporary slowdown in immigration and by the ability of receiving societies to find alternative ways of staffing essential functional groups. In some areas of the United States where the birthrate is low, for example, the need for foreign workers has been reduced by increasing mechanization, by making greater use of the energies of teenagers and senior citizens for such tasks as gardening and crop picking, and by increasing the pay for unskilled labor.

Problems that arise because of very high birth rates are more difficult to deal with. Many women may want fewer children but do not have access to the information and materials that are necessary for the practice of birth control. And unless the birthrate falls and the creation of new jobs and new functional groups of many kinds is speeded up, the imbalance increases with each generation. Mass starvation can be prevented by charitable aid from more prosperous nations, but food imports alone do little to prevent serious threats to peace and democracy. The more privileged members of developing societies that have very high birthrates are likely to support more and more repressive governments, which then take stringent measures to control the political activities of growing masses of poor, frustrated, and unattached young people.

In previous centuries, when population levels in a society increased to the point where existing natural and social resources were insufficient to satisfy needs, this did not necessarily lead to a severe imbalance between functional groups and numbers of people. The balance could be maintained if whole tribes were killed off by more powerful tribes, which then took over their hunting or farming territories, or if a previously flourishing society was reduced in size by starvation and epidemic diseases. As long as arable land was obtainable by discovery or conquest, large numbers of people could fairly quickly satisfy their needs by creating simple functional groups in these areas. One reason the huge population increases in North and South America during the 19th and 20th centuries, caused by both high fertility rates and massive immigration, could be accommodated was that the new arrivals, and also the abundant children of previous settlers, were able to quickly form homesteads and villages in fertile areas of the two continents. Family farms and small enterprises in the villages took care of both material and nonmaterial needs; indeed, large numbers of immigrants experienced an increase in the quality of life.

Another reason a more severe population/functional group imbalance did not occur throughout the world during the 19th and 20th centuries was that rapid industrialization was occurring in parts of Europe, Asia, and the Americas. The development of larger and more varied functional groups in these areas made it possible for more people to live well in the cities, too. Many nations were able to satisfy the needs of their growing populations by organizing new industries and businesses, building more schools and cultural institutions, and expanding their armed forces and government bureaucracies. Such complex organizations could be organized with amazing rapidity, inasmuch as the intellectual and scientific achievements of the 18th and 19th centuries—as well as the spread of democracy—had led to a rapid growth of conditions favorable to the establishment of new functional groups: namely, plenty of available ideas, better communication channels, and increasing numbers of qualified people. Whether current scientific advances will eventually lead to additional jobs is more doubtful, especially since some new knowledge enables more work to be done by smaller numbers of personnel.

The development of more and more complex and specialized functional groups in modern societies has weakened the tradition that large families should be encouraged. It has become evident that the survival and prosperity of a modern nation, family, or business depends less on numbers than on appropriate education and good use of human capabilities. Declines of birthrates in Europe, North America, and Japan have been hastened by this realization, and also by the opening of more career choices to women, by the increasing economic and emotional costs of rearing and educating children, and by pressures on parents to spend more and more money on goods and services that they see as necessary for a comfortable life. Government policies have also played a role. For example, China has slowed population growth by a "one-child-per-family" policy, and has also encouraged rapid industrialization that can take care of the needs of more people without more territory. Nevertheless, even in complex societies, the "more-babies-are-better" tradition lives on among members of some religious and ethnic groups.

Although the rate of population growth has begun to slow in less developed parts of the world during recent decades, there are still many nations where functional groups are being overwhelmed by growing numbers of young people. This is true especially in societies where religious and sometimes political authorities support traditions formed during the long period when survival and prosperity was linked to population size. Powerful pressures on both men and women, which have already been described, ensure that there will be many very large families. Meanwhile, birth-control information and materials are often unavailable.

In addition, many overpopulated traditional societies lack the economic influences that tend to restrict family size in complex societies Families in developed countries usually find that each child represents an additional expense and often causes loving parents to make major sacrifices. In very poor traditional societies, on the other hand, more children can mean more security and even more income for the family. A dozen children begging on the streets can bring in more money than one or two. Also, since it is often the case that each child receives a small allotment of food from the government or from international charitable organizations, a large family may be better fed than a small one. Nor do more children raise family expenses appreciably. There are few educational costs when schooling is not available, or when a simplified form of education is provided free or for a nominal sum by religious, military, or political bodies. And, when a dwelling can be constructed from mud or waste materials in an urban or rural slum, the costs of housing a large family and a small family are about the same. In addition, parents with many children have a better chance of being cared for in old age. As William Diebold, for many years director of economic studies at the Council on Foreign Relations, has described the situation, "with the birth of each child the family becomes a little richer and everyone else in the country becomes a little poorer."

Until the population/functional group imbalance in developing countries can be slowed and eventually corrected, the resulting mass misery is likely to cause continuing domestic unrest, to fuel terrorism, and to increase the danger of major wars. Since the needs of only a minority can be adequately cared for by existing or quickly created functional groups, there will be constant political and military struggles among the "haves" and "have-nots." One authoritarian government, nearly always protecting the "haves," will be followed by another. Wars may result if leaders in any country attempt to use their high birthrates to force other nations to surrender land or wealth.

A shortage of jobs and schools in most societies that have very high birth rates tends to strengthen the link between violence and rapid population growth. One student of international relations, noting that a very large proportion of people under 24 years of age live in developing countries and will be looking for (nonexistent) jobs during the coming decade, has written that terrorists "whether in Afghanistan or Colombia or Indonesia, are united by the fact that the vast majority of them were recruited from places where a burgeoning youth population sees hope as more of a taunt than a promise." (Rothkopf, 2004) And a *New York Times* correspondent in Africa reports that increasing numbers of youths from Sierra Leone, Liberia, Guinea, and Ivory Coast "are now schooled in nothing but the art of destruction." (May 5, 2003) Unless the very high rates of population growth in many developing countries decrease, and the organization of additional and more specialized functional groups in these countries can be speeded up, these population imbalances will continue to be serious threats to peace and democracy.

It can thus be argued that greater democracy throughout the world, a better life for everyone, and increased international cooperation are by no means guaranteed by present trends toward peace and democracy. Instead, countertrends fed by wars and terrorism, by deteriorating mutual trust, and by population imbalances point in a different direction. The world of the future, according to this pessimistic viewpoint, could be one in which most or all societies are dominated by small elites; and most people are severely restricted in the degree to which they can develop and use their potentialities. Widespread dissatisfaction in these societies, combined with the ambitions of their rulers, would lead to frequent domestic disturbances and international wars. New ideas that are unwelcome to the elites would be suppressed, and communication channels would be controlled. A downward spiral in the quality of life for most people would begin. Intercultural ties and international cooperation would decrease as simpler lifestyles and more limited aspirations reduced pressures to form additional specialized functional groups. The trend toward a peaceful and democratic world society would be reversed.

This doleful scenario suggests that the current era, in which more and more people are able to develop and use their talents and to lead satisfying lives, is a temporary blip in human history. For thousands of years it was considered normal—and sometimes God's will—for authoritarian or traditional leaders to control their people, for the strong to oppress the weak, for powerful societies to obliterate or absorb less vigorous ones, for little more than the basic needs of most people to be satisfied, and for the contending elites that dominated tribes or states to fight each other for resources and territory at great cost to their unhappy subjects. Why should we look forward to the arrival, sooner or later, of an era that would differ so markedly from nearly all preceding eras?

It could also be argued that the populations in a nondemocratic and unpeaceful world of contending political units would not really be so miserable. There are many people alive today who believe that most of us would be happier, and certainly more virtuous, if we could live in simpler societies where everyone would be compelled by pious and authoritarian rulers to adhere to the same strict moral codes. Such societies have existed and have prospered in the past, according to this viewpoint; and there is no reason they could not succeed even better today. They would be able to provide more adequately for human wants and needs than were past authoritarian societies, inasmuch as benevolent rulers could eliminate both vice and waste and, by taking advantage of modern science, could ensure that everyone had at least minimal necessities and comforts. Limited democracy might even be possible, as long as those chosen to rule adhered to the approved principles of morality. In short, perhaps reasonable living conditions for everyone could be guaranteed without allowing freedom of thought and communication and without opening opportunities for an advanced education to more than a relatively few children of privileged families. Such societies would consist, essentially, of a relatively small, virtuous, and enlightened elite group of leaders, on the one hand, and masses of happy, reasonably prosperous, and moral bureaucrats, professionals, farmers, and workers, on the other.

Some of today's political leaders, including both peaceful ideologists and terrorists, seem to have such a vision of the future, based partially on their visions of past history. They are convinced that, if they could persuade or force people to comply with certain behavioral codes, it would be possible to build stable societies free of contemporary vices and that virtuous people would have a better life in such societies. The Roman and Chinese empires of classical times may have conformed to this model in some respects. Everyone knew his or her "place," and was well advised to stay in it. Later, Muslim empires flourished under strict Islamic law, and Spain dominated much of Europe and the Americas in the days of the Inquisition. In the Soviet Union of modern times, where ideologists were expecting the emergence of a "new Soviet man," almost everyone had a job and enough to eat. Why should history not repeat itself?

Probability of a More Democratic and Peaceful World. Despite these visions of an attractive past, and the serious threats posed by war, distrust, and population imbalances, the conclusion of this essay is that the secular trend toward a peaceful and democratic world society will continue. There are at least four reasons for this relatively hopeful point of view. First, in the global environment that has been developing during recent centuries, democratic states have increasingly become more stable, prosperous, and powerful. If one accepts the propositions about functional groups that have been advanced in this essay, the general direction in which human societies are likely to move during the next few centuries is fairly clear. It is now rational behavior for a nation to be as peaceful and democratic as possible. If following these policies increases the probability of surviving and prospering by even a small degree the policies will pay off in the long run, just as a 51 percent probability of winning a game of chance guarantees a favorable outcome if one is able to play long enough. Contributing to the stability of democratic nations is the fact that they are better able to allow individuals who are so inclined to lead simpler lives and follow their own moral codes. States based primarily on authority or tradition are more likely to experience difficulties in allowing deviant minorities to live according to their own principles.

Second, competing forms of governance based predominantly on tradition or authority have been unable to offer benefits to rival those provided by democracies without undermining their own power bases. Under modern conditions, enforcement of old-established roles and rules of behavior often stimulates eventual change. For example, when women are restricted to child bearing and household duties, and when modern medicine is available at the same time, the resulting population growth makes it necessary for the societies in question either to search for new ways to feed and accommodate increasing numbers of people or to control the population by more police power. If the former path is chosen, the need for innovations will lead to the development and testing of new ideas. Creativity will have to be encouraged and freedom of communication is likely to be increased. Nor can solutions be implemented unless more and more people have access to a better education. All these measures are likely to undermine authoritarian controls. If, on the other hand, stricter controls are adopted, these are likely to engender violent outbursts and uprisings. Either way, the efforts of authoritarian regimes to avert disaster will make it more difficult for those in power to maintain total control of their populations and will increase the likelihood that more democratic political institutions will eventually develop.

Furthermore, the legacy of the past includes not only restrictive behavioral codes but also ideas that are unsettling to both tradition and authority. Some of these ideas can be traced to ancient Egypt and China, Palestine, and Greece. Reformers in predominantly Muslim nations can find precedents for many innovative proposals in the work of the 14th century North African historian and social scientist, Ibn Khaldun, among others. (Ahmed, 2003) Those who seek to modernize forms of governance in less developed countries can often present themselves as traditionalists if they wish to do so.

Third, technological developments have for the first time made a world public opinion possible, and this growing body of opinion is likely to exercise continuing pressure in favor of peace and democracy. Many of the same innovations, especially in the field of communication, have also facilitated the growth of international functional groups of many kinds. These new groups are not confined to business and intergovernmental organizations but include also professional and artistic societies, groups of friends, and even international families. Thus, large and growing numbers of people—many of them influential—have a substantial stake in preserving and enlarging a peaceful world where individual freedom is maximized.

Fourth, the last several thousand years—and especially the most recent five hundred—have disclosed the remarkable potentialities of human thought and the exciting achievements that are possible. Even in the face of draconian measures to revive the authoritarian or traditional past, there will be people everywhere who will remember a "golden period" when at least some societies were organized in such a way that more needs and aspirations of population members could be satisfied, and where more human capabilities could be developed. These memories will ensure that societies and functional groups based primarily on traditional or authoritarian principles will experience continuous internal pressures to offer their populations the benefits that are remembered as having been made possible by peace and democracy.

One cannot predict the speed with which changes in the present world order will occur, or forecast more than a few of the implications of humanity's transformation into a single gigantic functional group composed of individuals, nations, and societies. But several observations are possible. One is that progress toward a peaceful and democratic world society is likely to be delayed from time to time, even though not halted, by the threats discussed above: namely, wars, distrust, and population imbalances. Unfortunately, current United States government policies may have increased rather than reduced these threats, and may have already delayed the emergence of a more peaceful and democratic world society by several decades, if not generations. This is especially true of the use of military and police power in ways that stimulate the recruitment of terrorists, and the relative lack of emphasis on peaceful and cooperative efforts to control violence.

A further observation is that some mostly positive steps taken toward the development of a world society can also cause delays. Democracy and free trade have already exacerbated ethnic hatreds and have caused economic hardships in many developing countries, as pointed out by Chua (2003). Problems are caused by other implications of globalization, too. Lives can be shattered when people face the necessity of changing their jobs or careers. Parents are saddened when they see their children abandon old and valued traditions. Small businesses do not necessarily enjoy being gobbled up by international corporations. Devout believers in a religion will have difficulty accepting the notion that other faiths should be able to reach out to people who are likely to benefit from them.

It will take time to solve such problems, too, although it is also necessary to note that these problems differ in character from the wars, frauds, and population imbalances discussed above. The difficulties resulting from the gradual emergence of a world society are part of the costs of building a better future for the world's population, while the threats to a world society carry no such promise. Those who point out problems arising from the introduction of greater democracy and more free trade, and help to solve these problems, may actually speed up the emergence of a world society. On the other hand, those who start wars, undermine trust, and fail to recognize the problems caused by population imbalances can delay, even if they cannot stop the advent of a more peaceful and democratic world society.

Of course, conceptions of democracy may change as time goes on. This is because the various processes and structures now associated with democracy—such as elections, legislatures, courts that enforce the law, and executive agencies with limited powers—do not automatically ensure formation of functional groups that serve the greatest good of the greatest number. What is important is that the various forms of democratic governance have usually been reasonably hospitable to creative thinking, to the development of communication channels that allow full and accurate information flow, and to the establishment of institutions that enable people to discover and use their highest capabilities. If other systems of governance should prove more efficient at providing these basic requisites for human cooperation, then democracy as we know it today might become outmoded.

While the development of a more peaceful and democratic world society on Planet Earth will take time, there are measures by which its emergence might be hastened. Some of these are outlined in Part II of this essay. They include large and small actions by governments, educational institutions, and people in general. Whether these suggested measures and others that have been suggested elsewhere do or do not have merit can probably be determined by those who reach maturity during the next few decades. The 21st century should in any case prove to be a fascinating century in which to live.

Part II

Practical and Impractical Applications

The model of society outlined in the above chapters contains few surprises. Most people would agree that, if we are going to satisfy our material and non-material wants and needs, and build increasingly complex civilizations, there must be many specialized social groupings in which individuals and organizations are able to work together. These "functional groups" make the necessary coordination of effort possible. It is only common sense that ideas, communication channels, and qualified personnel (including skillful leaders) are essential if efficient functional groups are to exist. Nor is it unreasonable to conclude that, in times of rapid change, these social organisms must often be adapted to new conditions, and that some adaptations are better than others.

Our model, while simple, has a number of possible utilities, some of which will be outlined in the following chapters. (1) It suggests criteria that can help us judge whether the decisions we make in the course of daily life, both big and small, will advance or inhibit development of the kind of world we want to live in. (2) More specifically, the model points to policies that might enable governments at all levels—and leaders or managements of multifarious private functional groups—to serve more efficiently the needs and aspirations of their members, controllers, or the public. (3) Similarly, it may stimulate ideas about ways in which educational institutions might improve their ability to prepare people for roles in some of today's and tomorrow's functional groups. (4) It may be useful also to individuals who want to evaluate, and possibly redirect, their own participation in functional groups, so as to make better use of their talents and realize more of their goals. That is, it may suggest "do-it-yourself" ways of improving the quality of your own life. (5) Finally, the model may highlight questions and problems that could be of interest to researchers and others who are looking for ways functional groups and whole societies might better serve human wants and needs.

Some of the following ideas can be classified as old hat or as common sense; others may appear to be untimely, impractical, or fanciful. But please don't reject such suggestions on these grounds alone. The purpose of constructing the models outlined in this essay is not limited to stimulating ideas that are novel, feasible, and timely. A manifestly impractical suggestion can sometimes be useful in helping to define where we want to go, even though we don't yet know how to get there. One aim of this essay is to encourage consideration of a broad range of alternative actions and policies that might improve the quality of human life. Hopefully, some of the criteria suggested by the models of social organization that have been described will assist us in judging policies already on the table. Or, the models may stimulate ideas which, although of little use under present circumstances, will be applicable at other times and places.

Nor should notions that seem trivial, or represent slight modifications of familiar formulas, or smack of illogic, necessarily be excluded from consideration. As to triviality, all of us are frequently confronted with the cumulative importance of small things that add to or detract from the goodness of life. We know that a single vote is unlikely to decide an election, but are also aware that electoral majorities are built one vote at a time. Similarly, we realize that traffic delays that are annoyances to individual motorists can, if added together, cause huge losses to the economy of a city or even a whole country. Educators would probably concede that a teacher who can find an extra five minutes to make sure a child understands an arithmetic problem has no discernable influence on the future of the nation, but might well be convinced that a like investment of time by many teachers could affect a society's future standard of living. Small changes in individual behavior can, when cumulated, bring about major social changes.

Qualitative, as well as quantitative, changes in existing practices—sometimes very slight—can also make a big difference. This is emphasized by the frequency of questions that cannot be answered satisfactorily by "yes" or "no," but only by answers that specify "how much?" or "under what conditions?" One example is taxation. Very few people oppose taxes altogether. Rather, arguments are likely to be over who should pay and at what rate. Or, attitudes about immigration and population cannot be described meaningfully by labeling some people as being "for" and others as being "against." In this case also, differences of opinion tend to be about degrees of permissiveness and rates of growth. Even thoughts about the desirability of freedom tend to be nuanced. Few people are opposed to freedom in principle, but most would also agree that complete freedom for everyone is impossible.. The judicially-inspired axiom: "Your freedom to shake your fist ends where my nose begins," is often cited.

Lack of consistency, too, is not necessarily a valid reason for rejecting a strategy. Indeed, many desirable social processes may require contradictory qualities or behaviors. It is usually assumed that functional groups will work better if their members share similar goals and behavioral codes, but it is also generally acknowledged that some of these groups must include nonconformists, critics, and innovators if they are to survive. Similarly, cooperation or harmony among a society's functional groups is important for the well-being of a society, but many of these groups perform better if they compete with each other, and thus are extremely uncooperative at times. Civility helps to avoid violent conflict, but successful adaptation to change requires vigorous criticism that often is impolite and causes bad feelings. Racial segregation of educational institutions is illegal in the United States, according to a Supreme Court ruling of the 1950's, but the court also provided that desegregation need not occur immediately but should proceed with "all deliberate speed." Seeming inconsistencies of this type may be unavoidable in well-functioning complex social organizations.

A final word of caution is that the menu of suggestions presented here by no means exhausts possible courses of action—bold or trivial, new or old, logical or illogical—that may be suggested by the models of social organizations that we have tried to construct. Only a few of the possible implications can be pointed out in a brief treatment such as this. Readers who have stayed with the discussion thus far are invited to think about additional applications. They are also urged to adopt a critical role and to identify weaknesses and fallacies in the discussion, as well as deficiencies in the pictures of society on which the discussion is based.

7

Everyone Can Affect the Shape of Tomorrow

We may be able to anticipate some likely characteristics of the world of the future, but exactly what this world will look like and when it will arrive depend heavily on what is done today. We have to place our bets now! The journey to a peaceful world society consisting of interdependent individual societies, each of which serves the needs and aspirations of its members well, will be shorter or longer, smooth or bumpy, depending on decisions made by millions of individuals. A small proportion of these individuals will be people of power and influence. Their decisions will certainly affect many significant developments. Probably even more important, however, will be the cumulative impact of what large numbers of "ordinary" people do every day in their families, work places, and neighborhoods, as well as when they vote, discuss, or demonstrate. The effects of these decisions and actions by masses of anonymous individuals will become evident more gradually, and it rarely will be clear just who was responsible for causing which effects. Suggestions in this chapter are intended to be relevant to people in both categories—those who are important and those who are anonymous—who wish to help strengthen the capability of their society to offer a more satisfying life to everyone.

Hard-headed realists may object that most people are so concerned with their own survival and well being that they can devote little attention to improving the lot of their neighbors. Only small minorities are inspired by visions of a peaceful world society, and even fewer can do anything to turn this vision into reality, according to this way of thinking. Realists are likely to point out that the strong have always oppressed the weak, and history shows that wars and destructive conflicts among ethnic groups and national states are always with us. Critics may believe that it is a waste of time to appeal to small and weak publics consisting of altruists. A more sensible course would be to look for ways to increase national power, build strong leadership, and ensure orderly societies guided by law and by time-tested moral principles that have served humankind well in the past.

But, are the realists actually being realistic? One can acknowledge that most people are preoccupied with assuring their own comfort and happiness—at least most of the time—and that wars and destructive conflicts have occurred constantly throughout history. But one can also recognize that idealists, altruists, and people of good will can be found at almost all times and places, and that nearly every individual shows at least some traces of generosity and kindness. Utopians, idealists, and reformers have proved to be a tough breed. They are almost constantly ridiculed, persecuted, and rejected, but they do not appear to have ever been completely eliminated from a society. Nor is there any indication that they will ever disappear or give up. And they may be more prevalent in today's world than before.

The analysis in this essay suggests that those who believe in the possibility of more responsive societies, and a more peaceful and democratic world, should constantly be asking themselves three questions. First, how can I help create conditions under which functional groups that are more likely to satisfy human needs and desires will emerge? That is, can I do anything to encourage creativity, to improve communication channels, or to assure a supply of qualified personnel, whether for families, businesses, or other kinds of social organizations? Second, might I be able to improve the structure or operating rules of some functional groups with which I am concerned so that they would do a better job in giving people what they want or need? And third, might it be possible to alter the relationships of these groups with other functional groups so that they would complement each other or at least would not become involved in destructive conflicts?

In the real world, nobody can take the time to consciously filter all major decisions, let alone minor ones, through a multilayered sieve of considerations such as the above. Nevertheless, sometimes we welcome explicit criteria against which to test a choice—as when deciding which of several candidates to vote for in an election, or when selecting a few organizations from among innumerable good causes to which to contribute money. More often, we become involved (sometimes without recognizing it) in creating, or obstructing, infrastructures for certain functional groups; improving, or degrading, the use of available human resources; and finding, or ignoring, ways in which people can work together most constructively. We all have some influence, and those who care might as well try to use it.

Building Infrastructures for Functional Groups of all Kinds. When we defend freedom of the press, or support an adequate budget for public schools, or contribute to private research and education, we are helping to shape an environment in which functional groups of many kinds can flourish. The same thing happens when we honor creative artists, encourage children to think as well as to memorize, and learn to know and to appreciate people from a variety of ethnic and national groups. It is obvious that nearly all of us can play a role in activities such as these if we want to. Equally obvious is that many of us can help to shape public opinion. And unless public opinion favors original thinking, an open communication system, and educational opportunities for everyone, it is much more difficult for new businesses, innovative schools, or needed neighborhood organizations to form, or for existing groups to adapt to new conditions.

At the same time, some kinds of behavior by members of the public (all of us) tend to weaken the infrastructure for functional groups. This happens when we try to silence people with new and possibly disturbing ideas, sabotage our society's communication systems, whether intentionally or unintentionally, or fail to support educational opportunities that encourage people to make the most of their talents. There are so many ways in which each one of us can either help or hurt the functional group infrastructure that it is impossible to list them all.

To give one example, we tend to weaken our society's communication system when we use expressions and concepts that are likely to be understood only by people like ourselves. Senior citizens in today's complex societies frequently complain that there are some subjects on which they have difficulty conversing with their grandchildren. Different generations often use different vocabularies. Misunderstandings between the sexes occur when communications do not convey the intended meaning. Men who are trying to compliment a lady on her appearance, or who want to share a tasteless joke, run the risk of being accused of sexual harassment. And there are cases where unfamiliarity with the meaning of a single word can cause trouble. A member of the Washington, D.C., city government was almost driven from office because he used the word "niggardly" in referring to an effort to save money. Such misunderstandings can never be eliminated entirely, but we can avoid many of them if we are aware of the problems than can arise when members of different groups use different vocabularies

In complex societies, especially, people who belong to the professions and to specialized groups of many kinds find it more and more difficult to communicate with members of other groups, and with the general public. This is partly because each specialty develops its own technical terminology for internal communication, and this esoteric vocabulary is then used when speaking to outsiders who are unfamiliar with many of the expressions used. Those who write instructions on how to operate computers are especially likely to make this mistake. And not only outsiders are likely to be confused by specialized terminology. Misunderstandings within functional groups increase also, as more and more previously homogeneous groups include people from varying backgrounds. This has happened, for example, in enterprises that now include both traditional administrators and temperamental scientists—sometimes referred to respectively as "suits" and "blue jeans."

Good two-way communication involves not only agreement about the meaning of words but also the ability to interpret nonverbal communication. This can be significant when people from different backgrounds try to cooperate. For example, it often is important to recognize that styles of clothing and ways of wearing hair and beards serve as vehicles for communicating ideas. These styles, which are traditional among members of some communities, can cause unintended messages to be sent to members of other communities. A Muslim woman who covers her hair in a predominantly non-Muslim society is unlikely to realize that many of those around her may interpret the message she is sending as "I am different from you," or "I am more pious than you," or "I have no respect for your customs." Similarly, foreign men resident in predominantly Muslim rural societies have found that if they lack a beard, or at least a mustache, they may be regarded as not having much in the way of either learning or authority. When they shave their whiskers, these foreigners send an unintended message.

Nonverbal communication resulting from changing fashions in complex societies can also cause misunderstandings. Children may be ostracized in school if they wear clothes that their classmates regard as inappropriate. Adults who are similarly out of tune with prevailing fashions may not be invited to join certain clubs or to take part in community activities.

Whether based on religion, tradition, or fashion, rules governing clothing, hair, and sometimes diet, tend to have positive effects on communication and cooperation under some conditions, and disruptive effects on functional groups under other conditions. In homogeneous societies and groups, they may promote cooperation by reminding people of values they share with each other. But in complex societies, non-verbal communications often send disruptive message to those with other traditions and preferences. Prominent displays of differences can retard both intergroup and intragroup cooperation.

At the same time that members of the public can unintentionally affect the quality of their society's communication network, they may also help to determine whether or not suitable personnel will be available to staff functional groups of various kinds. If people living in complex societies place a high value on education, respect diversity of opinion, and resist discrimination against those who have different backgrounds, the specialized functional groups in these societies are more likely to find the personnel they need. Conversely, if there is widespread prejudice against members of any population category, this tends to weaken the society by preventing qualified people from occupying roles for which they might be well suited. Societies in which public opinion prevents or limits the education of women, or of minority group members, are unable to take full advantage of the capabilities present in these segments of their population. All of us, in the course of our daily activities, can have a significant effect on the quality of personnel available to functional groups of many kinds.

For example, the ability of people to work smoothly with superiors or associates in associations of many kinds is likely to depend in part on child-rearing practices, in which most of us are likely to be involved at one time or another. Parents who encourage the settlement of disputes by discussion and negotiation help their children develop skills that are valuable when it comes to taking part in almost all functional groups. Groundwork that facilitates acquisition of many other skills and interests, also, is often done within the family or neighborhood. Similarly, parents and neighbors can either encourage or discourage creativity. Even in highly complex societies that have specialized educational institutions for the very young, day-to-day activities in the family and neighborhood are important in determining how well a society's functional groups will be staffed.

A Second Universal Task: Critiquing Established Groups. Almost everyone can become involved also in helping to make sure that existing functional groups work as well as possible, and even in designing new ones. Such involvement is particularly desirable at the present time. One result of the rapid social and physical environmental changes now taking place in most parts of the world is that many of the most important functional groups we have inherited from the past have to be revised. And it often happens that brand new groups have to be developed if newly felt needs or aspirations are to be served. Leaders and specialists take a prominent part in revision and innovation of functional groups, but nearly all population members have some influence on the process.

The need for revisions or innovations in functional groups is particularly noticeable in societies that are trying to modernize. For example, anthropologists doing research in American Samoa in the early half of the 20th century found that there were strict rules governing behavior at meals, as there are in most societies. "Titled people of appropriate rank eat together," they wrote. "Women and untitled men eat separately, usually later, and children usually last on the remaining pickings." (Keesing and Keesing, 1956, p. 79) These deeply ingrained customs sometimes caused problems when specialists, both titled and untitled, tried to meet to discuss a specialized subject. "The writers have seen a Samoan chief ask a younger untitled man to join…in an informal meal on a modern egalitarian basis as being 'all educated people.' The younger man tried again and again to swallow food but it would not go past his throat so that he almost choked on his respect, and finally the chief said: 'You had better go and finish your meal with the women and young men.'" (*Ibid.*) One can assume that, as more and more young Samoan men and women went abroad to study, these rules governing mealtime behavior became increasingly troublesome, and were gradually revised.

Western journalists, writing about the famine in Ethiopia at the start of the 21st century, became aware of somewhat similar rules which, they suspected, explained why they encountered many healthy adult males who had severely undernourished children. Especially in rural areas, it was customary for the men in a family to eat first, and for the women and children to dine on what was left. Again, one can assume that famine conditions persuaded many Ethiopians that these ancient mealtime customs weakened both the family and the whole society and brought pressures for change.

As these examples suggest, members of current generations in all parts of the world, to a far greater extent than their forebears, face the problem of determining how functional groups can be adapted to changing conditions. Usually, one can find reasons for the old rules of behavior, or can at least propound likely theories, but this does not mean rules should not be changed in light of new conditions. In earlier times, most environmental changes, especially social and cultural changes, occurred slowly enough so that most people could follow examples set by their parents and grandparents with confidence that they were doing the right thing. Today, by contrast, decisions about revising inherited procedures or creating new functional groups have to be made frequently. Nearly all of us participate, directly or indirectly, in some of these decisions, and in this way we influence the quality of life in our societies.

Adaptation to new environmental conditions is made more difficult by the fact that there may be agreement that changes are necessary but no consensus on what the changes should be. In addition, there is always the possibility that new ways of doing things may prove to be worse than the old ones. Thus, fear of disaster has often delayed decisions by farmers in developing countries to experiment with new crops and fertilizing techniques. The old methods could provide only a minimum existence to the family, it is true, but the new ones being proposed by the government or by foreign advisors might not work at all.

There is one category of functional groups in which warning bells are likely to start ringing when inherited procedures no longer work well—namely, business enterprises, and especially those in a competitive environment. When a business is losing money due to changes in environmental conditions, it can't survive if it continues to follow the same procedures as in the past—unless it is supported by a government or a private philanthropy. Many businesses therefore, as a matter of routine, review their structures and procedures frequently to see whether they should change some of their practices. Entrepreneurs tend to be constantly on the lookout for environmental changes to which they might have to adapt. It would be incorrect to conclude that all functional groups should operate the way a business does, but all societies would benefit if a substantial proportion of their members were to adopt a critical stance and ask from time: Is this group in which I am participating accomplishing what it should, or would it work better if changes were made? The question is often difficult to answer with confidence, but societies in which it is frequently asked are more likely to survive and prosper.

In the case of families, religious bodies, and governmental institutions, especially, it is often difficult to determine when inherited structures and roles have become dysfunctional. Further, there are likely to be emotional, religious, or political factors that make people resistant even to discussing whether the structures of such groups or the rules and roles that govern behavior in them should be revised. Nevertheless, it is often apparent that changes even in such "protected" groups have been made. In most societies, the power of family patriarchs has been greatly reduced and the rights of women have been increased. Religious bodies, while retaining many ancient forms, less often use violence to convert or kill those having different beliefs. Governments still collect taxes, but governmental powers less likely to pass from older to younger generations of the same family.

The family or household is one of the most ancient functional groups, and continues to be one of the most important, but it survives in increasingly diverse forms. In complex societies, most families retain at least some traditional characteristics, while at the same time both family structure and the roles of family members are in a process of redefinition. One recent survey in the United States finds that, while many aspects of family life today would look familiar to colonial Americans, during the past 150 years, marriage has become a less and less central event for most adults. There are many reasons for this, including longer life expectancy, the sexual revolution, and changes in the experiences of youth. (Coontz, 1992, pp. 185 ff.) As a result, new behavior patterns within some families have to be established. For example, in industrialized societies, millions of women now keep working at jobs outside the household for years after their husbands retire. This represents "a stage of the marriage relationship that's occurring for the first time in history," according to University of Minnesota sociologist Phyllis Moen. (*New York Times,* March 23, 2004) One can expect that many people are asking whether adjustments in family relationships are desirable in light of this new development?

Among the many questions regarding family organization that societies throughout the world now have to face as a result of recent environmental changes, two are especially critical. One is how households can be constituted in such a way as to assure the "right" number of babies and so as to also provide these children with the most favorable conditions for development and learning. In some traditional societies most families are organized so as to follow the old rule, namely: Be fruitful and multiply! In most industrialized societies, on the other hand, birth rates are well below replacement level, as women assume more and more positions in the job market and families find the rewards of having many children are exceeded by the costs. Achieving a balance between number of children and the capabilities of functional groups to satisfy the needs of a society requires new patterns of family organization in both cases.

The second question has to do with the way people define the family to which they belong. Is it an extended family that includes several generations, cousins, in-laws, and perhaps others? Or is it a nuclear family, usually consisting of two adults and their children, if any? The extended family has been a vital mechanism in most societies for most of human history. But the nuclear family appears to be better adapted to modern, complex societies.

A search for solutions to the problem of assuring the right number of children has been hampered by widespread expectations that birthrates will go down in areas of the world where they are still very high, even without changes in family organization. In addition, opportunities for migration have enabled some societies with both low and high birth rates to survive without major disasters. Another factor slowing change is the commonly held belief that the number of children in a family is a private matter to be decided by parents, perhaps with the advice of relatives and religious counselors. While it is easy to find arguments supporting the position that number of children is a private matter, this point of view ignores the fact that every member of a population is affected by the birthrate, and is likely to suffer if that rate continues to be too high or too low. Emphasis on privacy also tends to overlook the strong pressures to increase the number of babies that are still being exerted on individual families by many religious organizations, as well as by some political authorities and interest groups. Employers and landlords in complex societies, on the other hand, may use their influence to persuade couples to have fewer children. Most of us insist that family size is a private matter without considering either the urgent public interest or the ability of powerful outside groups to intervene.

What to do? Solutions to population problems that are both effective and politically feasible are unlikely to be found unless all aspects of these problems are freely discussed. Yet failure even to mention, let alone confront, difficulties caused by unduly high or low birthrates is almost routine in major news stories about education, immigration, terrorism, and poverty, and especially in speeches about these subjects by political leaders. It is not clear whether both politicians and the mass media are trying to avoid controversy when they fail to explore the relationship between rates of population increase or decrease and other problems, or whether they feel that their audiences will not be interested. Whatever the reasons for resisting discussion of population problems, these problems are unlikely to be solved without wars, mass death, and widespread misery unless thoughtful members of all societies are aware of them and cooperate in the search for patterns of family organization that help to achieve a balance between birth rates and functional groups.

The second question about how to organize families—whether a society should emphasize the nuclear or the extended model—brings up the problem of assuring compatibility with other essential functional groups in a society. It is fairly clear that the traditional extended family often harmonizes poorly with other important functional groups in modern, complex societies. One reason for this is that traditional family patriarchs usually speak for several generations and exercise control over nearly all aspects of the lives of those in their clans. Another is that the obligation of family members to help each other is so strong that it seems to justify breaking the law and discriminating against those outside the family.

The system of extended family governance can also prevent family members from taking advantage of opportunities offered by specialization and industrialization. These people may be unable to make use of their unique capabilities at the same time that specialized functional groups are finding it difficult to secure the services of the best qualified personnel. Young people in extended families may be discouraged from leaving a particular village or area, or from taking a job that involves travel. A patriarch in Iraq, for example, told a visiting journalist in 2003 that men in his extended family were advised not to become involved with strangers, since there was enough for them to do right at home. Another reporter in Iraq quoted a tribal chief as saying: "I told my children [he had 21 children and 83 grandchildren] not to participate in any outside groups or clubs. We don't want distractions." (*New York Times,* September 28, 2003) The same journalist noted that Iraqis frequently described nepotism not as a civil problem but as a moral duty. They found the idea that people should sometimes put public service ahead of family obligations to be absurd.

Traditional extended families also tend to reduce some of the advantages offered by democracy. If most members of such families vote in elections according to the dictates of the patriarch (as the *Economist* reports is now the case among some immigrant communities in Western Europe) the viewpoints of younger generations are greatly underrepresented, and the interests of women may not be considered at all. Further, the tendency of each clan to demand its "share" of political jobs makes it less likely that government officials will be chosen on the basis of their qualifications and records.

In contrast, members of nuclear families can more readily assume roles in which they are expected to have individual opinions, where frequent travel is involved, and where they are in close association with people from other cultural backgrounds. And because nuclear families usually have fewer children, parents can spend more time (and money) on helping these children get a good education, both in the very early months and years and when the time comes for specialization.

Nuclear families are increasingly becoming organized in several ways, depending on the preferences of their individual members, job requirements, and the environments in which they are located. Much as law and medicine have broken into hundreds of differentiated specialties during the past few decades, many kinds of family organization are emerging from the present confusion. Some households consist of two employed adults and no children. In others, a third adult is brought in to care for children. Increasing numbers of females are principal family breadwinners, and more men are learning to play a part in child care. Members of nuclear families are under less pressure to follow tradition and more often can ask themselves which course of action will allow them to use their unique qualifications and which choice will facilitate cooperative endeavors.

But the traditional extended family can satisfy some needs and desires better than nuclear families, even in complex societies. For example, in the United States, families at or near the poverty level often retain strong ties with large numbers of relatives, and children in these families gain substantial emotional satisfactions from the security and warmth of large family gatherings. Such satisfactions are denied children of more affluent parents who regard ties with relatives as less important and who rush their children about from one enriching or educational experience to another. (Lareau, 2003)

Similarly, extended families often can take better care of their older members than nuclear families can, although this causes new problems, too. A relatively recent development in complex societies is the emergence of numerous "sandwich families," usually consisting of two middle-aged adults who try to care simultaneously for both their own parents (and possibly grandparents) and also their children. These distraught couples sometimes see the traditional expanded household as one way of easing their burdens. It is possible also that greater emphasis on the extended family would help to reduce the very high divorce rate in complex societies and thus tend to assure more stable environments for young children.

Population balance and extended versus nuclear family organization are only two of many questions about the family that face today's societies. The proliferation of households headed by individuals of the same sex, and pressures by homosexuals for the same marriage benefits as heterosexuals, also present questions about family structure and the roles of family members.

Religion is another area in which almost everyone in modern societies is faced with many choices, whether or not they are conscious of this and whether or not they are actively involved in a religious organization. Religious doctrines and the structure and practices of religious bodies affect the performance of functional groups involved in government, education, and elsewhere. Although some people have concluded that religion is unnecessary or even undesirable in today's world, and assert that they are quite comfortable as non-believers, even their indifference amounts to making a choice.

As has been the case with families, new political, social, and physical conditions have forced reexamination of functional groups based on religious belief and has led to decisions about how much of the old to maintain and which innovations should be adopted if these groups are to continue satisfying important human needs and aspirations, or to satisfy them better. Criteria suggested by our schematic models of various societies, and by the directions in which these societies are moving, may be helpful in identifying elements in a religious tradition that tend to increase the efficiency with which other functional groups serve human needs and aspirations? The model may also help to determine whether some inherited ideas and practices in religious traditions make satisfaction of human wants and requirements more difficult.

To start with a few negative observations, powerful religious groups have sometimes made adaptation to changing conditions more difficult by resisting new ideas and by discouraging criticisms of the established order. In Christian churches, old hymns sometimes suggest that existing social arrangements are immutable. To cite an example, one venerable hymn text reads: "The rich man in his castle/The poor man at his gate/God made them high and lowly/And ordered their estate." Religious authorities in many societies have sometimes weakened the infrastructure that makes certain functional groups possible. They have discouraged creativity, limited the content of communication channels, and restricted training for specialized roles—sometimes preventing all but the most elementary education for women.

Some traditional religious doctrines and structures have inhibited the development and use of the full range of human capabilities by disregarding or denying personality differences and by ignoring the widely varying talents among individuals. For example, in many religious communities all married couples are under pressure to have children, regardless of their qualifications for parenthood. And, until the last few centuries, it was almost universally accepted that, ideally, all members of a given political unit should adhere to a single religion. Minority religions, if not actively persecuted, were merely tolerated. At a minimum, the official or dominant faith would have special privileges.

While now greatly weakened in most modern and some developing countries, the assumption that all members of a society should share a single religion still dominates parts of the world. Even more widely accepted is the idea that an individual should automatically assume the religious beliefs of his or her parents. As a result of such traditions, established beliefs, rituals and practices have frequently been forced on all members of a population, community, or family. The result has been that some individuals have found it more difficult to make the best use of their unique capabilities. Within some Christian communities, for example, painting the undraped human figure has been discouraged. And Robert Burns could scarcely have found an environment less hospitable to his sensuous ballads and sensual life style than the one favored by the Presbyterian religious authorities of his day.

Persecution of deviants on religious grounds has limited the contributions that talented but nonconforming people can make to a society as a whole, especially as creative thinkers. Not only artists have been discouraged. Scientists are still condemned for deviating from traditional cosmologies in fundamentalist Christian communities of the United States that reject the theory of evolution. Many religious traditions, by stressing otherworldliness, inhibit those who are inclined toward business and manufactures. And unknown millions of people in all parts of the world, to whom elaborate ceremonies and liturgies are meaningless, have been forced to waste incredible amounts of time.

These observations lead to a suggestion that would be fiercely opposed in many contemporary societies, but might be seen by some individuals as a goal for the future. Namely, a society as a whole is likely to benefit if each person is encouraged to find the belief system and religious affiliation best suited to him or to her. This suggestion flies in the face of dominant practices throughout history, but is in line with what is now happening among minorities in quite a few complex societies. Many parents and educators, often adherents of smaller religious bodies such as the Unitarians, have followed such policies and have found them viable. These advocates of religious choice have tried to ensure that younger people are fully informed not only about the traditions of their families and communities but also about other religious traditions. Children who have been brought up in this way are likely to feel free throughout their lives to choose among available alternatives. Such an approach helps to assure that religious dogma is less likely to prevent a society from tapping human resources that otherwise might never even be discovered. Those who are concerned with building a world where all people can cooperate peacefully in the search for a better life should be encouraged to stress the positive aspects of religious diversity and to point to the added strength of societies where anyone can practice a minority religion without feeling like an outsider.

An even more extreme suggestion is that the clergy, or other professional leaders of religious bodies, should see themselves not only as advocates and expositors of specific doctrines but also as impartial advisors to people who are looking for a spiritual home. Such an advisor might say to an inquirer: "You are certainly welcome to join us, but, in view of your personality and talents, you might be happier in one of the congregations down the street." While it is possible to visualize such a clergy person, examples are difficult to find in the real world, and they may not yet exist.

When it comes to promoting cooperation among people with different beliefs, the record of most religious bodies is poor. They have often been successful in motivating their own members to work together constructively, and have created impressive organizations to relieve suffering and promote education, but they also have histories of exacerbating intergroup and international violence. Under current conditions, whenever religious organizations demand conformity from all members of a community or society, or seek to impose their structures and beliefs on other peoples, the probability of destructive conflict increases.

As populations of industrialized nations become increasingly heterogeneous, claims of any religious body to a monopoly or to a preferred position become more and more disruptive. Yet this is not a sufficient reason to ignore the virtues of even the most aggressive religious communities. The fact that they have survived for more than a few generations is a strong indication that they are providing benefits that their adherents see as valuable. One problem facing contemporary generations is how to preserve the enormous psychological (and sometimes material) values that all major religions bring to millions of people, while at the same time promoting active cooperation, as well as constructive peaceful competition, among those with varying theological preferences.

Sharply contrasting with possible negative effects of inherited doctrines and practices are ways in which religious traditions help to create more responsive societies and enable people to cooperate with each other more efficiently. Behavioral codes specified by a variety of religions stress honesty, reliability, kindness, and generosity as important components of morality. In communities and societies where such principles are widely observed, it becomes more likely that functional groups of many kinds, whether families, businesses, government agencies, or other, will do a better job in satisfying the wants and needs of both their members and the public.

Religious institutions and doctrines have frequently helped societies make good use of their human resources in many other ways, and continue to do so. By stressing the worth of each individual, they help to reduce the probability that the poor and the disadvantaged will be abandoned and deprived of opportunity. Faith-based schools and charities provide both economic support and education to millions, thus enabling them to develop and use a greater proportion of their capabilities. Religious and philosophical traditions and groups encourage and strengthen large numbers of those who might otherwise give up hope.

They enable even larger numbers of people to withstand hardships and disappointments, or to overcome drug and alcohol dependency. Secular functional groups, whether government or private, which help people make better use of their abilities, often follow precedents and practices previously established by religious institutions. For example, religious missionaries from industrialized nations started public health and economic aid programs in many areas of the world well before the local governments did.

Although past records of major religious bodies in resolving conflicts, eliminating violence, and preserving peace are less distinguished than their aid programs, all such religions have at least some traditions that tend to encourage tolerance and nonviolence, such as injunctions that people should be slow to anger and should obey the law. Present-day advocates of peaceful conflict resolution, both within and among nations, frequently try to strengthen and extend these religious traditions, especially by promoting understanding and dialogue.

Numerous theological institutions are currently cooperating in efforts to improve communication among leaders and members of different religious traditions and to reduce the extent to which religious doctrines tend to hamper cooperation among people belonging to different religious groups. For example, at one recent interfaith conference in New York City (sponsored by Temple Israel, Saint James Episcopal Church, and Auburn Theological Seminary), religious scholars representing many traditions agreed that it is not enough for adherents of each religion to insist that it favors peace and tolerance. These adherents should also admit that some of their fellow believers use interpretations of ancient texts to justify persecution and violence. These misinterpretations should be recognized, confronted, and overcome. A Muslim participant in the conference, which by chance was held shortly after adherents of *Al Qaeda* had demolished New York's World Trade Center, put it most dramatically when he said that: "I may denounce them (Bin Laden and his supporters)…and even pray that they die of piles and (are) infested with the fleas of 10,000 camels.... We cannot, however, disown them."—that is, deny that they represent a religious tradition. (*Auburn Views,* Winter 2002, p.6)

Whether or not current efforts to reduce the extent to which religious beliefs and institutions divide rather then unite people within and among nations are succeeding is an open question. Horrible examples of bigotry are much too frequent and easy to find. What is indubitable is that religious beliefs and institutions embody a large and influential part of our heritage. How we shape them so that they serve human needs and aspirations under constantly changing conditions will influence the future. As a multi-disciplinary social scientist puts it: "...religion survives science as it does secular ideology not because it is prior to, or more primitive than, science or secular reasoning, but because of what it affectively and collectively secures for people." (Atran, 2002, p. 278) Much earlier, anthropologists had noted that "primitive man recognizes both the natural and the supernatural forces and agencies, and he tries to use them both for his benefit.... He knows that a plant cannot grow by magic alone,.. or a fight be won without skill and daring." (Malinowski, 1948, p. 32)

A challenge to generations alive today is to find ways to preserve and develop inherited religious structures and roles that help people cooperate in building more satisfying lives, and at the same time to reinterpret or replace religious traditions that fail to serve human needs or frustrate human creativity.

Government is a third major area in which the public can play an important role in efforts to improve the ability of major functional groups (usually official agencies) to help people achieve the values they want and to encourage the development of a more peaceful and democratic world. As with families and religious institutions, almost everybody is involved directly or indirectly in governmental processes and has a stake in their responsiveness to human needs and desires. And we all have at least a tiny influence on the shape of governmental structures and the ways officials perform their duties.

In democracies all adult citizens are, in theory, expected to adopt a critical attitude toward governmental institutions and to take a part in improving them. We are reminded of this every time there is an election, and the news media provide frequent reminders also. In authoritarian and traditional societies most people are not encouraged to criticize government, but they often do this anyway—although usually in private—because of their perceptions of injustice or because of hardships for which they blame their rulers or the system under which they are living.

The models of society we have tried to construct in this essay suggest two questions with which citizens of complex democracies should be particularly concerned: Which jobs should be done by functional groups that are part of government or under government control? And how can these jobs be done so as to yield the greatest benefits to the public?

When it comes to deciding who should do what, the principal advantage enjoyed by private groups is that they can adjust more quickly and easily to environmental changes, including new desires on the part of the public. Nongovernmental bodies are also likely to be more receptive to new ideas, and they can experiment more easily. These are among the reasons why it is a responsibility of good government to do everything it can to promote the success and efficiency of private groups that provide useful services, and also to regulate them so as to ensure maximum benefits to the public—for example, by encouraging competition among businesses. If this principle is followed, it tends to reduce the size and cost of government, although not necessarily government's scope or authority. However, our model also suggests that government should perform essential tasks that cannot be done as well by private bodies, especially when it comes to public order, defense, and security. Reasons for assigning primary responsibility for these and some other tasks to government will be discussed in more detail in the following chapter.

The second question concerns the efficiency of official agencies. This depends in large part on management skill, but also is heavily influenced by the attitudes of both civil servants and members of the public. How public officials and agencies perform their duties, and whether or not members of the pubic are satisfied or dissatisfied with government's performance, is determined in part by attitudes inherited from the past.

These inherited attitudes affect official agencies in different ways than they affect households or businesses. In the latter groups, new patterns of behavior usually emerge *after* attitude changes in substantial sectors of the public. For example, large numbers of men began to provide significant help with household tasks only when public opinion began to approve of this, and profit-making enterprises are quick to respond when they sense a public demand. In governments, on the other hand, structural and role changes often come *before* new attitudes have taken hold among major sectors of the population. Forms of democracy may be adopted in previously traditional or authoritarian states, but many politically significant attitudes and behavior patterns that developed long before this continue to influence both government personnel and members of the public.

Even in fairly mature democracies, it seems probable that inherited stereotypes affect attitudes toward government agencies, and these attitudes can influence both voters and government office holders. For example, opinion researchers in the United States found in 1997 that only 5 percent of their sample said that they had a great deal of confidence in the quality of work done by career workers in the federal government. (Cantril and Cantril, 1999, p. 30) It's true that another 50 percent said they had a "fair amount" of confidence, while 37 percent had "not very much" confidence, or "none at all." Nevertheless, a self-respecting private corporation would be horrified if the work of its employees had been given a similar evaluation, and it seems unlikely that professional civil servants deserve such a low rating. The Cantril and Cantril study of attitudes toward government also found that a large proportion of the public had ambivalent feelings about government activities in general. That is, many people said they supported a wide range of officially-administered programs but at the same time agreed with the statement that government "does too many things people could do better for themselves." (*Ibid.*, p. 10) One has reason to suspect that this ambivalence, also, is due in part to traditions of rugged individualism.

It is difficult to locate empirical data, such as figures from public opinion polls, to document this hypothesis that inherited attitudes often govern opinions about contemporary government activities, but there are a number of studies that support it by inference. A fascinating investigation of democratic institutions in Italy suggests that the quality of the work done by some government agencies was strongly influenced by attitudes formed during the 12th and 13th centuries and passed down from one generation to another. (Putnam, 1993) Also suggestive are polls conducted in the United States in mid-20th century, which found that people who had negative opinions about government in general were often strongly in favor of specific governmental programs and policies. Indeed, many respondents who could be classified as opposed to government activities on the basis of their ideological position could also be seen as favorable to such activities if judged by their attitudes on specific issues. (Free and Cantril, 1968)

What has happened in many countries that have recently adopted democratic constitutions also suggests the influence of past traditions. Office holders of elected governments have often used their powers to accumulate enormous wealth for themselves and their families, while most members of their populations continue to exist at a subsistence level. In this respect, these officials are continuing practices established in times when it was customary for very poor populations to support the luxurious life styles of small elites. Even though some office holders and most members of the public in developing countries do not approve of bribery, nepotism, and other behaviors that characterized previous elites, they are unlikely to be surprised by such things. The idea that power carries with it many perks is a familiar one, whether the power is acquired through a democratic election, divine intervention, conquest, or skullduggery, "To the victors belong the spoils" was a widely cited aphorism in early days of the United States. Similar ideas can be found among both officeholders and many members of the public in other new democracies.

The behavior of citizens in both old and new democratic states who sabotage institutions on which they depend by doing everything they can to avoid paying taxes and by condoning tax evasion as moral or even virtuous behavior may also be explained in part by inherited attitudes. During much of human history taxation served primarily to benefit the tax collectors and small ruling elites. In medieval Europe, for example, taxes were used almost entirely to support the life styles of the warrior class—and their expensive squabbles with each other. (Wood, 1987; Ladurie, 1978) Taxpayers got little in return. Negative attitudes toward taxes on the part of the public were fully justified.

Stereotypes of bureaucrats and politicians fattening themselves at the public trough and convictions that money is wasted as soon as it passes into government hands persist even in democracies where budgets and expenses are open for inspection and are subject to stringent controls. Substantial numbers of people continue to behave as though taxes are collected mainly for the benefit of government officials and their families, or are used to perform functions that private enterprise could do better. Tax avoidance has remained respectable in many countries.

Such attitudes have been encouraged by the fact that in some democracies, especially newer ones, government officials at all levels have indeed continued many of their former practices, often using tax receipts to enrich themselves and their friends and supporters. News media in democratic societies help to reinforce stereotypes that portray government as stupid and dishonest by sensationalizing any irregularities that can be detected without at the same time indicating whether these occurrences are frequent or exceptional. There is also a tendency in all countries for people to focus their attention on taxes that are unfair, or fail to promote the public good, while taking for granted those that enable large numbers of society members to prosper. The possibility that well-considered public expenditures—for example, in early childhood education—might lead to smaller government and greater value at less cost is rarely appreciated. Nor is it easy to reassure taxpayers that enthusiasm about taxes as instruments for helping people help each other is not equivalent to favoring larger and more expensive governments. This disjunction between what we expect contemporary governments to accomplish and our willingness to provide them the means to do what we want constitutes a major threat to an improved quality of life in complex democracies.

Partisans of democracy thus have the task of simultaneously finding ways to achieve three goals with respect to taxes: prevent waste of public monies, collect taxes fairly, and make the benefits of taxation so clear that legislators do not feel they have to apologize when imposing a tax and citizens recognize the benefits of paying it. In all democracies there are at least some individuals and groups devoted to advancing the first two goals—economy and fairness.

It is more difficult, however, to find advocates who are able to focus the attention of mass publics on the benefits of taxation and the vital role it plays in supporting functional groups that are essential to a prosperous complex society. A few politicians with more than normal courage sometimes point out these benefits. Economists, political scientists, and other academics often do so more systematically in their professional work, but these efforts have not proved widely persuasive. There are also occasional popular movements that advocate taxes for specific purposes—for example, for improving transportation. Nevertheless, as public opinion researchers are fond of pointing out, many people who are enthusiastic about government programs that provide medical benefits, or pensions for aged retirees, are ambivalent when it comes to the taxes that support these programs. "Who should pay these taxes? Rich people, perhaps. But why me?"

The benefits of taxation thus receive less attention than do its negative aspects. Too many politicians in the United States and other democracies have found that one way to get elected is to promise tax reduction while ignoring or simply denying the negative effects this will have on essential services. The voices of those who point out the vital importance of taxes for the prosperity of a modern complex society tend to be weak, while advocates of tax reduction or tax avoidance (legal or perhaps legal) dominate the channels of public communication and much private communication. Prominent advertisements in American media frequently make such appeals as: "Don't let Uncle Sam take your hard-earned dollars. Let us show you how to avoid taxes." And the accusation that a politician has "voted five times to raise taxes" may be enough to defeat him or her in the next election. Whether or not tax increases would make it possible for a government agency to provide vital services or for new and profitable businesses to be created is treated as irrelevant.

How to level the playing field? Advocates of democracy gain nothing by attempting to hush those who are critical of tax policies—such critics are essential and merit encouragement. What is lacking is vigorous advocacy of other points of view. The question is therefore who might be able to reach the public with messages to the effect that we often get very good value for the taxes we pay, that a higher tax may sometimes enable us to avoid much larger expenditures, that waste and greed are problems in private enterprise as well as in government, and that many expert civil servants work hard for low pay. Bureaucrats cannot disseminate such messages without being accused of trying to increase their own power or the size of their paychecks. They are often prevented from doing so by law. Government contractors, also, are inhibited by suspicions that they are simply drumming up more business. Other private corporations would be likely to spark protests from their owners or stockholders if they devoted substantial resources to pointing out the merits of taxation.

One possibility is that in the more prosperous democracies one or more nonprofit foundations might find it possible and rewarding to take on the task of informing people about positive as well as negative aspects of taxation. Medium-size foundations frequently search for ways they can render a significant service with relatively modest funds. This role as tax analyst could provide such an opportunity. A small nonpartisan staff of economists, behavioral scientists, lawyers, and journalists might make an appreciable impact on public discussion by ferreting out and publicizing specific examples of "smart taxes" as well as of wasteful taxes. They could find numerous cases in which efforts to cut taxes led to greater costs to taxpayers. (A humble example is that of a municipality that discontinues trash collection in order to balance its budget, with the result that households and businesses have to pay higher charges to a private collector who has a monopoly in the area.) There are already numerous nonprofit foundations that represent viewpoints about taxation held by various ideological or commercial constituencies. A nonpartisan foundation that focused on the virtues and potentialities of taxes would be a welcome addition to the group.

Another ancient notion tending to degrade the quality of life in democracies, in addition to the idea that all taxes are bad, is that government is nearly all-powerful. According to this way of thinking, government should be blamed if it does not avert calamities of almost any kind—even calamities inflicted by the weather or other developments over which it has no control. Public officials occasionally do receive some credit for favorable developments, but not very much. Opinion polls over the years have shown repeatedly that when times are prosperous people tend to ascribe personal success to their own virtues, hard work, and sagacity. Bad times, however, are likely to be seen as the result of government mismanagement.

Outdated and unrealistic assumptions about governmental power—like erroneous beliefs about taxes—are often nourished by politicians and even by a free press. Politicians claim credit for anything good that happens while they are in office, while the opposition can be relied upon to blame the government for almost any adverse development. Attention is thus diverted from the extent to which nongovernmental groups and individuals, as well as such factors as climate, influence the quality of life. For example, people are less likely to reproach themselves for buying gas-guzzling vehicles or failing to cooperate in enforcing laws when they can convince themselves that it is government's responsibility to assure fuel availability, preserve air quality, and prevent crime—and that all citizens do not share this responsibility.

The picture of societies as systems of interrelated individuals and functional groups that have to be continually updated in view of rapid environmental change, which we have tried to present here, suggests that members of the public play an important part in evaluating the work of both official and nonofficial organizations. How well does any particular functional group serve the purposes it is supposed to serve? And how might performance be improved? Are optimum benefits (material and nonmaterial) being delivered at the lowest possible costs? Should inherited structures and roles should be revised, or are old attitudes are making it more difficult for new functional groups to do a good job?

Before leaving this area of discussion we should note that there are also cases in which old functional groups have come to serve new needs. Some organizations concerned with sports and athletics seem to fit into this category. The functional groups in question may have emerged long ago under very different conditions but meet a number of today's requirements even though the structure of these groups and the roles of their members have been modified only moderately.

Few of us realize that when we attend or participate in a sporting event we may be involved in a semi-religious ceremony that helped our distant ancestors survive. For millennia, many a tribe's well-being depended on having warriors and hunters who were stronger, faster, sharper-eyed, better organized, and more canny than those of competing tribes. It was important, therefore, that people should honor strength, speed, keen vision, teamwork—and above all the ability to win—whether the opponent was a rival ethnic group or a charging tiger. And, on second thought, the ancestors who benefited from sports may not be all that distant. British commentators have frequently observed that wars were won because of lessons learned on the playing fields of Eton and Harrow, while Americans have sometimes claimed that skill in throwing baseballs made hand grenades into more deadly weapons when they were used by U.S. soldiers.

Nevertheless, a nation's welfare now depends much less on keen vision, strength, and speed, although teamwork is still important. Our most important functional groups today require people who can understand complex problems, choose capable personnel, make wise decisions, and are able to cooperate with those who differ from themselves. Whether Team A or Team B wins makes little difference to the standard of living of those who spend a small fortune on tickets for the big game—unless they have also made substantial side bets. So why do we still devote so much time and money to sports? It would be more sensible to raise the salaries of social workers, teachers, and judges.

But one can argue that massive expenditures on sports are justified because sporting events satisfy needs that have emerged or increased in relatively recent times. While physical skills now have little to do with national survival, the entertainment value of sports has increased, especially in complex societies that are populated largely by sedentary indoor workers. More significantly, we can vicariously enjoy the excitement of combat and the delicious sensation of victory when we watch a football game. Some of us may also learn to overcome the bitter taste of defeat, and how to cope with disappointment by looking forward to a better outcome next time. Sporting events also emphasize teamwork and the necessity for long, arduous practice, self-discipline, and punctuality, all of which are increasingly necessary if today's major functional groups are to operate successfully. Most of all, winning teams are likely to include members of various national, religious, and ethnic groups, making it clear to thinking people that social organisms often have to draw on worldwide talent if they are to excel. You can't restrict functional group membership to those in your own tribe if you want a really good team, an outstanding university or, in many cases, a successful business.

◆   ◆   ◆

People alive today were born into an age where the speed and magnitude of environmental changes, both physical and social, force all societies to adjust constantly and to invent new functional groups or to modify existing ones in order to satisfy important desires and needs of their members. To follow ancestral traditions slavishly, without evaluating and occasionally revising basic institutions, can lead to the deterioration or death of a society. But to adopt unwise adaptive changes can also lead to disaster and destruction. Everyone, whether consciously or not, is involved in a search for a balance between the old and the new that will lead to the kind of world we want to live in.

This chapter has suggested some ways in which all those who wish to do so can take an active part in this search. When we make a decision of almost any type, we can ask ourselves whether this decision is likely to advance or retard the development of a peaceful world consisting of well functioning complex societies. We can help to encourage creativity, strengthen communication channels, and improve educational facilities—thus contributing to infrastructures that facilitate the formation and operation of efficient functional groups. We can make large or small efforts to see that human resources are not wasted, including our own capabilities. We can try to improve human cooperation by learning how to reach agreements and by finding ways of reconciling differences where agreements are not possible. And when we examine our inherited institutions we can try to find ways to strengthen or adjust them so that they will better serve the needs of ourselves and others.

The models of society sketched in this essay may be of use also to those with more specific interests—in government, or in education, or in social research. In addition, this way of looking at societies and functional groups may be helpful to individuals who wish to find ways of exploiting their own talents and reaching personal goals. The following chapters are devoted to these possible applications.

8

Implications for Governmental Operations

Individuals who take part in a government administration, or who seek to influence it, often look for ways in which it might be strengthened, or weakened, or guided in different directions. They also may be concerned with specific problems faced by individual government agencies. Whatever the scope of their interests, they may find it helpful to look at their society or nation, or the emerging world society, as a complex entity composed of numerous smaller, and interacting, functional groups.

The efficiency of a government can be evaluated from three points of view, much as is the case with a business, family, or voluntary association. Does it satisfy the expectations of its leaders and managers? Does it serve the needs and desires of its rank-and-file members—civil servants and others—who are then likely to be better motivated to do a good job? Does it provide services desired either by other functional groups or by members of the public, and at reasonable cost? The government in a rigorous dictatorship or authoritarian traditional society might be an efficient one only from the point of view of those who exercise power. A corrupt government might be seen as efficient by its rank-and-file employees, as long as they were able to profit from generous bribes and payoffs, but might be the despair of its leaders and would certainly be a burden for the public. In the following discussion, the most efficient government is the one that does the best job from the point of view of people in all three categories: policy makers, civil servants, and the public. This is the kind of government that should, in theory, exist in well-functioning democracies.

While sharing many characteristics with other functional groups, governments also have at least two unique characteristics. One is that communication channels connect them, directly or indirectly, with most (and ideally with all) individuals and groups in the political unit. The other is that governments can make laws governing the conduct of these individuals and groups, and usually claim the right or are given the right to use violence, as well as other kinds of pressure, to enforce these laws. The power to make laws and to use force—combined with access to a comprehensive communication network—enables governments to collect taxes and organize a variety of specialized functional groups, such as police, military establishments, courts of law, schools, and sometimes (especially in authoritarian states) luxury services for the governing elite.

A government's ability to get a bird's-eye view of a society or political unit is made possible by the two-way communication channels that ordinarily link official agencies directly or indirectly with everyone, or almost everyone, in a complex democratic society. Complaints and suggestions reaching these agencies often reveal unsatisfied needs as well as hopes and fears.

Governments are also more likely than other functional groups to have access to a wide range of information from both private and tax-supported sources about the social and physical environments. Private sources that may provide information usually include universities, think tanks (including individuals who publish thoughtful books), corporations, business and professional associations, and the news media. Additional data are assembled by official agencies that monitor the weather, international trade, population trends, financial transactions, employment, and many other matters.

Despite its power and the information at its disposal, a government must be able to get along with other functional groups, just as these other groups have to find ways to get along with the government.

Authoritarian rulers often can harmonize their activities with those of other functional groups by forcing the latter to adjust. In traditional societies, the various component social units can coexist with each other because they follow inherited rules that have allowed the society to coordinate its various parts well enough to survive in the past, usually for many generations. A democratic government ordinarily has to bargain and make concessions in order to get along with other functional groups. It is expected to use force only as a last resort.

This view of government as a body that has to adjust to other groups, a view that is held by most people who favor democracy, differs from traditional approaches. In ancient times, it was common for the supreme ruler to be worshiped as a god. His orders could not be questioned. Even in modern democracies, some of this awe of the ruler remains, and government tends to be regarded as having a higher status than other functional groups. Nevertheless, to treat government as a "superior" entity is unrealistic in a well functioning complex society. Governments are essential to the survival of a society, but no more so than functional groups that provide food and other necessities, and they may be less essential than families.

Democratic theory specifies that governmental power should derive from the governed. This is a realistic goal in modern complex societies, but doesn't go quite far enough. One should add that the less a government has to use its coercive powers to provide the best possible services to the pubic, the more efficient it is likely to be. Skill in negotiation, persuasion, conflict resolution and compromise are among the criteria by which the efficiency of a government's conduct of domestic as well as foreign affairs can be gauged.

What Should be Expected from Democratic Governments? To decide just what services should be provided by an efficient government has become a major bone of contention for citizens of democratic societies. At one end of the continuum are those who feel that governments, because of their unique capabilities and ability to function without showing a profit, can do a better job than private functional groups in providing for nearly all a society's needs—material as well as nonmaterial. At the other end of the continuum are those who believe that the best government is the one that governs least. Members of both groups tend to agree that governments should be responsible for assuring order and security, although there can still be sharp differences as to what is security and what is order, and how much of each is desirable.

The models of societies outlined in the preceding pages do not resolve the question as to the optimum extent of government in a complex democracy, but they do suggest a number of criteria by which the quality of a democratic government can be judged. (1) Does this government do a good job in assuring that the society has the best possible infrastructure—one that will encourage the development and operation of a wide variety of functional groups? (2) How well does it succeed in helping desirable functional groups to coexist, harmonize their activities, and support one another, and in controlling or eliminating groups that have been determined by democratic processes to be undesirable? (3) Is it effective in ensuring that necessary and desirable services are available to all members of the society at the lowest possible cost—whether these services are actually provided by government agencies or by other functional groups? (4) Does it provide desirable services that other functional groups cannot or will not make available at reasonable cost? (5) Is the government itself organized so as to perform the above four tasks as well as possible?

These criteria may appear to be self-evident, but they conceal any number of thorny problems. The very first requirement mentioned—that a democratic government should help to build and maintain an infrastructure favoring the emergence and operation of the widest possible variety of functional groups—conflicts head on with the almost universal desire of government policy makers to stay in power. For a government to nourish innovative thinking, comprehensive information, and quality education for everyone amounts, among many other things, to tolerating and sometimes even nurturing one or more political parties that oppose the party in power. Especially in fledgling democracies, it is very difficult for those in power to allow—let alone encourage—people who disagree with them to engage in public criticism. But if a government does restrict opposition parties, discourages its own officials from voicing independent opinions, and seeks to control communication channels, less information will be available to government decision makers. The quality of their decisions will inevitably deteriorate. Opposition groups will be deprived of information they need to propose alternative policies, it is true, but the society in question will become less able to satisfy the needs and aspirations of its members and may not remain competitive with other societies.

No completely satisfactory way of reconciling this conflict between a government's desire for privacy when making decisions and a society's need for a strong infrastructure that will facilitate functional group formation has been found. Even in countries where democratic government has become traditional, there is a strong tendency for an incumbent administration to emphasize internal secrecy, to keep its deliberations private until it is ready to make a formal announcement, and to minimize public differences of opinion among its officials. This ability to keep a secret and to display unity may confer political advantages in the short term, but in the long term lowers the quality of decisions. Nevertheless, governments often maintain—especially in new democracies—that if opposition political parties have advance information about government plans, or if officials are allowed to express alternative opinions, public order will break down.

The problem is to find the right balance, and this may differ from one country to another. Our model does suggest, however, that those who advocate restrictions on information about what a government is doing, or who want to limit the ability of opposing groups to organize, should bear the burden of proof. Will greater freedom and openness result in more serious damage than the contemplated restrictions?

Indeed, our model suggests that tolerance for dissent and for unconventional behavior is not enough. A basic task for all governments, even though they may refuse to recognize it, is to *encourage* free and comprehensive investigation and communication on all important subjects, *unless* there is a high probability that damage to the society will result.

One implication of a democratic government's obligation to nourish a strong infrastructure for all functional groups—as well as the capability to control or eliminate groups which, after due process, have been identified as destructive—is that it should do what it can to prevent interference with free thought, open communication and universal education. This often means breaking up monopolies, especially in the mass media, and fighting prejudice and discrimination in both the public and private sectors of a society.

A second basic obligation of all democratic governments is to help (and sometimes to force) major functional groups in a society to coexist peacefully and, when possible, to support each other. This task grows out of the obligation of democratic regimes to encourage a wide variety of social organisms, some of which—as well as their individual members—will inevitably compete with each other, quarrel with each other, or prey upon each other. A government cannot reasonably be expected to totally eliminate conflict from a society, but must provide facilities to regulate or resolve conflict, or must see that such facilities exist.

The most common way for governments to encourage both domestic tranquility and a wide range of groups that compete to provide people with things they want is to enforce a body of law. These laws aim to control or eliminate activities that violate the society's accepted behavioral codes and to make the community safe for "good" functional groups. It is especially important to discourage violence and fraud, since behavior that falls into these categories strikes most directly at the heart of human cooperation.

Public authorities must also see that systems for settling disputes and for maintaining public order exist and are doing what they are supposed to do. Some of these systems, such as courts, police departments, and factory inspectors may be part of government. Others, such as mediators, arbitrators, and self-regulating bodies, may be established under private auspices, often with encouragement from the state. Local governments sometimes take an active part in seeing that specialists are available to help keep the peace in communities. In a well functioning democracy, the net result of combined public and private conflict-settling arrangements should be to allow people and groups to compete in serving many needs and desires, some of which conflict with each other, without negative effects.

Democracies help to preserve internal peace and bring about cooperation among functional groups of different kinds in many other ways as well. For example, legislatures provide forums where representatives of widely differing interests can engage in discussions. Official and nonofficial leaders can call attention to values that are shared by people who may have varying points of view on specific issues. For example, politicians looking for votes may point out that whether or not we favor or oppose higher tariffs on imports we can all take pride in the skill of our workers, the achievements of our scientists, and the virtues of our ancestors. And both advocates and opponents of government subsidies to schools controlled by private functional groups are likely to agree that all children should have the opportunities afforded by a good education.

Governments are well advised to assign a high priority to domestic conflict resolution and to recognize that moneys spent in bringing about harmony or cooperation among diverse functional groups within a society are likely to be repaid many times over. Too many governments fail to ensure the availability of sufficient judges and court facilities; nor are governments always diligent in seeking ways to discourage frivolous law suits and the use of delaying tactics by disputing parties. The efficiency of a society's mechanisms for promoting conflict resolution and harmonious relations is directly related to the quality of life it can offer its members.

A third task of democratic governments is to ensure, to the extent possible, that all members of the population have access to, or are provided with, services and resources that will help them lead satisfying lives—and at the least cost in energy, time, and money. The government may not be the best functional group to provide these goods, services, or resources, but it is often the only body that can centralize information on what is needed and what is lacking, and that also can call attention to the opportunities and dangers of various courses of action. In addition, government may be the only functional group that can detect and restrain monopolies that impose unreasonable costs, interfere with free communication, or restrict development of new ideas. Officials should be able to take action that will protect competition when necessary.

Some democratic governments try to satisfy a large proportion of the population's needs themselves, as in countries where manufacturing, transportation and education are largely in the public sector. In other countries, the voters—or designated decision makers—have determined that nongovernmental functional groups should be the dominant suppliers. In nearly all cases, however, the government is held responsible for seeing that no vital goods or services are unavailable.

This responsibility—to step in as a *supplier of last resort*—is the basis for a fourth major function of democratic governments. They should try to supply desirable goods or services when these cannot be provided by private functional groups, or cannot be obtained by those who need them at a reasonable cost. In any society there are likely to be a number of essential requirements, both material and nonmaterial, that private bodies are unable to supply. These may include such ephemeral desiderata as a sense of unity or security, or such basic needs as food, sanitation, and emergency medical services.

Some would add "leadership" to this list of needs that democratic governments are customarily expected to satisfy, and not necessarily as the supplier of last resort. They point out that governments should be able to encourage a sense of national pride, rally the citizens in crises, and provide a sense of direction to the polity as a whole. However, within democratic societies there are likely to be differing definitions of good leadership. To some observers, the best leaders are those who are most adept in using persuasion. To others, leadership implies the ability to overwhelm the political opposition, wave the national flag, or dominate the news media. Some cultures prefer strong, silent types; others prefer top officials who can make a three-hour speech without notes. The model of a democratic society presented here suggests what may be an appropriate compromise: namely, a government that does a good job in executing the tasks listed in this chapter is providing quality leadership. Flamboyant personalities are not essential.

Mention of leadership reminds us of a fifth key governmental responsibility. This is to ensure that government itself, as an important and complex functional group, is honest, well organized and administered, and able to adapt to constantly changing conditions. Like other functional groups in the modern era, agencies of a democratic government must be able to revise and update their structures and operating rules, and also the roles played by their personnel, in a timely manner. This is most obvious in the case of military establishments, which are often accused of being ready to fight the last war but not the next one. But law enforcement personnel, tax collectors, diplomats, and other officials are just as likely to follow patterns established in previous generations and to be unable or unwilling to institute changes unless they are pushed. And in democratic countries structural changes in the executive branch of government are often dependent on action by leisurely and parsimonious legislatures. The ability of democracies to change their political leadership peacefully from time to time is especially important, in that the honesty, efficiency, and constant updating of a government becomes more difficult to assure the longer it remains in power. To "throw the rascals out" is far from a cure-all for weaknesses in a democratic government, but it can be a great help.

In addition to periodic elections, democratic governments, like other functional groups, constantly require creative ideas, comprehensive communication channels, and qualified personnel if they are to operate efficiently and adjust appropriately to changing circumstances. Partly because traditional attitudes toward government among both insiders and outsiders survive in all nations, it is especially difficult for official agencies to satisfy these requirements, even in democracies. Many government personnel resist new ideas and resent criticism. Internal channels of communication are often weak. Important information is frequently bottled up by top officials, who may also pay little attention to the advice and experience of their subordinates. Unqualified bureaucrats, including those in policy-making positions, are sometimes installed because of political pressures or family connections rather than because of their qualifications. Once in office, these less competent functionaries often display remarkable ability both to retain their jobs and to resist making any improvements in how these jobs are done. A constant effort to improve the capabilities of government organizations should be a preoccupation of both internal watchdogs and outside critics.

That there are many weaknesses in democratic governments is often easy to point out and belabor. This is in itself a danger. No examples are given here because they are unnecessary—everyone can provide their own. In contrast, good work performed by skilled or idealistic public employees is usually taken for granted. The picture of governmental inefficiency that is given by news reports may thus lead to the conclusion that nongovernmental organizations could provide the same or better services at a lower cost. Yet such a conclusion is often mistaken. Deficiencies in non-governmental functional groups may be easier to correct, but they are also more difficult to discover. Waste in a large corporation may exceed waste in a government agency of the same size, but is not equally obvious. And even glaring defects may not lead to improvements in a commercial organization that serves people's needs badly, as long as profits are good. As a result of the ease with which a government agency can be faulted, and the greater difficulty of detecting dishonesty and waste in private organizations, a valid determination as to which should provide given goods or services is frequently difficult to make.

Indeed, our model suggests that arguments about whether small government is preferable to big government, and whether taxes are too low or too high, are frequently meaningless. It would be more rewarding to discuss and explore how each desirable activity in a democracy can be conducted so as to achieve the best results at lowest cost. There are situations in which government agencies may be able to provide greater benefits at lower cost to the population as a whole than private functional groups could provide at the same or even higher cost. Medical insurance is one of many controversial areas in which the relative efficiency of government versus private providers is a major consideration. One body of opinion holds that a single government insurance agency could provide better and less expensive services than large numbers of competing private companies, each of which has to maintain its own administrative bureaucracy. Some (probably pro-government) partisans to this debate have reported that in the United States private health maintenance organizations have to spend 15 percent of their income on administration, while the administrative costs of the government Medicare program amount to approximately 2 percent. (*New York Times,* Jan. 28, 2004) A competing viewpoint is that government insurance programs provide medical services that are slower, less reliable, and of lower quality than those available from private insurance companies.

A related implication of the model described here is that cuts in government budgets frequently result in net losses for citizens and taxpayers when these cuts weaken the society's infrastructure for private functional groups, many of which satisfy important material and nonmaterial needs and desires. This is especially likely to be true in areas such as education, public health, libraries, research, conflict resolution, police protection, and transportation. Yet cuts in the infrastructure are often the first to be made. The negative results may not be immediately apparent, but the long term capacity of the private sector to provide people with what they want and need may be greatly reduced. More crowded schools turn out less competent managers and employees; more robberies occur when there are fewer police; and cuts in budgets for public transportation and highways result in longer delays for commuters. Citizens in a democracy are faced constantly with the problem of ensuring that restricting government expenditures does not result in net long term losses to the society.

Our model thus suggests a number of criteria for judging the appropriateness of government involvement in satisfying the needs and desires of population members. The suggested approach might be considered both liberal and conservative. It is liberal in the sense that it calls for constant reevaluation of existing institutions to determine whether government or private initiative can do the best job, but it is conservative in that it holds private initiative to be usually more efficient than government agencies in satisfying human needs and desires, at least in democracies.

Some Examples: Immigration, Taxation, and Terrorism. In addition to highlighting general principles about ways democratic governments might serve societies better, our model suggests actions public authorities might take with respect to specific issues. The following discussion will consider three policy areas where controversy tends to be vigorous—immigration, taxation, and terrorism. There are, of course, many others.

Policies regarding immigration have been affected profoundly by environmental changes that occurred during the past two centuries. In contrast to the situation only 100 years ago, most areas of the world are now abundantly populated. The age-old rule that a society should strive to increase its numbers as rapidly as possible is often inappropriate today, and the recent trend toward very small families in complex societies is also troublesome. How to maintain a balance between population size and the availability of functional groups that serve the needs of society members is a more pressing problem for most countries than it was several generations ago. A related change in recent times is that immigrants to the industrialized democracies now tend to be concentrated in urban centers where more and more jobs require specialized skills.

Throughout history, most immigrants came to new lands as colonists who brought at least some functional groups with them (families, religious bodies, local leadership, and sometimes defense forces), and then established new functional groups (farms, businesses, singing societies, and athletic clubs). They provided many of their own services and expected few benefits to be provided by the receiving society. In recent decades, countries that attract immigrants have had to devote more attention to helping immigrants fit into existing functional groups. They often try to estimate how many individuals, skilled or unskilled, should be admitted, and what actions should be taken to maximize the contributions the new arrivals make to the institutions of the host society and to minimize the damage they might inflict on these institutions. These plans may be vitiated by illegal immigration, which in Western Europe and North America is often estimated at about 50 percent of legal immigration. Even legal immigrants may bring functional groups with them that clash with institutions of the host society, such as some religious bodies and some extended families.

Previously, immigrant communities, especially in cities, served as bridges that helped people from other cultures to become integrated with the host culture gradually. This still happens, but less often. Now, the world is a smaller place. Developments in transportation and communication make it possible for immigrants to maintain close ties with their countries of origin. Many continue living according to the rules of the culture in which they grew up, while treating the host society mainly as a source of money, much of which is sent home. The distinction between immigration and colonization becomes blurred. Ironically, it thus happens that some industrialized nations, which previously established profit-making colonies that extracted wealth from less developed societies, are finding the situation now reversed. These former colonial powers are involuntarily helping to support poorer countries they once exploited.

The tendency for immigrants to retain many characteristics of the cultures from which they come brings advantages as well as problems to host countries. In the emerging world society, host countries find it advantageous when some of their component communities consist of people who understand foreign languages and cultures, and who still have contacts in the lands of their ancestors. To achieve acceptance and a good life, an immigrant no longer has to be assimilated to the point of being much like everyone else in the host society. Whether or not to step into the "melting pot" is more likely to be optional. What is important is not to lose a foreign accent, but to learn how to work in and with the host society's functional groups.

Massive environmental changes that have occurred within the past few generations thus make much of our past experience with international migration either misleading or irrelevant. In the United States, especially, one frequently hears statements like the following: "This is a country of immigrants. My grandfather arrived here with five dollars in his pocket. He didn't speak a word of English and had no friends or family in America. But he worked hard, bought his own farm, sent two of his six sons to college, and provided jobs for a dozen people. So let's encourage as many immigrants as possible. They make the country rich." Such observations tend to ignore the loss of open space, the much greater break with the "old country" on the part of former immigrants, the growing importance of specialized education as well as hard work, and the economic and social problems that arise when large numbers of unskilled workers crowd into a complex society.

Although anti-immigration movements have developed in many developed countries, informed discussions about immigration rarely find those who favor unrestricted immigration on one side of the table and those completely opposed on the other. Few people who have thought about the matter advocate unregulated international migration or oppose immigration entirely. Every nation has benefited from the ideas and skills that new arrivals have brought, and all receiving countries have also experienced difficulties.

Arguments about immigration thus tend to be over numbers, categories, and cultural influences. How can the countries to which immigrants flock balance the costs incurred against the benefits received? Should those who settle in another country be discouraged from establishing enclaves where they continue to use their own languages and observe their own customs? What responsibilities, if any, do the countries of origin have when it comes to regulating immigration? Should immigrants who wish to retain political affiliations with their countries of origin be allowed dual citizenship? To what extent do considerations of charity and humanity obligate the complex democracies, most of which are relatively prosperous, to assume new burdens by admitting those who are starving or are facing political persecution?

Our model of a democratic society suggests a number of ways to look at such questions. The first obligation of a government, according to this approach, is to do what it can to enable all members of the society, whether recent arrivals or old inhabitants, to work together in functional groups that serve everyone's needs and aspirations. This means, among other things, that each immigrant should be encouraged to participate in existing institutions of the host society at the same time that he or she may be part of an immigrant subculture. A government's policy regarding immigration might therefore include the following specifics:

#1. Do everything possible to ensure that new arrivals share a common language with native-born citizens, so that they will not be forced to depend almost entirely on a subculture. Immigrants who seek permanent resident status or permission to accept employment, or who wish to start their own businesses, should be required to have a minimum working knowledge of the common language, preferably on arrival. Those granted citizenship should be able to use the common language with sufficient fluency to follow the mass media and take part in political discussions with citizens of their new country. (Language requirements would of course not apply to tourists, diplomats, or temporary business visitors.) Without at least some familiarity with a common language, immigrants are prevented from participating in most existing functional groups, are subject to exploitation, and are more vulnerable to crime.

Without reasonable fluency, immigrants who become citizens are limited in the contributions they can make to democratic processes. For a democratic country to provide voting instructions in a foreign language is an oxymoron, and should be avoided in all but special cases. It does serious damage to the communication network of a democracy, especially by creating a barrier between office holders or candidates, on the one side, and citizens who are unfamiliar with the common language, on the other. The latter may become dependent on politicians who claim the ability to deliver votes from blocs of citizens who have little knowledge about what they are voting for or against. . .

#2. Try to see that immigrant populations do not increase more rapidly than the society's ability to create functional groups that can assure a good quality of life for them. This means either limiting immigration or encouraging different categories of immigrants at different times. It also may involve taking measures to ensure that decent housing, economical transportation, adequate medical care, and other amenities are available. For example, an industry that employs large numbers of unskilled workers from other countries might be required to build housing or provide bus services for them. Efforts to assure adequate housing for foreign agricultural workers provide a precedent in the United States, although not invariably a successful one. If families accompany the workers, then more money will also be needed for schools and playgrounds. Government involvement in planning support facilities is especially desirable in situations where employers reap profits from cheap labor while passing the "overhead" costs caused by educational, housing, or transportation requirements of these workers to tax payers in the host society.

#3. Use imagination in devising ways to bring new arrivals into contact with long-time citizens, so that each immigrant will have multiple ties to the host society. For example, one possibility would be to require that each immigrant have at least one sponsor whose parents had been citizens of the host country. Another approach might be to ensure that libraries, athletic fields, and other educational and recreational facilities are located so as to bring new arrivals together with older residents. Indigenous churches and other religious bodies could also be encouraged to reach out.

#4. Experiment with ways to anticipate, and if possible to moderate, problems that are caused by differing behavioral codes. At a minimum, receiving countries could make sure that new arrivals are aware of prevailing standards of conduct and values in the host society. Immigrants should know that in most complex democracies parents are expected to recognize the right of their children over a certain age to select their own friends, marriage partners, and jobs, even though the families may not approve of the choices. And those who intend to establish themselves in a new society should be informed about ideals that are generally accepted as goals, even though few people succeed in living up to them completely: for example, that an available job should go to the person who is best qualified, regardless of his or her social status, family, or other characteristics not related to job performance. In other words, immigrants should know that some behaviors that are not illegal may still cause their new neighbors or colleagues to distrust or dislike them. They should be aware that patriarchal extended families, a street-centered social life, and business practices based on membership in a particular ethnic group can prove devastating to existing political structures, neighborhoods, and small enterprises. At the same time, immigrants should also be aware that some traditions they bring with them are likely to strengthen their ties in the new country. These include respect for the law and hard work, family involvement in education, participation in athletic activities, a love for music and the arts, and a variety of tastes in food and literary styles.

#5. Encourage current citizens, most of whom are descendents of immigrants from previous decades and centuries, to help ensure that functional groups in all fields are open to participation by new arrivals with the necessary qualifications.

#6. Make it clear that the host country appreciates the languages, knowledge, and experience that recent arrivals bring with them. Efforts to help immigrants work constructively in a new environment should not discourage them from keeping up contacts with their former homelands, nor should efforts be made to persuade them to adopt all the customs of older residents. Immigrants should be aware that host countries tend to benefit when immigrants teach their children the language of their former country, as long as these parents also encourage their children to achieve complete fluency in the common language of the new society.

#7. Above all, try to protect the efficiency of functional groups that serve the needs and desires of society members as a whole. This is the most important job of national and local governments with respect to immigration. To achieve maximum possible freedom and opportunity for people from all cultures should be a goal of all governments, but a way to do this cannot always be found quickly. It may take more than one generation. Sometimes, existing functional groups can adapt in such a way that they serve the wants and needs of both older residents of the host society and also the desires of immigrants, who may have very different goals. When this proves impossible, however, the existing functional groups should be protected. The amounts of time, effort, and money that are required to build good educational facilities, voluntary associations, businesses, neighborhoods, government agencies and many other institutions are so enormous that humanity as a whole is the loser if these are damaged or overwhelmed, whether by immigration or for other reasons.

So, what should governmental authorities do when confronted with a dispute between a school and a family that insists, perhaps for religious reasons, that their children should not wear the school uniform or should be given special food? Our model suggests that the school's right to continue existing procedures should be protected if it can be shown that making exceptions to established rules would reduce the quality of its work. What the decision of a judge or arbitrator might be would depend on the circumstances in the individual case, but the conception of society advanced here would require the burden of proof to be on those who are asking for exceptions. Every civilization depends on efficient functional groups and will be damaged if it fails to protect its social organisms that work well. A democratic government should not try to uphold the right of an individual to engage in activities that have been found to degrade the quality of life in the host society.

Many immigrants experience a huge increase in their earning ability when they enter a complex democratic society. This is the principal reason why so many individuals who are trying to enter an industrialized country illegally will pay large sums to be smuggled across a border. Some undocumented persons have paid as much as $50,000 to be transported from Asia to the United States, and the fee for being smuggled from Mexico to the United States is reported to frequently exceed $1,000.

A Rand Corporation study made at the turn of the century, in which immigrants who had been given permission to accept employment in the United States were asked what they had earned both before and after they arrived, found that the average gain was about $20,000 per year. Immigrants to Western Europe, Japan, Canada, and Australia probably did well also. This substantial jump in income, which frequently occurs just after crossing from a less developed society to a more developed one, suggests an unconventional way of looking at the second policy area that will be considered here—namely, taxation.

If mere access to a different society can make such a huge difference to income, perhaps the society's social institutions should be treated, collectively, as a money-producing mechanism. Everyone (not only immigrants) who profits substantially from access to this mechanism should help defray the costs of maintaining the societal structure. Of course, most residents do this already by paying taxes, but it may be that the concept of social organization as a money-making instrument would make it possible to calculate more rationally *how much* various individuals and enterprises should pay. Economists, who are often persons of noteworthy acuity, could certainly calculate with a fair degree of precision what percentage of each dollar earned by any given society member should be plowed back into the public treasury to cover the costs of publicly-funded functional groups in education, transportation, communication, public order, public health, defense, and elsewhere. Welfare costs should also be included, inasmuch as businesses and other profit making enterprises can be organized and subsequently expanded only when potential workers have some way of staying alive until they are needed.

But not only income should be taxed. Those who have amassed substantial profits and possessions want to be assured that these gains are not snatched away by predators or consumed by environmental disasters. Wealthy individuals can be reasonably sure that they will be able to keep a substantial proportion of their winnings only because of the protection afforded by military establishments, diplomats, environmental services, police, and other agencies. Economists should therefore calculate, in addition to an income tax, fair insurance fees for each individual's net worth—perhaps totaling a fraction of a penny on each dollar over a given minimum. These fees should then be included with the taxes that are paid to governments at various levels.

According to this line of reasoning, families and individuals with income and net worth near or below designated poverty lines should not be taxed at all; and in some cases they should be subsidized. They do indeed owe something to the society as a whole, in the sense that they enjoy at least a modest degree of security, opportunity and wellbeing, but most of them pay their society back in nonmonetary contributions. Many of us benefit directly or indirectly from what they do, whether they are unskilled workers, members of the clergy, retirees, mothers and child-care aides, graduate students, or hand-to-mouth poets, artists, and musicians, or unemployed persons seeking work. In addition to their "in-kind" contributions to the economy, such non-tax paying members of society are major sources of intangible benefits that make life more pleasant and interesting for others. They frequently offer friendship, encouragement, information, and other intangible values to those who need support, and may also contribute to the beauty and security of the environment.

These suggestions about tax collection policy may be dismissed as visionary or impractical by tax experts, but that is not of great significance. The main reason for introducing unconventional ideas about raising money to cover the costs of operating complex democracies is to emphasize that new formulas governing taxation are urgently needed. Present systems are mainly piecemeal adaptations of older systems, unsupported by any central concept, with the result that even in popular democracies tax policies still disproportionately enrich small elites. Enormous progress has been made, in that taxes now also benefit nearly all members of complex societies in one way or another. Indeed, the fact that a substantial proportion of tax revenues in a democracy are spent to facilitate the operation of businesses and many other private functional groups is an important reason for the greater prosperity of democracies. Nevertheless, greater recognition of the enormous part played by a society's less affluent groups in making private profits possible could lead to a fairer allocation of the tax burden.

Although they follow a somewhat different reasoning, two authors, professors of philosophy and of law at New York University, have come to a similar conclusion in a recent book on taxes and justice: "Our main message throughout this book has been that societal fairness, rather than tax fairness, should be the value that guides our tax policy, and that property rights are conventional: they are to a large extent the result of tax policies...so they cannot be used to determine what taxes are just." (Murphy and Nagel, 2002, p. 173) One of the book's reviewers adds a concise example of the way taxes help to create wealth: "Peace is a boon to hoteliers, Conrad Hilton pointed out in his will. Without vast taxpayer investments in keeping the peace, as well as in building roads and airports, his fortune would have been much smaller." (*New York Times,* April 21, 2002)

Discussion of taxes leads by a circuitous route to a third area, namely, foreign relations, in which our model of contemporary societies suggests government initiatives. One reason tax policy and foreign policy are related is because the increasing mobility of capital in the emerging world society has made it easier for individuals and functional groups to avoid regulation and taxation by moving their assets and/or headquarters to whichever country makes it possible for them to maximize profits. This often frustrates the efforts of individual nations to devise and enforce fair and efficient tax policies. It also facilitates the concealment of illegal gains. Consequently, an important goal for international negotiations in the coming years should be to establish mechanisms that will enable all governments to help each other enforce their respective tax laws. Some major steps in this direction have already been taken. Switzerland, for example, has relaxed regulations that formerly allowed dictators in other countries to hide looted funds in secret bank accounts. It now maintains a list of foreign leaders suspected of corruption and money laundering. (*New York Times,* Feb. 25, 2004) What is needed now is a continuation of the process until all national governments are cooperating.

The desirability of international cooperation with regard to taxes is one of many indicators that a new era in relations among societies and nations is rapidly emerging. An important aspect of this new era is that the world can now be thought of as a single political/economic unit. Much as the globe came to be seen as a geographic whole during the 16th and 17th centuries, we have become aware more recently that political, economic, and cultural developments in any part of the world can, and often do, affect conditions in all other areas.

We also have some knowledge—and many more theories—about the causes and effects of these interactions. There is increasing awareness that a world society is emerging—that the long-term security and happiness of people in any nation are more and more dependent on the welfare of people everywhere. As a Senior Fellow at the Council on Foreign Relations pointed out in the 1970's, whether one looks at security, the economy, ecological problems, resources and technological capacities, or general social problems, "national autonomy is everywhere on the decrease and the need to rely on actions of others virtually ubiquitous." (Morse, 1976, p.680) No nation will achieve the best possible quality of life for its people unless all nations work together.

The gradual development of international polls and surveys during the second half of the 20th century reflects growing interest in relationships among populations of widely disparate nations. As of 1980, a World Values Survey, coordinated at the University of Michigan, was organized by an international consortium of research organizations. The survey was repeated in 1990, 1995, and 2000. (Inglehart, *et al.*, 2000) As many as 80 countries were involved in some aspects of this study. A more recent "Global Attitudes Project" was conducted in 2002 by the Pew Research Center for the People and the Press. This survey interviewed nearly 40,000 people in 44 countries on all continents except Australia. Regular regional studies of public opinion are now conducted in Europe and Latin America.

One result of the increasing linkages among all societies, and the growing awareness of and knowledge about these global interrelationships, is that many new international functional groups are being formed, as has been noted in earlier chapters. More than ever before, it is possible for people in various nations to find ways in which they can work together for their mutual benefit. This is true most obviously with respect to international trade, but in the long run intellectual collaboration, not only in the sciences but also in the arts and humanities may prove to be more important. This is not to say that collaborative efforts to improve the lives of people throughout the world will always be successful, but it does mean that it makes sense for democratic governments (and also private groups concerned with international relations) to take an active part in stimulating such efforts.

A major goal of contemporary diplomacy, public and private, should therefore be to build a gradually widening consensus about cooperative actions that can be taken to improve the quality of life for all the world's inhabitants. Even before substantial agreement can be reached on more than a few specific points, it would be possible to encourage a sense that, whatever their differences as of the moment, all nations should be committed to working together toward shared objectives—that they should be searching for policies that will benefit all parties, and for ways to overcome disagreements. The work of United Nations agencies and of other binational and multinational agencies deserves strong support. Efforts to assist developing nations in building strong infrastructures for functional groups of all kinds would be likely to have major positive effects on building a peaceful prosperous world in the long run. Independent mass media channels would be particularly important in this regard, especially if they were able to engage in "joint venture programming" with other countries, as recommended by a Council on Foreign Relations task force. (2003, pp. 38-39)

Efforts to increase international cooperation through official diplomacy and through international agencies such as the World Bank and International Money Fund should be supplemented by increased government action to stimulate and facilitate work by private groups that try to improve conditions of life for people throughout the world. Most governments already support student exchanges and international professional meetings, but the possibilities for expanding this sector of governmental activities are almost infinite. For example, small subsidies would enable a wide variety of think tanks and universities throughout the world to explore additional ways in which people from different nations could help each other in satisfying both material and nonmaterial needs and desires. Even without increased governmental funding of such activities a lot could be accomplished with very little money or no money at all. Vigorous encouragement by official agencies might persuade numerous private groups to organize and pursue their own programs.

A great many examples of relatively small but successful efforts by both local and international bodies to improve the conditions for life, especially in poorer countries, can already be found. A recent volume entitled *"How to Change the World: Social Entrepreneurship and the Power of New Ideas"* details some of these. (Bornstein, 2004) The author, an economist, gives particular attention to the "micro-credit industry," especially in Bangladesh. Fifteen years ago, only a handful of organizations were involved, but today there are more than 2,500 micro-lenders and more than forty million borrowers. The Grameen Bank of Bangladesh, founded in 1976, had by 2003 made small loans totaling about $4 billion to 2.8 villagers, mainly women. (*Ibid.*, p. 13) Most loans were used for starting small businesses, often in the home. Similar micro-lenders can be found in numerous countries of Asia, Africa, and Latin America.

Other types of successful self-help operations are frequently reported in the press. For example, in one Iranian village where all major decisions had traditionally been made by a small group of elders, young people asked to participate. As a result, a five-person local council was elected. It attacked what were found to be the community's 81 most pressing problems, including seasonal flooding and the position of women. (*Washington Post,* September 2, 2001) Instances of this kind suggest that it would be worthwhile for international bodies, public and private, to "cross-report" such local initiatives. That is, systematic efforts should be made to insure that efforts to improve the quality of life that seem to succeed in one area could be brought to the attention of similarly-motivated groups in many areas. It might also be worth while to provide outside assistance for the organization of community groups similar to the one noted in Iran.

An ingenious and self-supporting method for assisting people in both complex and simpler societies to improve their living conditions has been suggested by a Senior Fellow at New York's Council on Foreign Relations. He points out that persons retiring in societies where the cost of living makes comfortable retirement too expensive for them might be encouraged to find retirement homes in countries where the cost of living is low. This would reverse the present situation in which immigrants from more traditional societies now frequently provide personnel to take care of retirees in the heavily industrialized nations. To this end, the various governments involved could negotiate a "suitable legal framework for issues like taxation, insurance, property, and inheritance." (Mead, 2004, pp. 207-209) The fact that increasing numbers of retirees in complex societies have no family members who can help to take care of them makes this suggestion more and more relevant.

A major goal of both government and private efforts to improve conditions of life for all the world's inhabitants should be to persuade as many people as possible to become involved in such efforts, even if the involvement is limited to participation in discussions. The vision of a world society in which everyone can contribute to more satisfactory conditions is one that can capture the imagination. Yet, no government or private group has yet found a way to dramatize the new possibilities for international cooperation that are constantly opening up; most of the world's inhabitants still feel powerless and therefore tend to sit back and wait for benefits to be delivered. Well considered propaganda and information campaigns could make many more people conscious of the gains that might be made if new ways of cooperating within and among nations can be found and exploited.

Of course, even low cost efforts to stimulate discussion of quality of life problems and to develop new ideas about how to deal with them require some money, and additional financial support for international cooperation is often difficult to obtain. The proposition that what helps people throughout the world achieve a better life is also good for you and your country is a difficult one to sell to voters or to contributors to good causes. As is the case with the proposition that paying taxes can save you money, attitudes formed in past centuries tend to inhibit the adoption of policies that seem to benefit foreign lands. Politicians who promise benefits for voters in their own country, even at the expense of other peoples, are often viewed with more approval than are "do-gooders" who advocate giving money to people of other nationalities while there are still many needy people at home. Old style politicians benefit from memories of the past, when the way for a country to become rich and successful was to exterminate or subjugate other tribes and nations and take their land and natural resources. Even when voters or contributors are benevolent, some of them can be persuaded that foreign peoples are less intelligent or less virtuous and that it is therefore to the advantage of other countries to be conquered and civilized, or else to be left to their uncivilized ways and treated as a source of cheap labor and low-cost raw materials.

Nevertheless, changes in the world environment have made these traditional views unrealistic, and it is a primary obligation of national leaders to emphasize this. Constantly increasing international interdependency—and the resulting gradual emergence of a world society—means that the self-styled practical person who still insists that the way to national prosperity is to dominate other peoples is actually a romantic dreamer with his head in the past. The costs of war and other forms of conflict keep going up, while wealth and nonmaterial values are increasingly a product of cooperation—both national and international. The successful nation of the future will be one that finds new ways for peoples to work together, so that everyone benefits. Nations and societies will continue to compete, but the winners will be not the most heavily armed, or the ones with the most suicide bombers, or the ones with the highest birthrates, but will be those that find the most mutually beneficial ways of using the enormous human talents that are widely distributed among nations.

This does not mean that defense establishments will become obsolete in the near future. The world is in the middle of a change from a tribal to a universal perspective—not at the end of the process. What is to be hoped for is that there will be constant improvements in techniques for conflict resolution, and also that more diligent searches for constructive solutions to international problems will be conducted. Cases in which governments conclude that violence is unavoidable will then become fewer and fewer. Nevertheless, sick and irrational behavior on the part of occasional governments cannot be ruled out. The big change that could be accomplished in the near future is acceptance by as many official and nonofficial leaders as possible of the idea that the most important goal of a national foreign policy is to build mutually rewarding international cooperation.

At the same time that governments search for new ways of exploiting the new potentialities of international cooperation, and encourage private bodies to do so also, they should take vigorous steps to oppose the three major threats to a peaceful and prosperous world society: violence, fraud, and population imbalances. Governments of most complex democracies are doing this already, but even greater efforts would yield enormous benefits. In particular, more attention should be given to assuring that families in areas where there are very high birth rates are assisted in limiting their size. Until the huge imbalances between population growth and the functional groups needed to lift millions of people out of poverty and despair can be corrected, mass violence and starvation will be difficult to avoid. The failure of the current United States government to give its full support to international efforts to promote family planning is one of the more discouraging aspects of today's world.

The possible achievements of more vigorous and inventive efforts to improve the human condition are sufficient to capture the imagination of people everywhere. It is within the realm of possibility that the grandchildren of those now starting their adult lives, on whatever continent, will experience substantial improvements in security, well-being and material prosperity. They also could enjoy greater freedom to develop their individual interests and potentialities. Even though nirvana cannot be achieved within the space of a few decades, the possibilities of improvement justify major efforts by democratic governments to agree on realistic plans that will ignite hope, enthusiasm, and vigorous discussion. As more people everywhere become conscious of the benefits that could accrue to them, the prospects for implementing individual projects will improve. The search for shared goals, and for additional ways in which nations can work together to achieve them, can in itself have positive effects on human behavior.

One of the positive effects of these efforts would be better control of domestic and international terrorism. Worldwide involvement of individuals, groups, and governments in devising plans for achieving a fuller life for everyone is a promising way to motivate broad segments of publics everywhere to build and preserve conditions that facilitate both domestic and international cooperation. Small terrorist groups and suicide bombers armed with weapons of mass destruction, which are difficult for law enforcement agencies to detect, are more likely to be neutralized if broad segments of the public everywhere come to realize that terrorism and violence of any kind are more likely to lead to worse conditions than to better ones. The groups best able to control potential terrorists (many of whom are psychologically abnormal even if not clinically sick) are the family, the community, and the neighborhood. There always have been and always will be extremists who are willing to resort to violence, but in past centuries most of them have been constrained by people around them — not by the police.

Of course, violent extremists and mentally abnormal people cannot always be prevented from throwing bombs, even by their friends and relatives. In such cases, people who happen to learn something about these terrorists' plans are more likely to take the trouble, and risk the possible danger, of cooperating with the authorities if they realize that violence is likely to worsen the quality of life for their families, and to make improvements more difficult for their children. On the other hand, if they see defeating terrorism merely as a way of preserving a miserable status quo, they will have little motivation to cooperate with forces of law and order.

Strenuous efforts to catch the imagination of members of all societies with a vision of the better life that would be possible in a more peaceful and cooperative world deserve a prominent place in the foreign policy of every nation. And the terrorists themselves are more likely to desist if their conduct is described as stupid, sick, and likely to make things worse. Denunciations of terrorist acts as despicable or inhuman may help to convince them that their goals are being achieved.

◆   ◆   ◆

Some of the suggestions in this chapter, although applying primarily to governments, may also be relevant to problems people encounter in nonpolitical contexts. Most of us take part in the leadership or management of big or small functional groups where we have quasi-governmental roles, even though we may not realize it. Sometimes, for example, we are the only individuals connected by communication channels with all members of a group. Our powers to shape policies and to enforce rules may also be considerable.

Whether the "governmental" functions we exercise are in families, businesses, voluntary associations, churches, or other functional groups, they are likely to involve us in some activities that resemble those of government officials. Perhaps we will want to stimulate creativity on the part of group members, encourage them to communicate with each other or with people outside the group, and help them develop their capabilities. We may be able to increase a group's efficiency by establishing conflict resolution machinery, or by working out procedures that will stimulate cooperation between old and new group members (the latter could be thought of as immigrants). In addition, our responsibilities may include collecting dues (or "taxes"), and may extend to "foreign policy"—that is, promoting cooperative or harmonious relations with other groups in the larger society or in foreign countries. In other words, some of the functions that have been discussed in this chapter mainly as responsibilities of government officials may devolve upon us in our private lives also, and some of the suggestions advanced here may be useful in these nongovernmental contexts.

The specific suggestions outlined above may not be the most promising ones, but it is likely that life for everyone in all societies would improve if we were to take our quasi-governmental responsibilities more seriously. Perhaps we should try to behave in our private lives the way we think our elected and appointed political officials ought to behave in public life! This would be a welcome reversal of the situation in which some people insist that high officials be judged according to the standards they observe in their private lives, rather than by their performance in office.

Well, perhaps that's going too far. Such thoughts may be so general and moralistic as to be of little practical value. But this notion about the part we play in society can at least lead to consideration of related questions that may be more relevant: How might the capabilities and skills of each one of us be enhanced in such a way that we will be better qualified to assume roles in the increasingly complex functional groups of the future? And how can we ensure that as many of us as possible end up in roles for which we are well qualified? Such questions can serve as an introduction to the next chapter.

9

Education and Placement

At the same time that many people have quasi-governmental functions, even more of us are educators, although we may not think of ourselves this way. It is obvious that overwhelming educational responsibilities are carried by parents and by teachers, but they are far from the only ones who help individuals learn enough to navigate successfully in the sea of life. Employers, supervisors, fellow workers, neighbors, friends, journalists, and many others are also constantly contributing to the knowledge and skills of people with whom they come into contact. The ideas about education outlined in this chapter are intended primarily for consideration by those who participate in academic life, but these observations may be relevant also to some of us without formal educational responsibilities.

The viability of a society in today's world is dependent in large measure on the quality of the education of individual society members and also on whether they occupy roles where they can use their skills and knowledge. Education, broadly defined as the transmission and acquisition of knowledge, skills, and values, contributes little to a society's strength unless those who are educated find roles in functional groups that enable them to make a large or small contribution to the society as a whole. In complex modern societies, the enormous diversity of functional groups has made efficient placement in jobs and in noneconomic roles more and more difficult, and we have been slow about confronting the problem. Schools and other educational institutions, and also parents, should be doing much more not only to help people acquire knowledge, skills, and values, but also to help them find roles where they can use what they have learned to the best advantage of both themselves and others.

However, both parents and schools in modern societies are already overwhelmed. As social complexity has increased, more and more tasks have been assigned to families and to educational institutions. They still bear traditional responsibilities for preparing young people for participation in the society's common culture, but that culture has become more and more demanding. It now includes a greater variety of widely-shared economic, political, cultural, recreational, and other activities, such as buying and selling, voting, television watching, book and newspaper reading, talking about football or baseball, and health maintenance.

Educational institutions in complex societies are now called on not only to perform traditional educational tasks but also to equip millions of people with professional and technical knowledge they will need in order to occupy thousands of specialized roles in business and the economy, government, and the professions.

As schools have been given added responsibilities during the past decades, the costs of educating young people and the number of years needed for formal education have risen sharply. Schooling takes a larger bite out of most lives than ever before. Two or three generations ago, only small minorities in the adult populations of industrialized countries had more than a primary school education. In the United States, as of 1940, fewer than 25 percent of the adult population had completed four years of secondary school and fewer than 5 percent had finished college. By the end of the century, some 85 percent had a secondary school degree, and more than 25 percent had graduated from a college or university. During roughly the same period, the annual expenditure per student in American public elementary and secondary schools rose from about $1,500 to approximately $7,600, in constant dollars. (These statistics have been compiled from the *World Almanac* and other respectable sources, almost all of which differ slightly when it comes to specifics but agree on orders of magnitude.) Figures from other industrialized countries are comparable. Yet, despite these huge increases in time and money devoted to education, most professional educators complain that they cannot do everything they should be doing to help students acquire the knowledge and skills they are likely to need, and also to help them find roles in which they can use their knowledge and skills to best advantage.

Because of financial and temporal limitations on formal educational institutions, large-scale adoption of all the measures suggested by our model of modern societies is clearly not feasible at the present time. Nevertheless, it may be helpful to describe some of these measures. Perhaps a few can be combined with existing activities, and others might take the place of traditional programs that are no longer as essential as they once were. Additionally, some desirable policies that have little chance of being adopted at any time in the near future could still serve as goals toward which educational systems can gradually work. It is important to recognize that most (perhaps all) of the suggestions made below have been tried out by educators in various fields. The ideas are not necessarily new. Our conclusion is that they should be given more emphasis.

The most important (and very expensive) educational policy suggested by changes in social and technological environments during the past few generations is that every person should now have an education tailored to his or her individual capacities and requirements. Individualized education has always been desirable, since each person has different capacities and desires, and it has always been available to at least some degree. Especially in earlier times, when families and neighborhoods performed most educational functions, parents and friends could take into account the characteristics of each child, and could instruct him or her accordingly.

In the present era, the availability of both improved testing techniques and computers makes it possible in theory for schools to develop a separate educational program for each student. As a professor of cognitive science, formerly at M.I.T. and currently at Harvard, has put it, "the sciences of the mind can...provide a sounder conception of what the mind of a child is inherently good and bad at." The problem thus becomes how to find ways that educators can get children to use their natural abilities to master materials that they find difficult. (Pinker, 2002; *New York Times,* Jan. 31, 2003) For example, the child who is naturally good at persuading other people but slow at arithmetic might learn arithmetic faster if he or she can be shown how useful numbers can be in the process of persuasion.

To administer individual programs for each child would, however, take an enormous number of professional educators and would break most educational budgets. Nevertheless, it is now generally recognized that smaller class sizes are desirable, and most teachers try to give each student as much individual attention as they can. As time goes on, it may be possible to come closer to the ideal of adapting educational programs to the capacities and unique talents of each individual.

Regardless of the difficulties involved, the following are a few of the ways in which schools in complex societies might increase their contributions toward a more peaceful world and a better life for everyone.

Emphasis on Diversity and Cooperation. Some elementary schools in the United States have posters on their walls with pictures of children from different backgrounds, and the words: "We are each unique and special." These, and similar displays in schools in other countries, are intended to promote tolerance and reduce the tendency of children to persecute classmates who speak other languages, don't follow current styles of dress, come from minority ethnic groups, or are otherwise perceived as different from the norm.

In addition, such posters can carry several implicit messages—some of which may be obvious only to the teachers. One such implicit message is that individual differences in personality and abilities can be a great asset in complex societies, which require people with many different kinds of talents and training to fill an enormous number of different roles. It is a logical, although untested, hypothesis that modern societies will offer a better life to their members if they learn more about how to take advantage of the wide variations in individual skills and predispositions among human beings. And the need for diversity is increasing. As more varieties of functional groups are developed to serve new needs and aspirations, people with very specialized abilities and preferences are needed to staff these mechanisms. We are all increasingly dependent on people who are unlike ourselves. The moral for educators is that they should devote as much attention as possible to helping each student make the most of his or her special interests and capacities.

Another implicit message is that there is no longer a "best student" in the class, as was often the case in grandmother's era. Individual students all have their strengths and weaknesses, and complex societies offer opportunities for nearly everyone to be good at something and to be bad at many things. Children who have trouble with arithmetic, spelling, or foreign languages should be made aware that everyone learns at a different rate, and that there is nothing wrong with taking more time, as long as they do their best. Those children who are slow in one area may learn faster in other areas—some of which may not be represented in the school curriculum. In addition, the slow learner sometimes makes better use of the knowledge that he or she has managed to acquire. One goal of the education process in a modern, complex society should be to give each individual pride in his or her unique capacities and achievements..

A third message is that schools should make as much use as they can of techniques for discovering and measuring individual abilities and attainments. Research in the sciences of the mind is proceeding at a rapid pace, with the result that every year more instruments and techniques for determining what a person is likely to be good at (or bad at) are available. It is becoming clear that what an individual learns and remembers depends in part on electrical and chemical processes in the brain, and that these processes differ from person to person. Very small variations in a single gene can make the difference between a good and bad memory. Thinking, also, is made possible by channels of communication among brain cells, so that some individual differences in processing information are likely to be due to variations in biological makeup. As it becomes possible to measure these differences more and more accurately, educators will be able to use such measurements to help individual students find the best learning techniques, subjects for study, and roles for later life.

The exciting possibilities of new techniques that can be used to assist students, both in their academic work and in choosing which functional groups they might like to participate in later on, should not obscure the fact that most schools are unable to make full use of the knowledge about testing and evaluation that is already available. Nor should quantitative measures (such as scores on multiple-choice questionnaires) be allowed to replace qualitative methods of evaluation that have proved their predictive value (such as the opinions of teachers and other expert observers). Both approaches are needed. That available techniques are not more widely used is usually due to shortages of personnel and lack of money, although political factors sometimes enter in also.

Tests of talent, knowledge, or "intelligence," whether qualitative or quantitative, can be destructive, especially when they result in a stamp of inferiority being placed on a child. Extreme caution is necessary. Nevertheless, the risks are no reason to disregard the potential gains. Educational institutions that use both old and new knowledge about the mind constructively will be able to qualify students to make a greater contribution in their societies than schools that routinely follow traditional educational practices only.

Our discussion of functional groups, and the many roles available in them, suggests how some dangers implicit in testing can be minimized or compensated for. Most important is that tests and evaluations should be focused on discovering talents and strengths—and not only in academic subjects. The emphasis should be on learning what an individual does well, or could do well, so that he or she can be helped in choosing congenial roles in various kinds of functional groups, including groups that provide recreation, affection and sociability as well as income. Similarly, weaknesses that become apparent as a result of tests should be explored in ways that enable the individual to overcome or compensate for them. For example, people who know they are slow readers can learn to allocate more time for a given amount of material, and those who have trouble remembering names or instructions may be helped by memory games or note-taking practice. An aim of education, at all ages, should be to equip people not only with useful information about the world around them but also with knowledge about themselves that will enable them to choose roles they like and can perform well. Educational institutions should do everything they can to make certain that students are aware of their own strengths and weaknesses—and of the ways in which their unique capabilities can help them contribute to the good life in a society.

Educational institutions that emphasize the positive nature of diversity are also likely to help students learn to cooperate with each other. Some schools have tried to do this by encouraging young people from various backgrounds to sit together at lunch every so often, rather than socializing only with fellow members of their own social or ethnic groups. Other institutions have included in their curriculums material about how to make friends, and have taught children various ways to resolve conflicts before they degenerate into fights. Psychologists, lawyers, political scientists, and others have developed promising methods of teaching conflict resolution. Some private companies now offer instruction in conflict-resolution techniques. Nevertheless, as with educational testing, most schools have been unable to give more than superficial attention to teaching cooperation and conflict-resolution techniques.

Research and experience in this area have outstripped the ability of educational institutions to make use of it. The lack of emphasis on conflict resolution in most primary and secondary education is not due to lack of ideas about what might be done. Research has increased enormously in the past few decades. There are now peace studies programs at several hundred colleges and universities throughout the world, and a Peace Studies Association was formed in 1987 to facilitate communication among these programs. (Rich and Strand, 2002) The *Journal of Conflict Resolution,* edited at the University of Michigan, has been published since 1957. It provides an enormous body of information on ways in which disputes can be settled and cooperative behavior increased. In addition, there is a substantial amount of popular and semipopular literature by lawyers, diplomats, arbitrators, and others that provides information about negotiation, mediation, and arbitration. One highly readable book by two Harvard University Law School professors is entitled: *Getting to Yes: Negotiating Agreement Without Giving In.* (Fisher and Levy, 1991) "This book began as a question," the authors write. "What is the best way for people to deal with their differences?" (p. xi) One of the book's conclusions, which is especially relevant to the present discussion, is summarized in its subtitle. This is that securing agreement does not necessarily mean giving up potential gains or violating strongly held principles. Schools should make every effort to see that students are familiar with the content of this volume or of similar books. More knowledge about the many ways of avoiding controversy and coming to agreements would benefit most of us, as well as the societies and the world in which we live.

The Vital Role of Communication in Education. Much as communication processes make possible the formation and operation of functional groups, they are also basic to education. An individual's ability to absorb knowledge, to think, and to exchange ideas with other people all depend on that person's capacity to receive and understand information, to store and manipulate this information internally, and to express ideas and emotions to others. One of a teacher's main jobs is therefore to help each student develop his or her capacities for receiving and comprehending, for remembering and thinking, and for using various means of expression, including writing, speaking, touching, and gesturing. We all need these three capacities.

As experienced teachers know, individuals vary tremendously in their inherited abilities to perform these various communication processes and also in the extent to which such abilities can be enhanced by training. Some students have sharp ears, read fast, and can understand quickly. Some are good at remembering and at putting two and two together. Others are effective speakers and writers. Most of us are strong when it comes to certain communication skills and are weaker in others; a relatively few fortunate individuals have outstanding abilities in all three categories.

The director of the Clinical Center for the Study of Development and Learning at the University of North Carolina estimates that weakness in one or more of the communication skills causes 10 to 12 percent of school children to suffer from "output failure." For example, they may fail to hand in homework at school and, in spite of being both motivated and intelligent, may be labeled as lazy or stupid. It is the responsibility of schools to diagnose the problem, which frequently can be overcome, and to take into consideration the child's strengths, "which are much more important in the long run." (Levine, 2003) The professor adds, however, that while schools are responsible for teaching children how to learn, "parents are responsible for teaching kids how to work." He suggests that parents "organize an office for the child, set up certain hours of the day that are for brainwork and keep kids in cognitive shape." (*Ibid.*)

A case history of an American male, whom we will refer to as "Raymond," illustrates some of the ways in which very slight differences in communication abilities, and either ignorance or knowledge of these abilities, can affect the life of an individual. When Raymond started learning to read in school, he complained to his mother that he sometimes could not hear what the teacher was saying. His mother took him to a pediatrician, who tested Raymond's hearing by holding a watch at varying distances from the little boy's ear and asking him whether he could hear the "tick." The doctor concluded that Raymond's hearing was normal and that his difficulties at school were due to lack of attention. The teachers at school agreed.

Despite his apparent attention deficit, Raymond made satisfactory progress in primary school, but his record in the public high school was only average. He usually scored low on intelligence tests, and concluded that he could not compete with the "smart" students. His parents became worried that he might not be admitted to a good college. They therefore sent him to a private school where classes were smaller and students were given substantial individual attention.

Before the first term at the private school was over, Raymond's teachers decided that the boy must be getting outside help with his written work. Even worse, he apparently was cheating in tests and examinations. The teachers agreed that his classroom work was poor; he frequently misunderstood questions; and he often failed to give the right answer even when it turned out that he had understood the question. In view of these obvious weaknesses, the relatively good quality of his written papers and his high marks on examinations were sufficient reason for suspicion. (Unlike the public high school, the private school did not use true/false or multiple-choice examinations.)

The school's headmaster summoned Raymond to his office and asked the boy why there was such a big difference between his classroom performance and his written work. Raymond explained that when writing essays and examination papers he had time to think, while in the classroom everything happened so rapidly that he had trouble keeping up with what was going on. The headmaster concluded that this explanation did indeed account for the disparity between Raymond's oral and written performance, and advised him to ask for clarification when he needed it in the classroom, and to take his time in answering questions. The boy's grades improved, and he was admitted to an excellent college.

While in college, Raymond learned that, although he read slowly, he had a better than average ability to recall what he had read and also that he had a facility for organizing and presenting this remembered information. With the aid of sympathetic faculty members, he also confirmed what he had suspected as a small boy—namely, that he had a slight but measurable hearing problem. It was not noticeable in personal conversation, but did indeed mean that he missed much of what was said in large class rooms. He learned also that his response time to many stimuli was longer than average. He was, literally, a slow learner. These deficiencies no longer caused serious difficulties after he became aware of them. He simply allocated more time to each task. Raymond graduated near the top of his class and embarked on a generally successful professional career. Probably because of his slow response time, however, he continued to score low on aptitude tests—especially those that required numerous decisions on multiple-choice questions within a limited time period.

A similar story, although more dramatic, is told by a mother writing about her son, Louie, in the *Washington Post*. (Carr, 2004) She explained that Louie had experienced increasing difficulties in school as he progressed through the grades. By the time he reached high school he was falling badly behind. A school counselor asked his mother to come in for a conference and explained to her that Louie's record and various standardized tests suggested he was suffering from dyslexia as well as attention deficit disorder. What happened after that is best told in the mother's own words: "When I told Louie about the diagnosis, he didn't look hurt or confused. Instead, his face relaxed and he shouted, 'You mean I'm not stupid?!' I was so taken aback that I started to cry. Louie said, still very relieved, 'Were you worried, too?' I cried harder."

Armed with knowledge about his disabilities, and with the benefit of a specially-designed education program that addressed his unique needs, Louie began to learn how to compensate for his difficulty in absorbing information. As of the time the article quoted from was written, he was doing well at a good college.

Most students are not as fortunate as Raymond and Louie were with respect to getting help in identifying and overcoming deficiencies in their ability to communicate, especially if these disabilities are relatively small or easily concealed. They end their formal educations without more than a general and frequently mistaken impression about their own personal strengths and weaknesses when it comes to receiving, arranging or storing, and transmitting ideas. Schools in complex societies do indeed offer some training in how to receive and understand communications (e.g., courses in reading and languages), how to remember and make use of information in various academic disciplines and day-to-day life, and how to express ideas (writing and public speaking). Mathematics neatly encapsulates elements of all three processes.

Nevertheless, many educational institutions are unable to ensure that each student receives a thorough evaluation of his or her communication abilities, and is informed about what might be done to compensate for deficiencies. Students graduate without knowing how their reading speed and ability to comprehend rapid speech differs from the average, whether their poor enunciation or unduly high or low voice placement lessens the ability of others to comprehend what they say, or if they have above or below average ability to make use of what they know.

Exploitation of individual differences for the good of both the individual and the society as a whole will be facilitated if we give greater attention to each person's inherited talents and acquired skills in communication. As Raymond's case history suggests, tiny differences among children in the ability to hear and interpret sounds may be responsible for large differences in what is learned and how rapidly it is learned. One child can tell from a tone of voice that a parent is angry, or sad, or happy—and another cannot. Jane may hear the voice of one teacher clearly but have trouble with the voice of a second, while for Dick the situation is just the reverse. These tiny differences have cumulative effects, and can influence the child's relationships with family members and playmates, the grades she or he receives in school, and even whether the graduating student will get a good job and build a happy marriage.

Nor is diversity in communication abilities a matter of interest only to individuals and their families. All of a society's functional groups will benefit if each person learns how to make the most of his or her abilities to hear, think, and speak as clearly as inherited physical capacities will allow. Far too many people perform their roles less well than they could, or end up in inappropriate roles, because they are unaware that their skills in one or more types of communication are above or below average. Raymond, in later life, expressed regret that he had never taken advantage of speed reading courses or of opportunities to develop more skill in public speaking.

Similar observations can be made about the importance of educational institutions in identifying and exploiting other individual differences, in helping people learn techniques of cooperation and conflict resolution, and in assisting students to find roles they can perform both happily and well. Small advances (or declines) in any of these areas can affect the performance of functional groups of many kinds and may influence the extent to which a society is making good use of its human resources.

Although professional educators are not alone when it comes to preparing people to work together and to relate harmoniously to each other, the importance of schools and other specialized educational bodies tends to grow as societies become more complex. Educational institutions provide increasingly indispensable linkages between the talents of each person and the functional groups on which the society's welfare—and ultimately its survival—may depend.

10

Notes on the Individual's Pursuit of Happiness

The thesis to be presented in this chapter is that greater familiarity with ways complex societies are organized, and with reasons why functional groups satisfy human wants and needs well or poorly, can help people lead more satisfying lives. More specifically, it will be argued that we can make better use of our time and energy if we:

- periodically inventory our group affiliations and satisfy ourselves that they are helping us achieve values we consider most important

- monitor changes in our social and physical environments, and also in our own talents and capabilities, and learn how to adapt to both—or simply decide not to adapt

- are aware of our own hierarchy of goal values and also of changes in this hierarchy that may occur as we grow older and environments change

- maintain frequently updated plans for lifetime education, based on our goals and on what we know about our individual strengths and weaknesses

- make use of the increasingly available opportunities for further learning

But is there documentation to support the thesis that better understanding of the role functional groups play in our lives will help us to reach our individual goals? More specifically, why should the five very general suggestions summarized above be helpful in the pursuit of happiness? A critic who kindly agreed to read this essay prior to its publication had the following to say about the suggestions: "I would ask for evidence, for empirical studies, (or) a convincing record of experience...."

This criticism highlights the fact that there have been very few (if any) systematic studies that are principally concerned with the ways that knowledge about social organization in general can be useful to the individual. One reason for this was noted by Robert Merton half a century ago when he pointed out that relatively few efforts had been made to provide models of large-scale social organization, and that sociologists had been more successful in formulating theories of the middle range than in building grand theory. (Merton, 1957) This paucity of ideas about how different social processes within a society are linked to each other, and how the individual is pushed and pulled in several directions at once, have made it more difficult to understand the relationships between social organization and happiness. Numerous popular "self help" books are based largely on psychological research (e.g., Goleman, 1995; and Sheehy, 1976). In contrast, there has been little use of sociological research in this literature.

Yet, there are impressive numbers of publications that deal directly or indirectly with the influence of particular functional groups on behavior. Many of these provide anecdotal evidence that people benefit from knowledge about and participation in a wide variety of organizations. Therapists who are helping people overcome substance abuse frequently refer their patients to Alcoholics Anonymous or similar bodies. (Diamond, Jonathan, 2000) Consulting psychologists and psychiatrists nearly always try to learn about families and other functional groups that play an important part in the lives of those they are treating. Social workers often put their clients in touch with community organizations that can provide help or encouragement. Many therapists organize encounter groups and support groups. (e.g., Berne, 1964) As one therapist has noted, people trying to recover from an addiction often are driven by a desire to recover a lost spirit of community. (Treadway, 1990)

Also relevant are numerous books and articles (mostly written for mass audiences) on how to get ahead in business enterprises or how to improve your marriage. Dale Carnegie's *How to Win Friends and Influence People, 1936,* was one of the first in a long series of self-improvement volumes that attracted millions of readers. Most of these books make at least some references to the utility of knowledge about social organization, although they make much more use of popular psychology.

Even earlier there appeared substantial numbers of books and articles that were often collectively described as treatises on *How to be Happy Although Married.* With the benefit of hindsight, one can argue that the popularity of these writings (and the inclusion of the word "although" in the phrase used to describe them) implied acceptance of the notion that marriage did not necessarily bring happiness. This should have given advance warning of the flood of divorces in complex societies that was to build up during the 20th century. Many such publications made it evident, whether intentionally or not, that inherited ideas about family structures and roles harmonized poorly with the new social environment that was taking shape. During the 19th and early 20th centuries, especially, increasing numbers of married people suffered bitterly. Law and tradition were strong enough to keep them together, but the family roles they had inherited provided them with few satisfactions in the changing environment. Women, especially, were developing new expectations, two-income families were becoming more common, and parents were feeling pressures to play new roles in their children's education.

There is thus an impressive amount of literature that suggests the usefulness of knowledge about certain categories of functional groups, especially families and businesses, when it comes to achieving personal goals. But there have been few efforts to focus on the ways in which information about social organization in general can help the individual lead a more satisfying life.

This essay cannot make more than a small contribution to filling the gap in the literature, but it may at least suggest questions that can be asked about functional groups with which we are involved, or would like to become involved. Even though tendencies to take existing social organization for granted are deeply rooted, in a time of rapid environmental change many of us can benefit if we pause to consider whether our present affiliations and relationships are really serving us well. It may also prove useful to formulate questions about our personal goals and to consider the extent to which various functional groups are helping us, or might help us, to achieve them. These questions may lead to decisions about which way to turn at the next fork in the road.

Making Better Use of Functional Groups. If we want more out of life, one of the first things we can do is to find out whether we might derive increased satisfactions from the functional groups to which we already belong, or with which we frequently have to deal. Can we get a raise at the office? Are there ways we might do our job better? Does the family provide us with the security and affection we had hoped for? Might we increase the happiness of other family members by giving them more love and respect—and what would happen then? How can we maintain and increase the good will of our neighbors? Are the charities to which we contribute time and money really helping to build the kind of world we would like to live in? Is there any way we can learn more from what our school or university has to offer? How about the circle of friends with whom we play bridge or drink coffee? Is the time well spent? Greater satisfactions are likely to flow from participating in these and other functional groups if we look at each as a mechanism that satisfies some of our wants and needs, and ask whether there is anything we can do to make it work better.

Many of the same questions we ask about organizations in general, when trying to judge their efficiency, are relevant to groups with which we are affiliated in our personal worlds. We want to know whether the ideas on which they are based are sound, whether they have the best possible communication channels, and whether the personnel who operate them are well qualified. Thus, most of the observations about improving the working of functional groups that were made in Part I of this essay apply here also. It is unnecessary to repeat them. The big difference is that, in the context of our personal lives, when we talk about qualified group members we are first of all talking about ourselves. One way to increase the efficiency of functional groups to which we belong is to educate ourselves so that we will do a better job or can play a more constructive role. We may also be a source for promising ideas, and may help develop a better structure or communication network.

The search for a more satisfying life involves us not only in attempts to improve the performance of functional groups to which we already belong, but also in making choices among many different groups. We are sometimes founding members of new collectivities, as when forming a household or starting a business or recreational group. In other cases, we become new employees of existing businesses, join active religious institutions, or move into established communities. Whatever courses of action we decide on, we may have to evaluate several different groups and roles to see which ones are most likely to satisfy our own needs and aspirations. Which affiliations might yield the benefits we want the most and which might lead to frustrations and hardships? We should look also at our own characteristics and capabilities. Am I qualified for that role, or is there any way I could become qualified?

In today's world, people have to engage in these evaluations of functional groups and have to choose among them more frequently than has ever been the case before. This is partly because the past is now a less useful guide to behavior in the present than it once was. Knowledge of the ways humans have been able to satisfy their needs and desires throughout history is still extremely important, but because of increasingly rapid rates of environmental change we more often have to stop and consider whether patterns of behavior established by our forebears are still the most appropriate ones for us.

We are thus forced to carry an increasingly heavy burden of choice. The societies in which we live are more complex than those in which our parents grew up. There are many more categories of functional groups that have to be staffed. People are living longer. We have to choose among different functional groups even when we are very young, especially among groups of playmates and school friends. As we grow older we discover new interests, aptitudes, needs, and desires that can be served by many different kinds of groups. To find rewarding roles in these varied groups, we often need more specialized skills than did our parents or grandparents, and at the same time probably will require a broader range of knowledge about the world in general. We have to know how to operate computers and cell phones, and also to be aware that events occurring on the other side of the globe can affect our day-to-day lives.

At the same time, we find it necessary or desirable to learn how to interact with more people who are unlike ourselves than was true in previous eras. Functional groups to which we belong, even families, are now more likely to include individuals who have learned behavioral codes that differ from the ones we have acquired. People with whom we frequently interact may pursue a wide variety of interests, some of which we do not share. The importance of learning communication skills and techniques of conflict avoidance and resolution has therefore increased. One should know how to coexist with and often to work with other people who have different customs and different values.

As we grow older, we usually have more influence on the structure, composition, and activities of some of the groups in which we participate. But many of us take only limited advantage of our opportunities to choose and to influence. We allow chance, tradition, or more purposeful people to determine our affiliations. The results of behaving like driftwood in a stream are not always bad; indeed they can be very good if one has intelligent and loving family and friends. On the other hand, it is also possible that many of us would experience more satisfying lives if we were to take a careful look at the various functional groups with which we spend so much time, and to which we devote so much energy.

It is often helpful to inventory the most important functional groups to which one belongs, or with which one spends time, whether they are formal organizations or informal gatherings of friends. Our fellow group members may be in one place or widely separated. They can be participants in a chat room on the internet or they may belong to our immediate families. Within a formal organization, such as a school, a church, or a business, there may be several sub-groups that should be listed. Group size doesn't matter; a two-person family may be the most important entry on our list. It is sometimes useful also to inventory groups to which we would like to become affiliated if possible. How long either list will be depends partly on how we define "important." Some people would end up with a hundred or more entries if they tried to be exhaustive. It is probably more appropriate to try and identify the top ten or fifteen.

The next step is to ask why we are affiliated, or would like to be affiliated, with each of these groups. What do we get out of them, or what benefits do we expect? This question is sometimes easy to answer, but more often is quite difficult. Functional groups can provide not only material benefits but also important nonmaterial satisfactions. Sometimes we are unaware of the latter, or we take them for granted. A job, for example, is often not only a source of income but may also provide sociability, self-respect and even entertainment. Families may supply their members with affection, information, and a sense of security, as well as with room and board. A tennis playing or hiking group, whether or not formally organized, is likely to be not only an asset to good health but also a source of sociability and friendship. In order to evaluate participation in any collectivity one has to consider all the advantages and disadvantages before deciding whether net benefits justify the investment in time, money and energy.

This focus on the bottom line can help us avoid mistakes. Many people become so conscious of what is wrong with their jobs, their marriages, or their communities that they fail to consider what is right with these affiliations. In such cases, they are likely to make decisions they later regret. Countless children, feeling oppressed and confined by parents whom they see as demanding or unreasonable, have considered running away from home. Fortunately, before packing their most prized belongings in a pillow case and exiting by the back door, most of these children become aware that the benefits of staying with the family outweigh the indignities or deprivations against which they are rebelling. Adults should try to be equally reasonable.

Nevertheless, the unhappy children remind us that it makes sense to examine periodically the rules and structures of functional groups to which we belong. Whether we see a group's bottom line as a plus or a minus, we should consider whether changes in the way the group is organized, or in the roles of its members, might significantly improve benefits. If these changes are feasible, an unattractive group may turn into an attractive one, and an affiliation that we already enjoy may become even more desirable.

Restructuring an organization so as to realize larger profits is common in the business world, especially as environments change. It can be equally desirable for functional groups in other sectors of a society. Some retirement communities, for example, have found that, as they grow in size, publication of a "house" newsletter tends to increase the average number of friends that residents have. Marriage counselors have noted that relatively minor role revisions—perhaps in connection with making love—can sometimes turn a shaky marriage into a good marriage, and a good marriage into a deliriously happy one. And communities in which neighbors learn to know and to cooperate with each other may have lower crime rates as a result, at the same time that neighborhood residents enjoy more affection and sociability.

In addition to thinking about improvements that could be made in the functional groups to which they belong, people are well-advised also to consider from time to time whether these groups harmonize well with each other. Perhaps some of these affiliations conflict and thus reduce the benefits of belonging to one or more organizations. During the second third of the 20th century, for example, many voters in the South of the United States became conscious that their traditional identification with the Democratic Party harmonized poorly with their economic interests. More and more of them began to support Republican Party candidates. At the same time, African-American voters throughout the country found that identification with the Democratic Party was more likely to be consistent with their other affiliations than was the party of Abraham Lincoln, author of the Emancipation Proclamation. Legal authorities often refer to simultaneous participation in two or more organizations that have opposing purposes as "conflict of interest." Many of us experience such conflicts even when no legal questions are involved.

Some incompatibilities may not be obvious, however. Teen-agers often fail to realize that their efforts to play roles prescribed by their friends of the same age can put them at a disadvantage when it comes to getting a good education and a good job. Some people in all parts of the world struggle to retain traditional religious affiliations that make it difficult for them to play their roles in business or professional groups to which they also belong. Efforts to reconcile these conflicts are occasionally amusing. The story is told that the American financier Russell Sage (1816-1906) once attended a religious revival meeting at which the preacher's eloquence persuaded Sage to contribute more money to charity than he later concluded he could afford. But Mr. Sage subsequently reported that the very next day the Good Lord had shown him how to get all that money back from other traders on Wall Street. When he made this unusual observation about the importance of divine guidance on Wall Street, the fabled financier may have been quite serious. As Max Weber explains in his *Protestant Ethic and the Spirit of Capitalism,* some Calvinist theologians held that God may help a deserving business person make a profit because the money is needed for a good purpose. (Weber, 1904-05, p. 109)

A systematic inventory of almost any individual's group affiliations frequently makes it obvious that there are frictions among them. Most commonly, the family and the job compete for time and attention. Often, merely being conscious of these frictions can help to lessen them, or at least may moderate their destructive effects. Thus, when people who belong to one political group get together with friends who identify with an opposing group, all those present may decide simply to avoid certain controversial topics.

In other situations, negative influences from one group may be reduced by positive influences from another. For example, therapists who are trying to help a member of a dysfunctional family may encourage this person to join an outside organization that will provide him or her with social support. One therapist notes that "involvement in an active and politically conscious social network" may be a significant factor in recovery. For example, he found that several of his patients had benefited from their affiliation with a group that assisted mothers of girls who had been sexually abused. (Diamond, Jonathan, 2000, p.178)

Many of us fail to take advantage of affiliations with the potentially helpful groups that are available to us. Lack of time and energy, or preoccupation with making a living and satisfying current responsibilities, or commitment to established habits and routines, or just shyness, may make us reluctant to even think about becoming involved with a new group. Two additional difficulties may restrain even those who are eager to explore opportunities for enriching their lives or coping with difficulties. One problem is in finding out what functional groups are actually accessible and what these groups really do. Most informal organizations—especially those consisting of a few individuals who share a particular interest—are small and not easily located, even when they are close at hand. The other difficulty is that many people are not sure what they want. They have a sensation of emptiness or dissatisfaction, of being unfulfilled, but are not sure what it is they are looking for.

When one wishes to locate possibly congenial or helpful functional groups, the opportunities are legion. The internet is the most convenient source for many people. Libraries are also usually accessible, although encyclopedias of associations and other written sources ordinarily restrict themselves to formal organizations that have officers and addresses. Local newspapers and newsletters that report on meetings and activities of many kinds are another good source. Social workers and clergy often know what is going on in various neighborhoods, and are usually happy to help people find groups that will satisfy some of their needs.

In many cases, the most promising sources of information are friends, relatives, co-workers, and casual acquaintances. Those who make efforts over a period of time to find out what other people they know do for amusement, edification, or advancement are likely to uncover a range of fascinating opportunities. Whatever sources are used, exploring one's environment for possibly interesting or helpful groups of people can be a rewarding activity.

An example of how a neighborhood organization can help a person satisfy one or more needs or interests has been provided by a New Jersey journalist who covered activities of local government bodies for a township weekly newspaper. She gradually became aware of a pleasant young woman who often attended public meetings of the zoning board, planning board, or township council. This woman mingled with others who attended the meetings, and occasionally asked questions, but didn't seem to have any official or unofficial responsibilities. The reporter finally approached the other woman and asked why she came to so many meetings, especially since they were often long and dull.

It turned out that the mysterious attendee was a suburban housewife whose family had recently moved to the neighborhood. She and her husband had two small children but few acquaintances in the area; they had to live on a tight budget, and he had to travel almost constantly on business. So, one evening every week, she hired a baby sitter for a few hours and came to whatever township meeting was scheduled for that evening. During and after meetings she was able to get acquainted with interesting people (of whom the reporter was one), and sometimes free refreshments were available. Her most important consideration, however, was that in the following year, when both children would be in school or day care, she intended to apply for a job with the township government. By that time she would not only know personally many of the town's officials but also would be familiar with the kinds of problems they faced. People who volunteer for jobs with social service organizations or political groups often have similar long-term strategies.

Contrasting with the volunteers, and the woman who attended so many township meetings, there are many individuals would like to enrich their lives but are not sure what it is they are looking for. Nor are they conscious of the range of rewards that are possible as a result of group membership. These people can sometimes be helped by a check list of the gratifications that nearly all human beings seek. Such a list may allow them to visualize the various benefits that particular affiliations are likely to bring. It can also be useful when it comes to anticipating disadvantages. A job, for example, might look interesting and pay well, but it might also lack security and respectability. A listing of the various gratifications that group membership may or may not bring can thus facilitate comparisons of alternative courses of action.

There are other uses for such a list of potential gratifications also. Those who wish to evaluate existing group affiliations, which they may have inherited or fallen into by chance, sometimes find the list helpful. Systematically reviewing the rewards associated with various affiliations can be a factor in deciding whether to invest more time and effort in a particular group or to do something else. In addition, an inventory of the diverse needs and desires that can be served by group membership may contribute to a better understanding of other people's behavior.

We may ask ourselves: Why does she stay with such a stupid husband? Or, we may wonder why he doesn't just resign from the club if he doesn't like so many of the other members. In such cases, a look at possible gratifications can lead to new insights.

What Nearly Everyone Wants out of Life. There are various lists of the material and nonmaterial values sought by most people, but all these lists have deficiencies. Some are more complete or detailed than others, and some include overlapping categories. The list I find most useful is based on (although not completely identical with) a series of categories developed by Harold D. Lasswell, an innovative scholar of the 20th century who contributed substantially to psychology, sociology, and political science. He found that almost all people seek the following desiderata, which he called goal values: Well-Being, Power, Wealth, Affection, Safety, Respect, Enlightenment, Skill, and Rectitude or Justice. (Lasswell, 1976, p. 17) If one is looking for a job, the ideal position might provide a measure of all these values. It would be in a healthy environment, give authority to the incumbent, pay well, and allow one to work with friends, as well as provide security, prestige, and interesting information. Further, it would enable one to use and develop one's skills, and to always be on the side of justice or virtue. Many functional group affiliations provide several of these rewards, but few affiliations (whether or not income-producing jobs) offer all of them.

One can add or take away from the list. Some critics, for example, feel that entertainment should be included as a separate category. Others disagree, holding that the wish to be entertained is one aspect of the desire for well-being. The latter point out that people want to be entertained in order to feel relaxed, escape from worry, and have time pass pleasantly. Or, it might be that a category called beauty should be added, since it's a quality that everyone desires. But then we have to confront the problem that what is beautiful to one person may be ugly to the next. At which point the critic may observe that the same objection could be made to including justice in the list. Different people don't necessarily agree on what justice consists of.

The position taken here is that such a list does not have to be perfect in order to be useful, and that this one is an instrument that can be helpful in comparing the benefits offered by different social groups. It can also be useful in highlighting personality differences. For example, people vary enormously in the importance they attach to the various goal values. When one asks students to rank the values according to their importance, "enlightenment" is likely to be high on the list. For senior citizens, "well-being" and "security" tend to be near the top. In poor neighborhoods, "wealth" receives a higher score than in more affluent residential areas

Despite such differences, nearly everyone wants at least some amount of each value, but we all tend to have different ideas about what this amount should be, and which values are the most important. People who focus disproportionately on any one value are likely to be regarded unfavorably. Those who seem to want nothing but money can be seen as greedy misers; those too eager for power tend to be regarded as tyrants or bullies; those who value safety most highly are cowards; those who insist on justice in all cases without exception are likely to have little capacity for mercy. And so it goes.

Some of these categories can be defined more easily than others. Well-being refers to good health in a very broad sense. We not only want to be free from illness; we would like to be comfortable and to feel good "A book of verse beneath the bough/A flask of wine, and thou..." suggests an idyllic state of well-being, in addition to the enjoyment of other values. The ultimate denial of well-being is loss of life. The highwayman who demands "your money or your life" is capitalizing on the fact that most people prefer life to wealth when forced to decide between the two. A less drastic choice among values is posed by the airline that offers you a narrow and uncomfortable seat at a low price or a luxurious armchair at much greater cost.

Power includes the ability to influence as well as to command—to dispose of people and things as one wishes. We all want power, just as we all want good health, but some are more eager for it than others; many individuals are content with relatively little, while others can never get enough. One person may leave a highly paid job to take a political post with less pay but more power, while a second will rank affection higher than either pay or power, and will resign an important position in government or industry to spend more time with spouse and children. Those who value power highly may resort to unapproved methods to obtain it, perhaps by becoming schoolyard bullies or by assassinating rivals.

Wealth is something almost everyone wants, but we all make different decisions about what to sacrifice, and how much to sacrifice, in order to get rich. The way a desire for wealth competes with other values can often be seen when a person is trying to decide which of several jobs to accept, or which line of work to prepare for. Salary may be a deciding factor for some, but others will choose an occupation that pays less well and provides more of other values. Professions that rarely promise wealth, such as journalism, teaching, or theology, have nevertheless usually been successful in attracting able personnel. Yet, at the same time, it is a rare journalist, teacher, or member of the clergy who will refuse a larger salary—although he or she may later give away the additional money.

Affection includes love, both passionate and platonic, and friendship. Few of us can be happy, or even survive in the long run, without a measure of both. But some people give and/or receive a lot of affection; others make do with very little. The news media typically pay attention to situations where affection plays either an unusually large role, or a strikingly small one. A king who abdicates his throne to be with the woman he loves and the parent who shows wanton cruelty toward a child are both likely to be written up and talked about.

Respect is more difficult to define, in that it shades into other values, some of which almost everyone wants, and some that are less universally desired. Nearly all of us like to be esteemed, to know that others have a good opinion of us. Most people like attention, too, which often is an indication of respect. To appear on television, or to have one's name in the newspaper, is usually regarded as a mark of distinction. Even notoriety is occasionally welcomed; there are those to whom being ignored is worse than being criticized. This seems to be true of many small children. The prominent part that flattery, both genuine and counterfeit, plays in political and social life testifies to the importance of respect, as do the extremes to which people will go to "save face." Almost all of us want self-respect; those who seem to be completely without a desire for respect are sometimes classified as sick.

Safety is a condition in which one is protected against loss, usually loss of well-being or wealth, although some people also seek assurances that they will not lose power, respect, or affection. Safety is more than this, however, because it is associated with the feeling of being secure—a feeling that is pleasurable in itself, regardless of the type of deprivation that is forestalled. A lock on the door, a financial hedge against inflation, tenure in a job, a public relations counsel to protect one's reputation—they all can promote a feeling of security.

Enlightenment is a little like respect, in that it covers a spectrum of desiderata. Is satisfying one's curiosity a response to the same desire as mastering a science? How about keeping informed? The desire for information or knowledge takes many forms, and can be experienced as an inconsequential velleity or as a passion. The weary commuter who turns on the television news in the evening to see if anything noteworthy has happened that day and the scientist who stays up all night to complete an experiment are both seeking enlightenment, and both may have difficulty staying awake, but the resemblance usually ends there. There are some people, including many journalists and scholars, who organize their lives around a search for information; others devote little energy to it. But we all have to keep on learning about the essential aspects of our changing environments in order to survive. We often seek out information that will help us achieve one or more of the other goal values important to us. Information that is not relevant to some other value we cherish is easily forgotten, or may not be perceived at all. At the same time, the fact that we often just want to satisfy our curiosity suggests that the desire for enlightenment can be independent of other goal values.

Similarly, skill covers a range of motivating factors, but they all have to do with the urge to do something well, or with the appreciation of something that is very well done. The athlete and the devoted fan both admire skill, and their behavior is influenced accordingly. One devotes long hours to training and practice; the other pays a large sum for a good seat at a sporting event. The artist and the museum patron, the master craftsman and the discriminating consumer, the famous surgeon and the apprehensive patient—all are concerned with the development of skill, or with the enjoyment of its fruits.

Rectitude is the final goal value on this list. It includes justice, doing the right thing, and having the right thing done by others. Nearly all of us approve of justice in principle, and we are likely to love it most if we are the ones who will benefit from its application. Some people will devote almost any amount of time and money to the pursuit of justice—perhaps to right a wrong—and there are also those for whom it is of paramount importance to do what they conceive of as right, even if it is painful, expensive, risky, or embarrassing. Most people, however, do not seem to rank rectitude near the top of the value scale, unless they themselves are affected by its absence. If my neighbor suffers an injustice, I may feel unhappy, but I am also likely to think that it is the responsibility of someone else to right the wrong.

Anything we do is ultimately in pursuit of one or more of these goal values—at least, that is the theory. You may rake the leaves in front of your house to gain the good opinion of your neighbors (respect), or because you love neatness and order for itself (skill); or perhaps because the doctor has advised you to exercise (well-being). Most likely, you are seeking more than a single benefit. One person will take a job because it pays well, is prestigious, and offers security. Another person may prefer a position that makes it is possible to work with friends, to promote social justice, or to acquire knowledge. If you are trying to persuade someone else to do something, you usually point out to him or her which goal values will be achieved by doing it, or will be lost by not doing it.

An inducement that will satisfy a desire for a particular value in one person may not do so in another. The familiar phrase, every man has his price, suggests that the attractiveness of a reward will vary from one person to the next. A few ounces of gold may make some feel wealthy, but others require many pounds of the precious metal before they see themselves as affluent. Often, a feeling of wealth, or of poverty, depends on whether one has more wealth, or less wealth, than others in the community.

Similarly, conditions that will satisfy the desire for security, or respect, or affection in one person may leave another feeling insecure, unappreciated, and unloved. Nearly all of us want much the same satisfactions from life, but we want them in different amounts, and our desire for them can be satisfied in different ways. It's usually a sense of satisfaction we are looking for, not a specific amount of a particular value.

Each person's life is a struggle to achieve just the right mixture of the different goal values. Most of us have to incur deficits in some so as to gain more of others. The artist may sacrifice wealth and well-being in order to achieve skill, and the scholar may do the same for knowledge. An idealist may forfeit respect or safety in order to satisfy a desire for justice or rectitude. Most commonly, people endure deficits in such values as well-being, affection, and rectitude in order to achieve more power and wealth. The hard-nosed executive may sacrifice his health, make his family and employees miserable, and engage in shady deals in order to increase his bank account or to rise higher in the company.

Recent attitude studies have found a growing emphasis on nonmaterial values in the modern world. The coordinator of the World Values Survey writes: "In economic behavior, we find a gradual shift in what motivates people to work: emphasis is shifting from maximizing one's income and job security, toward a growing insistence on interesting and meaningful work" (Inglehart, 1997, p. 327)

This finding suggests, paradoxically, that one reason power and wealth are still sought by so many people is that they can be used to acquire and enjoy other values. The much-maligned money grubber may actually be a person who wants a substantial bank account so that he can retire comfortably, learn to paint, and study philosophy. In other words, he really wants well-being, skill, and enlightenment. The schoolboy who uses his superior strength and fighting ability to dominate his peers and disrupt the classroom may be trying to impress an attractive girl. He wants respect and affection.

Power and wealth can often, even if not always, be used to gain respect, well-being, safety, and justice. Skill, affection, and enlightenment cannot be bought, or gained by force alone, although enough power or money can usually assure membership in an expensive athletic club, an attractive spouse, and admission to a good school. Most wealthy people are willing, even eager, to trade substantial wealth for material and non-material rewards they want more. The fact that wealth can be traded for other values is one of the bases for philanthropy. You can become well-known by having your name on a building, and may also enjoy the affection and respect of those who benefit from your gifts. In former times, a substantial gift could buy you a ticket to heaven issued by an ecclesiastical authority. Value trading helps to explain conspicuous consumption and, indeed, a large proportion of economic activity. Other values can be traded, too, but less easily than power and wealth.

The phenomenon of value trading, in which we all engage, may make it difficult to determine what other people really want. Sometimes it is not easy to decide what we most want ourselves. Considerable introspection may be necessary. This is another occasion on which a list of goal values may be useful. One can go down the list and often identify values that may be relevant in a particular situation.

We all establish our own hierarchies of values—sometimes easily and sometimes with difficulty. These gradations of what we want most usually change somewhat as we go through life, but they are always there. We are happy when we can enjoy what we consider the right amounts of the good things the world has to offer. And, despite what cynics have to say about human nature being dominated by greed for money and power, for most people other values are more important. At least, at many points during a lifetime everyone is likely to give up some power and/or wealth in the pursuit of good health, affection, justice, or another nonmaterial value

Education as a Lifelong Preoccupation. Once we have decided what it is we really want, whether or not we get it often depends heavily on our formal and informal education. This is because training and experience are usually necessary to qualify us for roles in functional groups that can satisfy our wants and needs. We may end up in these roles because of good luck—it is especially convenient to be born into an affluent and caring family. But it also helps a lot if we have acquired the knowledge and skills that are needed to do good work in one or more occupations, or to function well as a spouse, neighbor, parent, friend, or football player. To be qualified for any role we need to learn how to do it.

As mentioned earlier, families, communities, and sometimes elementary schools in simple societies were able to train most people for the roles that they would play in their later lives, whether as parents, farmers, warriors, or members of the nobility or of religious communities. There were not many functional groups among which a person could choose, and behavioral codes changed very slowly. Consequently, education was something that happened while one was still young. Relatively little additional education, except for on-the-job experience, was needed in later life.

In modern, complex societies the situation is very different. If we want to be satisfied, we have to continue learning as we grow older. As we have seen, the numbers of functional groups and roles from among which a person has to choose is constantly growing and many roles are becoming more specialized. Not only are more kinds of jobs available, but there are more categories of families, communities, recreational groups, religious organizations and voluntary associations of all types. Furthermore, most of these functional groups are changing fairly rapidly. We die in societies that differ in important respects from the ones in which we grew up. Lifelong education and training are usually necessary if one is to perform a series of changing roles well enough to satisfy one's personal hierarchy of values.

Furthermore, the models of complex societies that have been presented in this essay suggest that, in modern settings and especially in democracies, each individual bears primary responsibility for seeing that he or she is qualified for roles that are likely to prove satisfying. Parents, schools, churches, and friends can help, especially in one's early years, but members of complex societies should as soon as possible develop their own plans to get the education they think they will need in order to do what they want. Then they should periodically review this plan as their environments and their own hierarchies of values change.

To keep personal educational agendas up to date is not always easy. Each individual is likely to have several different jobs and to occupy many different roles during his or her lifetime, and may need new knowledge and skills at any age. And we often learn things about our personalities and innate abilities that motivate us to try new roles and to abandon old ones long after we have left school. It is not uncommon for people to discover previously unsuspected interests and talents after retiring at 65 or 70.

Fortunately, opportunities for lifelong learning in complex societies are available and are constantly increasing. More and more people are taking advantage of courses that educational institutions offer to students of all ages, and governments frequently sponsor retraining programs for those who want to qualify themselves for new careers. It is often possible to participate in these activities via television, computers, or mail. Some individuals make it a policy always to be enrolled in a course or program that stimulates them to keep up with new developments, even if they devote only a few hours every month to these formal educational activities. As of 2004, the American Association of Retired Persons reported a statistic that seems almost incredible: namely, that 87 percent of employed adults, ages 25 to 64, in the United States were benefiting from financial support offered by their employers for work-related education! (*Live and Learn,* Winter, 2004)

For most of us, it is also feasible to make use of informal sources of continuing education. Of these, the mass media and the internet are the most accessible. Those who recognize the importance of lifetime learning are well-advised to get in the habit of mining the media for information and advice. (The benighted folk who regard the mass media and the computer only as sources of entertainment are wasting time and valuable resources.) The quality media—both print and electronic—in most complex societies provide substantial coverage of cultural and scientific developments, as well as news about politics, sports, and entertainments. Those who make a point of maintaining familiarity with the vocabularies that are used in all major categories of news stories, and with the subjects being discussed, are likely to become aware of gradual environmental changes that may affect them. Subscriptions to thoughtful weekly or monthly publications that try to cover a wide range of ideas—and preferably present different viewpoints—can also help people find where they are and where they want to be in a changing world.

Examples of environmental developments that have affected the happiness of many individuals can be found in almost any aspect of contemporary civilization. The sudden emergence of the computer as a device for learning and communication tended to isolate middle-aged and older people who didn't want to take the time and trouble to become familiar with this new device. Those who have ignored new styles of music and art have had more difficulty communicating with younger age groups. Changes in the ways medical services are delivered have baffled many members of both older and younger generations. International political developments and the lowering of confidence in the ethical standards of the business and financial community have diminished many people's sense of security. The list could be continued almost indefinitely. We cannot always avoid the effects (whether negative or positive) of such contemporary changes, but those who are better informed are more likely to cope successfully with new environments. They will enjoy a greater share of such goal values as safety, enlightenment, and well-being.

Day-to-day social activities, as well as the news media, offer opportunities for continuing education. Book clubs, community organizations, dinner parties—indeed, almost all functional groups in which one participates—can be fertile sources of information and new ideas, if one knows how to use them this way. This is because everyone with whom we come in contact has not only a unique supply of information and misinformation but also has memories of unique experiences. You will get more out of life if you can learn from other people's knowledge and experiences, as well as from your own. The trick is to somehow identify the specialized knowledge each person has, and then persuade him or her to talk about it. That is not always easy. Some of us seem to have an inborn talent for drawing others out, but we all can develop this skill to at least some extent. One way to improve your ability for this kind of informal interviewing is to watch how the experts do it. The most important thing is not to regard participation in a discussion as an opportunity to hear yourself talk.

Participation in social groups of all kinds also makes it possible to learn how to operate both formal and informal organizations, and especially to develop skills in getting along with other people. This is perhaps the most important part of the lifelong learning experience that we all have. If everyone could improve, even to a small degree, his or her skill in reconciling disputes and ability to coexist and cooperate with many kinds of people, almost all functional groups would operate more efficiently. The quality of life in all societies would be significantly improved. Learning how to reconcile disputes and solve organizational problems without destructive conflict, and without giving up important goals, is a major key to greater satisfaction of most human wants and needs. It is also a major qualification for many leadership positions.

It is significant that the word "compromise" has acquired a primarily positive value in English, while in some languages it more often carries a negative tone and suggests betraying one's principles or placing something valuable at risk. The word retains these negative meanings in English, but they are secondary. When Henry Clay (1777-1852), the legislator and orator from Kentucky who played a large part in the early history of the United States, is described as "The Great Compromiser," it is usually intended as a compliment.

The United States Constitution, which has proved to be a surprisingly durable document, resulted from many compromises. Disputes among the contentious Constitution writers could seldom be settled by appeal to a higher political or religious authority. Nor was there agreement on a body of doctrine or tradition. Protestants and Roman Catholics had been killing each other in Europe for many centuries, but in North America they learned to live together more peacefully, even though there were still tensions. Those who wrote the U.S. Constitution became convinced that unless the various colonies and diverse interests could find ways of cooperating the new country would be unable to function. This conviction was one reason for their success in building a viable society.

More recently, social scientists in the United States have expressed alarm at the rapidly declining rate of social and political participation during the second half of the 20th century. Not only do many fewer people now take the trouble to vote in elections, but members of the population devote much less time to attending meetings of community organizations, church groups, social clubs, and other voluntary associations. (See especially Putnam, 2000.) This finding causes apprehension, in that the declining participation in voluntary associations may mean that fewer Americans are learning the skills of group membership and leadership. They may be creating less "social capital," among the major components of which are expectations that people will cooperate with each other in the pursuit of mutual or compatible goals. One can hope that there are other ways of building social capital that compensate for this decline in participation, but just what they might be has not been established.

Lifelong learning involves introspection as well as monitoring the environment and participating in a variety of functional groups. To know as much as possible about one's own inherited talents and capabilities should be an important item on every educational agenda. Our capabilities are partly biological and partly acquired. The biological characteristics with which we are born don't necessarily determine how much we can learn or do, but they greatly influence how easy or difficult it is to hear what other people are saying, to learn to read, to remember, to relate one piece of information to another, and to express ideas so that other people will understand. These characteristics also have a strong influence on whether we will be especially good or especially bad at music, mathematics, creative writing, love making, long distance running, pantomime, and many other specialties. Even at an early age, a person can become aware of his or her strengths and weaknesses and can start to build on the former and to compensate for the latter. (Pinker, 2002)

Throughout life, we should periodically review our capabilities, and should try to keep our knowledge of them up-to-date. As with our hierarchies of values, our talents and skills tend to change as we grow older—hearing, vision, memory, and speed of reaction may deteriorate, but empathetic and deductive skills may increase. Collectively, these changes will affect our abilities to function effectively in families, hobbies, recreational activities, politics, and in informal groups throughout the neighborhood—as well as in paying jobs. However, self-evaluation is a difficult task. We need outside help not only because we are all biased when it comes to thinking about ourselves but also because specialized techniques of testing can provide information that is otherwise not available to us.

Nevertheless, making good use of biological and psychological testing facilities is often difficult. While specialized tests are usually helpful in giving us a picture of our own personalities and capabilities, they can be destructive if regarded as infallible. In particular, we should try to base conclusions about ourselves, and about our children or students, on many tests of different kinds that are conducted over a period of time. Some of these tests yield numerical scores; others may lead to more qualitative conclusions about abilities. Even when we have the results of several tests over a period of years, we should still be skeptical if the results seem to contradict the judgments of those who know us best. And self-evaluation, while nearly always biased, is not irrelevant. We all are aware of some things about ourselves that other people have never noticed—or will not tell us if they have.

One thing most of us can do is to consider whether we should take advantage of the testing opportunities offered by educational institutions or commercial laboratories, especially during our student years. Most schools and universities have facilities, even if not necessarily outstanding ones, for measuring "intelligence," speaking ability, aural and visual acuity, reaction time, memory, aptitude for various occupations, and other characteristics that may affect our participation in functional groups. ("Intelligence" is in quotes because the term can be used to embrace so many diverse qualities that it becomes difficult to be sure what intelligence really is.) Testing results should be discussed with such specialists as are available, inasmuch as these results are nearly always more meaningful if interpreted by experts. In addition, specialists can usually recommend steps that might be taken to compensate for weaknesses and take advantage of strengths.

After leaving school, we should consider whether to take advantage of psychological and biological tests periodically. Not only do our own capabilities change, but testing is an area where improved techniques are constantly being developed. In addition, we may find new interests and therefore will want to know whether our capabilities are such that we are likely to do well in new roles. Should we start playing the stock market, or would this probably be disastrous? Perhaps we should learn to play the piano instead.

Inherited biological predispositions, as well as acquired skills, massively affect our abilities in many games and recreational activities. For example, good memory, a talent for mathematics, keenness of vision, and other personal attributes are associated with high scores in poker, bridge, or scrabble. Psychological testing may help to predict whether or not you are likely to be a winner or loser in particular types of games. This information may allow you to find ways to benefit from strengths and compensate for weaknesses. It may also motivate you to learn how to be a good loser—a skill that is often more valuable than the ability to win.

◆ ◆ ◆

The foregoing chapter may seem to conflict with one of the central theses of this essay, which is that societies should be organized to serve the wants and needs of all their members as well as possible. To some readers, the chapter may suggest instead that people should use knowledge about social organization and individual capabilities not to seek social improvements but to pursue their own selfish goals and thus achieve greater personal happiness. Would it not be logical to conclude that more people must be turned into altruists before societies can be significantly improved? Is it not true that defects in all societies are caused by the tendency of most individuals to put their own interests ahead of the general welfare? So why encourage people to be selfish?

This objection is well taken insofar as it reminds us that individuals sometimes do their fellow human beings great damage when they are guided only by their own interests. One possible interpretation of the analysis presented here, however, is that the pursuit of individual happiness is likely to have net effects that are positive for most society members.

Such an optimistic conclusion cannot be proved, but there are several lines of reasoning that support it. First, people may not be as selfish as they often have been painted. Psychologists researching the brain have found that the "pleasure zone" is likely to be stimulated when a person cooperates with or assists somebody else. This might mean, according to researchers at Emory University, that "we're wired to cooperate with each other." (*New York Times, July 23, 2002*)

Also, much of our selfish activity (although by no means all of it) clearly does benefit the larger society, as economists have frequently pointed out. One of Adam Smith's often cited observations is that people are rarely more innocently engaged than when making money. The entrepreneur who is intent on a profit often offers us good products or services at reasonable prices. And should those who have a passion for justice, a love of knowledge, a need to feel respected, or a desire for affection necessarily be classified as selfish? Individuals who allow these values to determine the nature of their personal goals often do things that increase satisfactions for society members in general.

Further, most of the world's societies have through the centuries learned more and more about how to control activities that benefit only a few and damage many others. This is not to say that knowledge about control of crime, how to reduce corruption, and the administration of justice is always used. But the knowledge is there, and with the spread of democracy the likelihood that it will be used is greater. Some activities that prove to be harmful to the larger society can be and often have been controlled or—as in the case of human sacrifice, for example—largely eliminated.

Most importantly, as a result of many years of experience, the numbers and proportions of people who realize that their own happiness depends on the satisfaction of people around them have gradually increased. For these people, selfishness and altruism conflict less often. This consciousness of human interdependence has been hastened by the emergence of complex societies that depend on the cooperation of large numbers of people with varying characteristics. Such complex societies are capable of satisfying more wants and needs than have ever before been served; they thus make it worthwhile to cooperate with others. As a specialist on "neighbor law" has observed, when people have to live in close proximity, it's in the interest of everyone to make the relationship as friendly as possible. To love your neighbor shows enlightened self-interest. (Jordan, 2001)

For these reasons, greater awareness of how knowledge about social organization may benefit the individual can be seen as a step toward happier societies. There probably are other reasons, too. In any case, the author would like to think that readers who are able to make use of any ideas in this essay to help satisfy some of their needs or desires will thereby be contributing to the general welfare, as well as to their own satisfaction.

11

Where do We Go from Here?

Studies of human behavior, like many inquiries in the natural and social sciences, often end by raising more questions than they answer. This one is no exception. The models of different societies outlined in preceding chapters consist primarily of interrelated hypotheses that try to account for a variety of historical developments. Some of these hypotheses are widely held and might be classified as common sense; others are more controversial. But all of them, whether seemingly obvious or possibly inane, would benefit from further refinement and confirmation. In the writer's opinion, they all are more likely to be true than false, but others may differ. Whether or not one accepts these hypotheses as probably correct, it would be desirable to test them more rigorously.

For example, is it reasonable to assume that increasingly complex societies will continue to develop? Perhaps there is an optimum level of complexity that has already been reached, or surpassed. Is it possible that, in the long run, simpler forms of social organization may serve human needs and desires better and may prove more durable than the ones now common in industrialized democracies? And does this mean a reversion to societies dominated by tradition and authority, or a mixture of the two? It may be that simpler patterns of social organization, which might possibly emerge in the future, will not be identical with those that prevailed in any of the less complex societies of the past; innovation is not incompatible with greater simplicity.

Similarly, will there always be a critical mass of people who want to make greater use of human capabilities and develop these capabilities further? Is space flight really desirable, and would humanity really benefit from the creation of energy by nuclear fusion? A large proportion of the world's population shows little enthusiasm for trying out new ideas. Might novelty and creativity come to be regarded more as vices than virtues? Troublesome minorities—radicals and visionaries—have usually been responsible for proposing new forms of social organization and keeping these ideas alive until there is an opportunity to test them. (Less than one hundred years ago the notion that women should vote was regarded as ridiculous by substantial majorities almost everywhere.) Is it possible that in the future defenders of the status quo, or advocates of simpler forms of social organization, may find ways to contain or eliminate these troublesome minorities?

Many key hypotheses that are part of the picture presented in preceding chapters are difficult to prove or disprove. How can one test the hypothesis that violent conflict, whether domestic or international, is steadily becoming less rewarding to people in complex societies? Can it be convincingly demonstrated that cooperative behavior is likely to be more cost effective than force or violence when it comes to satisfying human needs and desires? While the hypothesis that peaceful cooperation is likely to be more profitable than war has found an increasingly large number of adherents, especially during the past century, the difficulties of proving it conclusively are enormous.

Problems of measurement are especially troublesome. Is it possible to assign a quantitative value to an increased sense of security, or to feelings of national pride? And what is the cost to a society of losing a life? Does the amount lost depend on roles already played by the person in question, or on his or her capabilities and the prospects for using these capabilities in the future? Until it is possible to total up gains and losses that accrue to individuals and to the component functional groups of a society, as a result of either cooperation or conflict, conclusions about the relative profitability of peace or war remain wobbly. And no matter how destructive wars and other forms of conflict may be, there are always likely to be some people who benefit—just as improved cooperation is usually not without costs for somebody.

The difficulties of answering such questions do not make it unreasonable to ask them. Even though none may be resolved with complete certainty, further thought and observation can add or detract from our confidence that a particular hypothesis is correct. And the degree of confidence in the truth of one hypothesis or another may make a large difference in the way people and functional groups behave. If the notion that war (or conflict in general) has become stupid should find even more widespread support this will affect policies of nations and large organizations, as well as what many of us do on a day-to-day basis.

In addition to formulating and then questioning broad hypotheses such as these, an equally important step in constructing improved models of social organization would be to focus intensively on three more specialized questions. How might key functional groups be constituted so as to better satisfy human needs and desires? What can be done to help people with differing behavioral codes work together more productively? Are there ways to reduce frictions among a society's functional groups and increase harmonious relationships?

When it comes to improving models for individual functional groups, each person is likely to have a different list of groups that deserve priority attention. In theory, we are all in a position to make unique suggestions about the structure of groups in which we participate, and about the roles that should be played by group members, so the number of possibilities that might be considered is very large.

A few ideas about how families might be organized so as to better serve the needs of parents and children and of the complex societies in which they live are mentioned below. These may serve as examples of the kinds of thought and experimentation that might also be applicable to other kinds of functional groups. One of the anomalies of current complex societies is that we are likely to encourage new ideas about organizing businesses so that they will be more profitable, while we often resist and even excoriate those who suggest revised structures and roles for functional groups that provide nonmaterial values such as security, affection, respect, or justice. It is usually accepted as a matter of course that corporations must be reorganized periodically, but similar approaches to families, governments, and religious bodies are much more controversial.

A second area where further thought would be likely to improve the quality of life for many people is that of comparative behavioral codes. It would be valuable to evaluate critically the prevailing rules that govern the ways in which people belonging to different functional groups and cultures treat each other. We should try to learn more about how behaviors prescribed by religions and philosophies affect the efficiency with which people play their roles in various kinds of functional groups. It would be valuable also to learn more about past experiences that led to these rules of behavior—such factors as control of a society by a very cruel authoritarian government, or periods of famine. Some of these rules persist to the present day, in spite of environmental changes that may have made them unnecessary or undesirable. It may be possible to formulate new rules that would be more appropriate under modern conditions. Some illustrative speculations about behavioral codes, and how they might be changed, are also presented below.

How to find means of improving relationships among functional groups is a third major question that is proposed as a focus for further inquiry. What might be done to reduce friction among the various groups to which an individual is likely to belong? Some ideas about extended families are mentioned in this connection. And how can the different social organizations in a society complement each other in such a way that they all are likely to benefit? The solidity and comfort of the societies in which we spend our lives, as well as of the houses in which we live, is determined very largely by the compatibility of various components. Do the walls support the roof, does the roof keep the interior dry, and is there sufficient space for the activities in which we wish to engage?

Thinking About Households (and Other Collectivities). Some fifty years ago, a Swedish sociologist, Alva Myrdal, wrote to friends in the United States: "We have the idea to build a 'Kollektivhus,' an ideal family hotel with cooperative organization to take care of all your material needs and unload your responsibility also for your offspring!…The children will be in nurseries in another wing, tennis courts in the park…everything you can dream of…and for a rent that will save us about half of our costs for the household." (Bok, *1991, p. 106)*

Alva Myrdal's suggestion, although she apparently never went on to turn it into a formal proposal, illustrates the diversity of ideas that might be relevant when one starts thinking about possible alternatives to traditional family structures and roles. Her daughter, who wrote the volume cited above, provides a moving account of problems that arise when both parents have demanding jobs. Both Alva and her husband were key members of the Swedish government during much of the period when their children were young. At one point, Alva Myrdal was in charge of the police when her son was arrested while participating in a political demonstration. How could she reconcile her obligation to uphold the law with her role as a mother? The family tensions that resulted from this instance of competing demands from two very different functional groups were never resolved.

New ideas about parental roles in complex industrialized societies are especially desirable at the present time. Birth rates in most of these societies have fallen so low that rising generations are too small to satisfy the personnel requirements of the society's functional groups. How might the birth rate be increased? One possibility is that parenting could become more and more a full time career for adults in specialized families. Responsibility for ensuring that a society had a high enough birth rate would no longer be shared by nearly all adult females and males, as prescribed by tradition. Instead, the society as a whole would depend mainly (although not exclusively) on specialized families to supply needed personnel. Such a development would in some respects parallel what has happened in agriculture, where an occupation that at one time was pursued by nearly every family has become the preserve of many fewer families and corporations, some of which operate very large enterprises.

Just what the roles of people in "baby farming" families might be would depend on creative ideas and on extensive experimentation. One possibility is that women and men who are particularly interested both in children and in education might be encouraged to have double-digit families and to pursue careers in "human development." These careers could be designed in such a way as to allow their practitioners to become specialists in various aspects of both childhood and education at the same time they are involved with bringing up their own children. A couple interested in careers of this kind might receive long-term loans that would enable them to have generous household help for the years when they were inundated with small children and were also studying. During this period in their lives, they would become specialists in branches of medicine, psychology, education, and other fields relevant to their interests in children. Those who wished to pursue advanced degrees would be assisted in doing so. As their own children aged, the parents would gradually move into full-time educational and medical work, with a percentage of their gross earnings dedicated to repaying the original loans. Then, as grandparents, they would help take care of children again. Baby farming parents who were not interested in an advanced education for themselves might specialize in providing for material and recreational needs of children—furniture, toys, reading materials, television programs, or sports.

This, of course, is only one of many, many possible models for specialized child-rearing families that might be considered, elaborated, and then tried out initially on a small scale. Other models might be derived from the experiences of cooperative experiments in different countries, such as the Israeli kibbutzim, or from a variety of practices that have been observed in other cultures and described by anthropologists and historians. The Head Start program in the United States, and similar programs in other countries, might also be sources of ideas. Unconventional approaches to family structures and roles are likely to be controversial, but the controversies themselves would in the long run probably help to ensure that viable models are found.

Consideration of various structures and roles that might be appropriate for households in complex societies inevitably brings up a question that is as controversial as it is elementary. Why have women never been paid for performing some of society's most vital and demanding roles—namely, having children and caring for them? And, for that matter, why have fathers, who often help take care of children and train them in farming or fighting, never been compensated for these services? The answer probably is that payment was not necessary in either case. Women were compelled to have children, and these offspring were able to help their fathers on the family farm at a very early age. Later, the children would be expected to care for their aged parents. But the traditional inducements don't seem to work well in modern societies. New motivations must be found. Should some of these motivations be financial?

The necessity of remodeling families so that they can adjust better to the requirements of industrialized societies has other controversial implications as well. One such implication is that attempts to turn the clock back and somehow try to enforce family structures and roles that seemed to work well in earlier times may prove disastrous. For example, a proposal has been made in the United States that the government should devote substantial funds to counseling married couples about how to stay together and thus ensure a more stable environment in which children can grow up. Other proposals are to the effect that divorce should be made more difficult. If such programs should fail to address reasons for the high divorce rates, including new requirements for extensive travel in connection with employment and diminished financial dependence of wives on their husbands, the efforts to make marriages more stable could boomerang and result in fewer marriages.

Similarly, efforts by some religious bodies to revive a patriarchal system, in which the senior male household member is expected to make all major decisions, could seriously weaken a whole society by failing to take advantage of the capabilities of wives who are more intelligent than their husbands. Inasmuch as intelligence seems to be randomly distributed between the sexes, assigning decision-making to the less intelligent partner in 50 percent of all households would seem to be a wasteful policy. Or, if efforts to stabilize families by mandating male supremacy were to result in a situation where only less intelligent women decide to marry, the negative results might be even worse. Babies in each succeeding generation would be influenced during their most formative period of life by those who were least competent to prepare them for their future roles in complex societies.

At the same time, controversies about whether or not lesbian and gay couples should be forbidden to marry have raised questions about the structure of single-sex households and their relationships with governments, other families, and religious bodies. Thought and analysis of available experience is desirable here, too.

Speculation about possible structures for functional groups and about various roles people might play in them is one of the requirements imposed upon all of us by rapid rates of environmental change. Leaders in business enterprises are usually more conscious of these requirements than are people in other social organisms. Many educational institutions try to be responsive to new conditions, but are often frustrated by budgetary problems. Governments sometimes attempt to modernize their administrative mechanisms, but nearly always find it difficult to secure the agreement of diverse and powerful interests. Religious bodies, many of them hampered by the belief that all necessary truth has been revealed to them in the past, are the least likely to see the necessity for adaptation, but even here there is considerable speculation and experimentation. The difficulty in finding the best possible models for all these diverse functional groups is, however, somewhat compensated for by the fascination of trying to do so.

Defining, Evaluating, and Reconciling Behavioral Codes. Let's start with what looks like a supremely unimportant question! In societies where it is customary for men to wear beards, does this have implications for organizational efficiency?

The reason for raising such a seemingly silly query at this point is to emphasize that even minor rules about behavior, whether embodied in fashions, religions, laws, philosophies, or customs, can affect the performance of functional groups—sometimes positively and sometimes negatively This is an enormous area where additional research and experimentation would be desirable. In the course of our interactions with other people, how much emotion or affection should be displayed, and under what circumstances? Which functional groups are strengthened by demonstrative behavior and which are penalized? When a popular fashion forces employed women to wear shoes with very high heels, does the cumulative impact of this rule have a negative impact on both the gross domestic product and happiness of individual families? (I think it does!)

But, to return to the question of beards and possibly mustaches, we know that for most organizations to function well extensive communication among their members and also with outsiders is necessary. We also know, from a large body of psychological research, that facial expression is important in conveying meaning, and often takes the place of speech, or even writing. So the question is whether beards and mustaches can interfere with nonverbal communication by facial expression to such an extent that the efficiency of functional groups will decrease as the amount of facial hair worn by male group members increases. Or, does the relationship of facial hair to misunderstanding depend on whether the organization in question is based mainly on traditional, authoritarian, or democratic principles? It may be that in authoritarian and traditional societies beards and mustaches can be a positive factor in some functional groups.

The importance of knowledge about styles of communication and different hierarchies of values is illustrated by a story from the 1950-51 war in Korea, when armed forces from several nations were trying to help South Korea repel an invasion from North Korea. One section of the front line, which was defended by three units from different countries—South Korea, England, and the United States—was under particularly strong pressure, but the commander at higher headquarters had enough reserve forces to help only one of the units. So he called the three front line commanders on a field telephone in an effort to find out where reinforcements were most needed. The South Korean officer reported heavy casualties, but said that his unit might be able to hold out without reinforcements. The American officer said the fighting in his sector was at a critical stage and that reinforcements would be a great help. The British officer said he had to admit that the situation was indeed "becoming a bit sticky." Analysis after the battle showed that the British unit had suffered by far the heaviest attack, and also that the British commander thought he had properly informed higher headquarters that his unit was in desperate circumstances. The story does not tell which unit actually received the reinforcements, but it does reflect the high value that English tradition has put on understatement and maintaining "a stiff upper lip."

The ranking of values, and the ways in which each person is expected to behave toward other people, differ from society to society and even from one community to another within the same society. Conduct and goals that are accepted as appropriate or even virtuous in one country or community may be condemned in others. It's convenient to consider behavior and values together, because what we do is so often explained by what we most want. In some societies, for example, the family is valued so highly that theft and deceit tend to be judged leniently if they appear to be in the family interest, while in other societies respect for the law is so strong that parents who steal to give their children a better life are trundled off to jail. Similarly, some societies and communities expect persons of high rank to behave in a domineering manner, while in other circles it is important to emphasize that everyone is equal—even though this is may be a fiction.

Knowledge and understanding of different behavioral codes and values are particularly desirable in today's world. We all are increasingly likely to participate in functional groups that include people from many backgrounds. The volume of migration, both international and domestic, has produced a situation where many neighborhoods are increasingly multicultural, where colleagues on the job may have grown up in other societies, and more and more families consist of people with different values and styles of conduct. In addition, the gradual emergence of a world society has resulted in the formation of thousands of new functional groups composed of people from different parts of the world who somehow learn to work together. How can we achieve the best possible cooperation and avoid needless friction in multicultural groups? Which values and behaviors are most strongly held in different cultures? Which rules about conduct are most likely to be shared by people from all societies? What kinds of behavior most frequently cause misunderstandings and frictions in today's world, and what are the most successful means of resolving these impediments to good cooperation?

International business personnel, diplomats, and social scientists have already accumulated vast quantities of information about behavioral codes and values in different communities, and also some information about how to bridge the differences among cultures. Public opinion researchers, too, increasingly address these subjects. In the World Values Survey, for example, respondents were asked whether suicide, cheating on taxes, lying, euthanasia and other controversial modes of conduct were ever justifiable; what the most important goals of their countries were; what they thought about the value of scientific advances; and how they would rank the importance of work, family, politics, and religion in their lives. (Inglehart, 1997; Inglehart, Basañez and Moreno, 1998) As expected, large differences in the responses from people in different societies were found. These data, as well as large quantities of data from other sources, are now available for further analysis.

Administrators and researchers interested in learning how people from varying cultural backgrounds can cooperate most efficiently in functional groups are faced with several practical problems. Which items within behavioral codes are most likely to affect the work of groups that include people from different communities and nations? What are the best ways of reconciling conflicting modes of behavior? How can knowledge about hierarchies of values and differing patterns of behavior be kept up-to-date in a rapidly changing world? To take an often encountered situation as an example, how can a dialogue be conducted most successfully between people who place a very high value on politeness and sensitivity and those who pride themselves on being forthright and outspoken? Cataloging and arranging the enormous quantity of potentially valuable information in a form that will make it useful to as many people as possible is a major challenge.

The problem of how to reconcile behavioral codes based on different religions and religious interpretations is a particularly difficult one. A first step might be to learn more about the effects of specific religious beliefs and practices on the ways people treat each other. In particular, how do these beliefs and practices affect people's behavior in functional groups outside the field of religion, and what are the psychological benefits (or losses) that accrue to believers? With more insight on such questions it may be possible to formulate rules of behavior that are acceptable to adherents of various religions who are cooperating with each other in intercultural functional groups.

Some of the ways in which adherence to particular religious doctrines and interpretations can affect people's performance of their roles in non-religious functional groups were explored by the German social scientist Max Weber. In *The Protestant Ethic and the Spirit of Capitalism* (1904-05) Weber showed how Protestant, and especially Calvinist, interpretations of Christian doctrine led believers to be especially careful about how they used time and how they spent money. Time and money were gifts from God, according to this interpretation, and waste of any kind was sinful. People should not be diverted by the search for pleasure. They should try to lead sober, systematic and ascetic lives. One could not know for sure whether one would go to heaven after death, but success on this earth might be an indication that one had been chosen by God for salvation, and was among the "elect." As Weber put it, "...a vocational calling was defined as absolutely the highest of all ascetic means for believers to testify to their elect status, as well as simultaneously the most certain and most visible means of doing so." (*Ibid.*, p.116)

Worthy achievement in any field, but especially in business, was therefore reassuring to Calvinists, and greatly to be desired. Weber concluded that beliefs of this kind were in harmony with the spirit of capitalism and encouraged behavior that stimulated the growth of capitalistic institutions, even if unintentionally. But not all devout Calvinists were about to become rich. Although business people who worked hard, led ascetic lives, and spent little money were likely to accumulate capital, Calvinists working in other fields might not make much money. Nevertheless, their devotion to the "calling" to which God had assigned them made them especially conscientious teachers, employees, or civil servants.

In contrast to Weber's work, most of the information that social scientists have gathered about religious bodies describes religious beliefs and practices but has little to say about the impact, if any, that these beliefs and practices have on functional groups outside the field of religion. It would be desirable to know much more about ways in which religious doctrines and traditions affect behavior not only at work but also in politics, in the household, and in the community. The 2004 Chairman of the Sociology of Religion Section of the American Sociological Association suggests that more attention be focused on religion "as a robust cultural and organizational complex, in actual societies, alternately shaping and being shaped by other social institutions, structures, and processes." (Warner, 2004)

It would be especially useful to distinguish between effects of religion on the individual, on the one hand, and its implications for the operation of various functional groups, on the other. We know that all religions that have persisted for more than a few generations offer something that many individuals find valuable and important—for example, hope, confidence, or inner peace. Otherwise, these religions, most of which have faced both persecution and competition, would not have survived. At the same time, a religious body or doctrine is unlikely to prosper unless it also is at least minimally compatible with other functional groups in the same society. If a religious belief inhibits the formation of families, or of financial institutions, or of medical services, both the society and the religious body are likely to suffer.

It would also be useful to see if religious and philosophical belief systems could be classified according to their value to individuals and their value to societies. One religion might be associated with societies that have happy people but low standards of living, while another religion might dominate in societies where people are less satisfied but more prosperous. The goal of such research could be to help the adherents of all religions find interpretations that allow for greater personal happiness and prosperity while also strengthening the societies in which they live.

Functional Group Interrelationships. A third, and related, area where further knowledge is particularly desirable has to do with improving relationships among different kinds of functional groups. It has previously been noted that schools and families often make competing demands on the same people and resources, as do churches and governments; industries and farmers. The discovery of ways to reduce frictions or to increase harmony among institutions, without loss of efficiency, can lead to better lives for large numbers of people. Here again, the number of cases in which conflict or friction among different groups can be found is almost infinite.

One example of the kind of thinking that would be desirable has to do with problems that arise when extended families are established within industrialized societies. Superficially, it would appear that the extended family makes the development of specialized functional groups more difficult and, in particular, degrades the quality of government in complex societies. But it is also clear that extended families bring enormous advantages to their members when it comes to affection, security, self-respect, and sometimes other values as well. The problem for creative thinkers is to find out how people in extended families might continue to enjoy these benefits and at the same time contribute to the quality of life in the societies to which they belong and advance the prospects of a peaceful world order.

Some examples of individuals and families that have experimented with models that probably benefit both individuals and the complex democracies in which they live are available. It is not uncommon for extended families in India and elsewhere to pool their resources so that younger family members who do especially well in school can pursue a higher education either at home or abroad. (This is the opposite of families that force older children to stay at home and take care of the younger ones.) A friend from Africa has pointed out to me that members of his family are attending schools and colleges in various parts of the United States and were thus learning about opportunities in several areas of the country. All his family members were also encouraged to help each other make contacts with a variety of people and groups in the host society. They were outward looking, rather than inward looking. This family has thus become a mechanism that helps its members to widen their horizons rather than to restrict them. There probably are many other models of this sort.

It would also be possible for extended families in different countries to "adopt" each other, much as many cities have adopted "sister cities" in other parts of the world. This would offer new educational opportunities for members of both families and would facilitate the development of behavioral codes that would help people from different cultures work together. One can hope that social scientists and others will explore the possibilities of interrelationships among extended families, much as Alva Myrdal speculated about the design and functions of the nuclear family.

In addition to searching for ways in which conflicts and frictions among functional groups might be minimized, it is even more important that we learn more about how various combinations of these groups tend to enhance, or degrade, the life styles of people in complex industrial democracies. Increasing varieties of functional groups confront the individual not only with more and more choices about what he or she wants to do, but also with decisions about how these choices will relate to each other. The old adage to the effect that the best way to get ahead in business is to marry the boss's daughter illustrates one way different functional groups can complement each other even in very simple societies. In complex societies the numbers and varieties of possible combinations become impressive. A person choosing a career line may want to consider how this is likely to combine with a love for a particular sport, participation in politics, the children's education, the prospects for making good friends, and probably many other interests. Little is known about these various combinations.

Similarly, nearly everyone has to decide how much time, energy, and money to devote to family, job, recreation, hobbies, public affairs, and other interests. Some people feel forced by circumstances to become workaholics, or slaves to their families, but others have considerable latitude in deciding. The continuing increase in the number and categories of possible activities open to people in modern societies means that most of us will be faced with such decisions more and more frequently.

Even more important is to learn more about various combinations of functional groups that affect a society as a whole. A major example of this kind of thinking and research is provided by a well-known volume entitled *Bowling Alone: The Collapse and Revival of American Community* (2000) by Robert D. Putnam of Harvard University.

Reviewing vast quantities of data about participation by Americans in political, social and recreational groups of many kinds during the second half of the 20th century, Putnam found that there has been a sharp and rather sudden decline in certain categories of group activities. In recent years, people have devoted much less time to meeting with their friends, neighbors, other members of their churches, and fellow citizens in general than they had in previous decades. Why was this? Putnam does not find a complete explanation for the phenomenon, although he points out that the advent of television accounts for some of it. He also offers numerous fascinating comments.

The significance of the question is enormous. Many scholars and observers, possibly starting with the 19th century French traveler, Alexis de Tocqueville, have concluded that democracy in the United States depends in large measure on dense networks of social organizations at all levels of American society and the discussions that take place in and among these various groups. These functional groups have helped Americans learn how to cooperate with others in the pursuit of common objectives and have done a great deal to prepare them for participation in democratic political institutions. In addition, these various social organisms—small and large—enable people in all parts of a society to communicate with government. "When people associate in neighborhood groups, PTA's, political parties, or even national advocacy groups, their individual and otherwise quiet voices multiply and are amplified." (Putnam, 2000, p. 338) Does the decline of such participation in the United States indicate a weakening in democracy?

One possible explanation for the decline in group participation is suggested by the model of industrial societies presented in this essay. If we assume that people become affiliated with functional groups in order to satisfy some need or desire, perhaps we should ask whether there were significant changes during the 20th century in how Americans satisfied these wants. One explanatory factor may be the sexual revolution that occurred at about the same time as the decline in group participation. Attitudes about relations between the sexes changed fairly suddenly after World War II. People became much more open. The subject could be discussed frankly in the mass media. A larger proportion of young people became involved in "trial marriages." The sexual revolution led not only to different relationships among young people, but also to changes in countless established households. It is possible that more people satisfied their desires for affection and sociability at home, or in extramarital relationships, and were less likely to seek it in community activities. The felt need for husbands to spend a night out each week "with the boys," or for wives to do the same "with the girls" may have become weaker.

An alternative or supplementary explanation may be that there has been a change in personal hierarchies of values. Perhaps people became more greedy, or more competitive and ambitious, as a prosperous and complex society opened up new opportunities for affluent life styles. Desires for power and wealth led them to spend more time working, or in upgrading their qualifications for higher positions, and less time in sociable activities.

A third possibility is that the growth of specialization in complex societies led to the formation of new types of formal and informal organizations that did not exist or were uncommon until the middle of the twentieth century. These organizations may have satisfied various needs formerly served in other ways. "Support groups" and new interest groups of many kinds flourished after World War II. Some of these grew out of communication links that emerged when nearly everyone had a telephone (and later a computer); others were made possible by rapid urbanization, which drained the countryside and brought together huge populations in relatively small geographic spaces. In the cities, and even in some suburbs, one didn't have to attend a meeting of an organization to see friends and neighbors; they were available just outside your door. Many very efficient support groups consisted of people who lived near each other, met very informally, and kept no records of their existence.

If any of these explanations is even partially correct, then declining participation in traditional community groups doesn't necessarily indicate a weakening of either democracy or community, although this still might be true. The fact that fewer people were getting experience in administering or even belonging to formal organizations might well lessen the efficiency of democratic institutions.

Whatever the explanation for the declining participation, the point here is that we know relatively little about the effects of different kinds of functional groups on each other. Family structures and roles must have substantial impact on the efficiency of businesses, government agencies, educational institutions, and other functional groups, but just what these influences are and how they are exerted remains uncertain. There are probably substantial effects that we know little or nothing about, and it may well be that some of the effects often taken for granted are weak or nonexistent. For example, do societies where families exert strong pressures on children to work hard in school tend to have more efficient institutions than societies that place less emphasis on classroom work and encourage children to develop their own talents and interests? In the increasingly complex societies of today it is important to learn more about such interrelationships.

Systematic research by social scientists and the daily observations and experiences of others will probably help us find answers to questions both about effects of functional groups on each other and about the various mixes most likely to satisfy different kinds of individuals. This is an area in which everyone who would like to do so can add to the existing stockpile of knowledge. Each human life is a laboratory in which important discoveries may be made. Not everyone tries to write books about their thoughts and experiences, but we can all share information and opinions with friends and other interested parties. Good ideas sometimes grow feet and reach millions of people even before they are incorporated into the mass or class media. In the interest of both ourselves and our fellow human beings we should constantly examine our own experiences to see what can be learned from them.

Some words of Walter Lippmann, written in 1914, are even more applicable to the situation today than they were at the beginning of the 20th century: "We are not used to a complicated civilization.... There are no precedents to guide us, no wisdom that was not made for a simpler age. *We have changed our environment more quickly than we know how to change ourselves.*" (Quoted in Putnam, 2000, p. 379)

And environmental change will continue, probably at an increasing pace. Each generation will have to face the central question considered by this essay, namely: How can we combine our energies and the enormous array of talents that are available in the human population so as to not only enable our societies to survive and prosper, but also so as to ensure that everyone has a better chance of leading a more satisfying life?

One possible answer is suggested by the somewhat unconventional dedication at the very start of this book, for which I hope my former colleagues will forgive me. We might try to organize the adult members of the world's population as though they were all members of a college faculty. Well, not exactly; institutions of higher education have frequently been described with good reason as anachronisms surviving from a medieval era. Nevertheless, some of their features deserve imitation in other functional groups. The characteristics of college faculties that I would like to see become more widespread in all societies include encouragement of the expression of many different opinions, toleration of fierce rivalries and intense disagreements that rarely come to blows, productive collaboration among individuals with varying behavioral codes and lifestyles, and a common dedication to helping future generations realize their highest values.

References and Further Reading

(Page numbers given in text are those appearing in the most recent edition listed below)

Ahmed, Akbar S. 2003. *Islam Under Siege: Living Dangerously in a Post-Honor World.* Cambridge and Oxford: Polity Press in Association with Blackwell Publishing, Ltd.

Almond, Gabriel A. and Sidney Verba. 1963. *The Civic Culture: Political Attitudes and Democracy.* Princeton: Princeton University Press.

Angier, Natalie. 2003. "Is War Our Biological Destiny?" *New York Times,* November 11.

Atran, Scott. 2002. *In God We Trust: The Evolutionary Landscape of Religion.* New York: Oxford University Press.

Atran, Scott. 2003. "Who Wants to be a Martyr?" *New York Times,* May 5.

Baird, Zoë. 2002. "Governing the Internet: Engaging Government, Business and Nonprofits." *Foreign Affairs,* November/December.

Barro, Robert J. and Rachel M. McCleary. 2003. "Religion and Economic Growth Across Countries." *American Sociological Review,* October.

Barron, Frank. 1968. *Creativity and Personal Freedom.* New York: Van Nostrand.

Berne, Eric. 1964. *Games People Play: The Psychology of Human Relationships.* New York: Grove Press.

Black, Matthew and H.H. Rowley. 1985. *Peak's Commentary on the Bible.* Nashville: Thomas Nelson.

Bok, Sissela. 1991. *Alva Myrdal: A Daughter's Memoir.* Reading, MA: Addison-Wesley.

Bornstein, David. 2004. *How to Change the World: Social Entrepreneurship and the Power of New Ideas.* New York: Oxford University Press.

Breasted, James H. 1933. *The Dawn of Conscience.* New York: Charles Scribner's Sons. NOTE: This is an old and fat volume. Those who are able to find a copy are advised to read the "Foreword," Chapter XVII ("The Sources of Our Moral Heritage"), and the "Epilogue." Also, with the aid of the index, one can skip through the insightful sayings of Amenemope. Many will seem familiar.

Callahan, David. 2004. *The Cheating Culture: Why More Americans are Doing Wrong to Get Ahead.* New York: Harcourt.

Cantril, Albert H. and Susan Davis Cantril. 1999. *Reading Mixed Signals: Ambivalence in American Public Opinion About Government.* Baltimore: Johns Hopkins University Press.

Carnegie, Dale. 1936. *How to Win Friends and Influence People.* New York: Simon and Schuster. NOTE: This popular work has sold more than ten million copies. A revised edition was published in 1981. Carnegie also wrote *How to Stop Worrying and Start Living*, 1948.

Carr, Martha Randolph. 2004. "My Son's Disability, and My Own Inability to See It." *Washington Post,* January 4.

Chua, Amy. 2003. *World on Fire: How Exporting Free Market Democracy Breeds Ethnic Hatred and Global Instability.* New York: Doubleday.

Cohen, Bernard C. 1963. *The Press and Foreign Policy.* Princeton, NJ: Princeton University Press.

Cook, Michael. 2003. *A Brief History of the Human Race.* New York: Norton.

Coontz, Stephanie. 1992. *The Way We Never Were: American Families and the Nostalgia Trap.* New York: Basic Books.

Council on Foreign Relations. 2003. *Finding America's Voice: A Strategy for Reinvigorating U.S. Public Diplomacy.* Report of an Independent Task Force. New York.

Davison, W. Phillips. 1987. *Mass Media, Civic Organizations and Street Gossip: How Communication Affects the Quality of Life in an Urban Neighborhood.* New York: Gannett Center for Media Studies.

Diamond, Jared. 1999. *Guns, Germs, and Steel: The Fates of Human Societies.* New York: Norton.

Diamond, Jonathan. 2000. *Narrative Means to Sober Ends: Treating Addiction and Its Aftermath.* New York: Guilford Press.

Easterbrook, Gregg. 2003. *The Progress Paradox: How Life Gets Better While People Feel Worse.* New York: Random House.

Encyclopedia of Associations. 2003. Foster City, CA: Gale Group.

Evans, M.D.R. and Jonathan Kelley. 2002. "National Pride in the Developed World: Survey Data from 24 Nations." *International Journal of Public Opinion Research,* Autumn.

Fisher, Roger and William Levy (with Bruce Patton). 1981. *Getting to Yes: Negotiating Agreement Without Giving In.* New York: Penguin. (Second Edition, 1991)

Florida, Richard. 2001. "The New American Dream," *Washington Monthly,* March.

Florida, Richard. 2002. *The Rise of the Creative Class: And How It's Transforming Work, Leisure, Community and Everyday Life.* New York: Basic Books.

Free, Lloyd A. and Hadley Cantril. 1968. *Political Beliefs of Americans.* New Brunswick, NJ: Rutgers University Press.

Frum, David and Richard Perle. 2004. *An End to Evil. How to Win the War on Terror.* New York: Random House. NOTE: A publication by knowledgeable authors who differ sharply from the point of view presented in this essay. Perle and Frum see military force, police power, and political pressure as major instruments for the defeat of terrorism, while placing less emphasis on the usefulness of negotiation and collective action.

Gans, Herbert J. 1967. *The Levittowners: Ways of Life and Politics in a New Suburban Community.* New York: Pantheon Books. (New Edition by Columbia University Press, 1982)

Gates, Robert M. 2004. "International Relations 101," *New York Times,* March 31.

Gilkey, Langdon B. 1966. *Shantung Compound: The Story of Men and Women Under Pressure.* New York: Harper and Row.

Golding, William. 1960. *Lord of the Flies.* Harmondsworth, England: Penguin Books.

Goleman, Daniel. 1995. *Emotional Intelligence*. New York: Bantam Books.

Gordon, Thomas. 1970. *Parent Effectiveness Training: The Tested New Way to Raise Responsible Children*. New York: Peter H. Wyden, Inc.

Hoffer, Eric. 1951. *The True Believer: Thoughts on the Nature of Mass Movements*. New York: Harper & Row.

Hoffmann, Stanley. 2002. "The Clash of Globalizations." *Foreign Affairs*, July/August.

Huntington, Samuel P. 1996. *The Clash of Civilizations and the Remaking of World Order*. New York: Simon & Schuster.

Inglehart, Ronald. 1997. *Modernization and Postmodernization: Cultural, Economic and Political Change in 43 Societies*. Princeton, NJ: Princeton University Press.

Inglehart, Ronald, Miguel Basañez and Alexander Moreno. 1998. *Human Values and Beliefs: A Cultural Sourcebook*. Ann Arbor, MI: University of Michigan Press.

Inglehart, Ronald, *et al.* 2000. *World Values Surveys and European Values Surveys. 1981-1984, 1990-1993, and 1995-1997* (Computer File). ICPSR version. Ann Arbor, MI: Institute for Social Research (producer), 2000. Ann Arbor, MI: Inter-University Consortium for Political and Social Research (distributor).

Jordan, Cora. 2001. *Neighbor Law: Fences, Trees, Boundaries and Noise*. (Fourth Edition) Berkeley, CA: NOLO.

Keesing, Felix M. and Marie M. Keesing. 1956. *Elite Communication in Samoa*. Stanford, CA: Stanford University Press. NOTE: Provides a far more inclusive picture of Samoan society than its title suggests. Extraordinary in its clarity and informality. Copies are difficult to find, but are very much worth reading.

Kennedy, Randall. 2003. *Interracial Intimacies: Sex, Marriage, Identity, and Adoption.* New York: Pantheon Books.

Ladurie, Emmanuel LeRoy. 1978. *Montaillou: The Promised Land of Error.* New York: George Braziller, Inc. (Translated by Barbara Bray) NOTE: A charming account of life in the south of France during the Middle Ages, based on remarkably detailed written records. Gives a feeling for the overwhelming power of tradition, as well as glimpses of forces that eventually would lead to modernization.

Lagos, Marta. 2003. "Support for and Satisfaction with Democracy." *International Journal of Public Opinion Research,* Winter.

Lareau, Annette. 2003. *Unequal Childhoods: Class, Race and Family Life.* Berkeley, CA: University of California Press.

Lasswell Harold D. 1927. *Propaganda Technique in the World War.* New York: Alfred A. Knopf.

Lasswell, Harold D. 1948. *Power and Personality.* New York: Norton. (Reprinted by Greenwood Press, Westport, CT, 1976)

Lasswell, Harold D. and Abraham Kaplan. 1950. *Power and Society: A Framework for Political Inquiry.* New Haven, CT: Yale University Press.

LeDoux, Joseph. 2002. *The Synaptic Self: How Our Brains Become Who We Are.* New York: Viking.

Lerner, Daniel. 1958. *The Passing of Traditional Society: Modernizing the Middle East.* Glencoe, IL: Free Press.

Lester, Toby. 2002 "Oh, Gods!" *Atlantic Monthly,* February.

Levine, Mel. 2003. "The Myth of Laziness." *Washington Post,* December 16.

Malinowski, Bronislaw. 1948. *Magic, Science and Religion and Other Essays.* (Reprinted by Waveland Press, Prospect Heights, IL, 1992.)

Mandelbaum, Michael. 2002. *The Ideas that Conquered the World: Peace, Democracy and Free Markets in the Twenty-first Century.* Washington: Public Affairs Press.

Massey, Douglas S. 2002. "A Brief History of Human Society: The Origin and Role of Emotion in Social Life. *American Sociological Review,* February. NOTE: A concise and readable overview of the development of human societies and the influences of emotion and rationality in human affairs.

McCombs, Maxwell E. and Donald L. Shaw. 1972. "The Agenda-Setting Function of Mass Media." *Public Opinion Quarterly,* Summer.

Mead, Walter Russell. 2004. *Power, Terror, Peace, and War: America's Grand Strategy in a World at Risk.* New York: Knopf.

Meier, Deborah. 1995. *The Power of Their Ideas: Lessons for America from a Small School in Harlem.* Boston: Beacon Press.

Merton, Robert K. 1957. *Social Theory and Social Structure.* Glencoe, IL: Free Press.

Micklethwait, John and Adrian Wooldridge. 2003, "Rebuilding the Alliance to Rebuild Globalization," *New York Times,* April 13.

Morse, Edward L. 1976. "Interdependence in World Affairs." In *World Politics,* edited by James N. Rosenau, Kenneth W. Thompson and Gavin Boyd. New York: Free Press.

Murphy, Liam, and Thomas Nagel. 2002. *The Myth of Ownership: Taxes and Justice.* New York: Oxford University Press.

Nalebuff, Barry, and Ian Ayres. 2003. *"Why Not."* Boston: Harvard Business School Press.

Noelle-Neumann, Elisabeth and Renate Koecher. 2002. *Allensbacher Jahrbuch der Demoskopie, 1998-2002.* Munich: K.G. Saur und Verlag der Demoskopie.

Norris, Pippa (ed.). 1999. *Critical Citizens: Support for Democratic Government.* New York: Oxford University Press.

Pinker, Steven. 2002. *The Blank Slate: The Modern Denial of Human Nature.* New York: Viking Penguin.

Putnam, Robert D., with Robert Leonardi and Raffaella Y. Nanetti. 1993. *Making Democracy Work: Civic Traditions in Modern Italy.* Princeton, NJ: Princeton University Press. NOTE: Should be included in any list of the most exciting social scientific investigations of the 20th century. The authors show how behavior patterns formed during the Middle Ages influence the performance of functional groups in modern Italy—and find amazing amounts of quantitative empirical data to back up their inferences.

Putnam, Robert D. 2000. *Bowling Alone: The Collapse and Revival of American Community.* New York: Simon and Shuster.

Quillian, Lincoln and Mary E. Campbell. 2003. "Beyond Black and White: The Present and Future of Multiracial Friendship Segregation," *American Sociological Review.* August.

Rawls, John. 1971. *A Theory of Justice.* Cambridge, MA: Belknap Press of Harvard University Press. (Revised edition published by Belknap in 1999)

Rich, Meghan and Kerry Strand. 2002. "Sociologists Central to Peace Studies," *Footnotes* (Newsletter of the American Sociological Association). March

Rostow, Walt W. 1960. *The Stages of Economic Growth: A Non-Communist Manifesto.* Cambridge: Cambridge University Press. (Third edition published by Cambridge University Press, New York, 1990)

Rotberg, Robert I. 2002. "Failed States in a World of Terror," *Foreign Affairs,* July/August.

Rothkopf, David J. 2004. "The Coming Battle of the Ages," *Washington Post,* February 1.

Ruthven, Malise. 1984. *Islam in the World.* New York: Oxford University Press. NOTE: Second Edition, published in 2000, includes extensive suggestions for further reading.

Seabright, Paul. 2004. *The Company of Strangers: A Natural History of Economic Life.* Princeton, NJ: Princeton University Press.

Schell, Jonathan. 2003. *The Unconquerable World: Power, Nonviolence, and the Will of the People.* New York: Metropolitan Books/Henry Holt & Co.

Schoenherr, Richard A. 2002. (Edited and with an introduction by David Yamane) *Goodbye Father: The Celibate Male Priesthood and the Future of the Catholic Church.* New York: Oxford University Press. NOTE: An exhaustive study of the way environmental changes, especially during the past century, have affected a major international organization.

Sheehy, Gail. 1976. *Passages: Predictable Crises of Adult Life.* New York: Dutton.

Shils, Edward A. 1997. *The Virtue of Civility* (Edited by Steven Grosby). Indianapolis: Liberty Fund.

Sutton, Francis X. 1968. "Technical Assistance," in *International Encyclopedia of the Social Sciences* (Edited by David L. Sills), Vol. 15. New York: The Macmillan Company & The Free Press.

Tocqueville, Alexis de. 1835. *Democracy in America.* Translation by George Lawrence published in 1966. New York: Harper.

Treadway, David. 1990. "Codependency: Disease, Metaphor, or Fad." *Family Therapy Networker,* Vol. 14, No. 1.

Turnbull, Colin M. 1972. *The Mountain People.* New York: Simon & Shuster.

Varshney, Ashutosh. 2002. *Ethnic Conflict and Civic Life: Hindus and Muslims in India.* New Haven, CT: Yale University Press.

Warner, Steve. 2004. "From the Chair." *Newsletter,* Sociology of Religion Section, American Sociological Association, Winter.

Weber, Max. 1904-05. *The Protestant Ethic and the Spirit of Capitalism.* Originally published in German. New translation by Stephen Kalberg, who also contributed a useful introduction and extensive notes, was published in 2002. Los Angeles: Roxbury Publishing Company.

Wells, Spencer. 2002. *The Journey of Man: A Genetic Odyssey.* Princeton, NJ: Princeton University Press.

Willis, Jan. 2001. *Dreaming Me: From Baptist to Buddhist, One Woman's Spiritual Journey.* New York: Riverhead Books.

Wood, Michael. 1987. *In Search of the Dark Ages.* New York and Oxford: Facts on File Publications.

Wright, Robert. 2000. *Nonzero: The Logic of Human Destiny.* New York: Vintage Books.

Zakaria, Fareed. 2003. *The Future of Freedom.* New York: Norton.

Index

A

affection, as a value 280
Africa 14, 21, 95, 145, 179, 309
Ahmed, Akbar S. 97, 182
al Qaeda 172, 209
Alcoholics Anonymous 267
Algeria 172
Ali, Abdullah Yusuf 111
Almond, Gabriel 119
Amenemope, 316
American Association of Retired Persons 287
Angier, Natalie 19, 20, 166
Anan, Kofi 159
Anti-Saloon League 122
Argentina 129, 130
Atran, Scott 172, 210
Auburn Theological Seminary 209
Australia 154, 156, 158, 164, 240, 244
authoritarian governance 23, 82-83, 91, 119, 131-144, 182, 295; definition, 131

B

Baird, Zoë 315
Bangladesh 246
Basañez, Miguel 163, 305
behavioral codes, 32, 87, 99, 102-118, 124, 158, 168, 170, 181, 182, 208, 238, 271, 285, 295, 298, 303-308
Belgium 54, 158, 164
Bible 106-110
bin Laden, Osama 209
birth rates 93, 95, 173-184, 201; *see also* population imbalances

black death 125
Black, Matthew 111
Bok, Sissela 299
Bornstein, David 246
Breasted, James H. 106
bribery 104, 213
Buddhism 114, 155, 162
Burns, Robert 206
Bush, President George W. 28, 159
business 115, 122, 124, 137, 198-199, 273
Butler, Robert N. 37

C

Callahan, David 316
Calvinism 274, 306
Cambodia 159
Campbell, Mary E. 156
Canada 36, 151, 162, 164, 240
Cantril, Albert H. 212, 213
Cantril, Hadley 213
Cantril, Susan Davis 212, 213
Cao Dai 155
Carnegie, Dale 268
Carr, Martha Randolph 263
Catholic clergy 56, 57, 58, 62
censorship 22, 97
Center for Immigration Studies 154
Chechnya 118, 151
Chile 145, 158
China 156, 157, 162, 165, 177
Christianity 106-110; *see also* Judao-Christian tradition
Chua, Amy 165, 184

327

citizenship 21, 154, 236, 237
City University of New York 154
civility 100, 104, 190
Clinical Center for the Study of Development and Learning 261
colonization 234-235
Columbia University 11, 21, 318
communication channels 4, 9, 22, 26, 69-85, 134, 194-195, 226, 260-265
competition 22, 44, 142-143, 208, 211, 229
conflict resolution 17, 30, 44, 209, 224, 228-229, 259-260
Confucius 110
Congress of World and Traditional Religions 17
Coontz, Stephanie 299
Council of Graduate Schools 156
Council on Foreign Relations 150, 178, 244, 245, 247
creativity 33, 66-70, 205, 251. 315
Croatia 146
Czechoslovakia 151

D

Dalai Lama 19
Davison, W. Phillips 68
Dawood, N.J. 111
democracy 131; communication in 82-83; adaptability of 133-136, 143-46; personnel for 119, 120, 136, 138, 140, 311-313; popularity of 163-64; future of 148, 181-185;
attitudes toward 212-217; services provided by 224-233; as destabilizing factor 165
Diamond, Jared 18, 19, 95
Diamond, Jonathan 267, 275
diversity, positive aspects 16, 29-30, 161, 207, 253, 257, 259
dual citizenship 21, 154, 236
dyslexia 263

E

East Asia Barometer 145
East Germany 136, 171
education 29, 67-68, 253-265; lifelong 89, 285-287
Egypt 182
enlightenment, as a value 281
entertainment, as a value 278
Ethiopia 197
European Union 160, 166
Evans, M.D.R. 161
experimentation 22, 25, 64, 144
extended families 31, 43-44, 113-114, 202-204, 309

F

families, structure of 38-40, 65, 94, 199-204, 299-302; family planning, 249; *see also* extended families *and* nuclear families
fashion 115, 122, 125, 170, 195, 303
feminism 121
Fisher, Roger 260
Florida, Richard 138
foreign policy 27-29, 243-252
foundations, philanthropic 217
France 39, 156, 320
Free, Lloyd A. 213
free trade 152, 159, 165, 184
Freedom House 132, 144, 163, 164
Friedman, Thomas 21, 50
functional groups, definitions of 9, 37-38; structure of 37-43; formation of 51-98; efficiency of 42-43; compatibility 43-44; adaptability 124-147, 198-199, 205, 302 interdependence 118-121; as global phenomenon 150-151

G

Galbraith, J. Kenneth 76
Gates, Robert M. 156

genocide 18-19
Germany 74, 171; *see also* East Germany
Gilkey, Langdon 53-62, 114-115
Global Attitudes Project 244
global government 160
global warming 128
globalization 21-22, 150-162, 165-166, 183-185
Golding, William 52
Goleman, Daniel 267
Grameen Bank of Bangladesh 246
Great Britain 151, 156, 158, 304
Greece 157, 182
Group of Eight 153
Guinea 179

H

Harvard University 255, 260, 310, 322
Head Start Program 301
Hinduism 114, 162
historians 71, 300-301
Hitler, Adolf 74
Hoffer, Eric, 172
Hoffman, Stanley 319
Hohenberg, John 11
Hussein, Saddam 28, 146, 159

I

Ibn Khaldun 182
Iceland 164
Ik 14-15
immigration 174-175, 233-240
India 50, 76, 154, 156, 157, 162, 309
Indonesia 172,179
Inglehart, Ronald 163, 169, 244, 284, 305
Institute of International Education 156
interethnic friendships 156
International Criminal Court 158
international law 158

International Monetary Fund 245
International Institute of Islamic Thought 97
Internet Corporation for Assigned Names and Numbers (ICANN) 157
Iraq 20, 24, 28, 60, 146, 159, 172, 202
Ireland 154
Islam 114, 162, 315, 323
ITC, Ltd. 157
Ivory Coast 179

J

Japan 93, 139, 155, 177, 240
Jesus 106, 107
Jewish tradition 107
Jordan, Cora 294
Journal of Conflict Resolution 260
Judao/Christian tradition 110
Jugoslavia 151
Justice, as a value, *see* Rectitude

K

Kazakhstan 7
Keeley, Lawrence 19
Keesing, Felix M. 197
Keesing, Marie M. 197
Kelley, Jonathan 161
Kennedy, Randall 155
Khmer Rouge 159
King, Martin Luther 68
Koecher, Renate 171
Koran (Holy Qur'an) 111
Korea 20, 304
Kosovo 118, 151

L

Ladurie, Emmanuel LeRoy 214
Lagos, Marta 145, 146
Lareau, Annette 204
Lasswell, Harold D. 152, 278

leadership 85, 101-102, 119-120, 139-141, 230, 251, 289-290
League of Nations 152
Lenin, Vladimir Ilyich 142
Lester, Toby 155
Levine, Mel 261
Levy, William 260
Liberia 154, 179
libraries 71, 85, 276
Lincoln, Abraham 118, 274
Lippmann, Walter 314

M
Malinowski, Bronislaw 210
Mandelbaum, Michael 19, 164, 166
Maori 18
marriage 21, 31, 112-114, 155, 268, 273, 301, 312
mass media 70-84, 134-135, 150, 227, 287, 311-312
Massachusetts Institute of Technology (M.I.T.) 56, 255
Massey, Douglas S. 15, 168
Mead, Walter Russell 247
Medicare 232
Meier, Deborah 67-68
Merton, Robert 267
Mexico 154, 158, 162, 240
Micklethwait, John 152
missionaries 54, 56, 59, 155, 209
Moen, Phyllis 200
morale 99, 100-102, 110. 123-124
Moreno, Alexander 163, 305
MORI 145
Morse, Edward I. 244
Murphy, Liam 242-243
Muslim 17, 97, 111-114, 181, 182, 195, 209-210
Mussolini, Benito 152

Myrdal, Alva 299, 310, 316

N
Nagel, Thomas 242-243
negotiation 196, 224, 260
nepotism 202, 213
Netherlands 54, 164
New York University 242
Noelle-Neumann, Elisabeth 171
nonverbal communication 195, 303
Norris, Pippa 163
North American Free Trade Agreement 159
Norway 164
nuclear families 14, 34, 47, 94, 201, 310

O
Olympic Games 136
Orwell, George 82

P
Palestine 172
Paul ("Apostle to the Gentiles") 106-109
Peace Studies Association 260
Pew Research Center for the People and the Press 244
Philippines 165
Pinker, Steven 255-256, 290
Plato 141
Pope John Paul II 17
population imbalances 24, 31, 93, 167, 173-184, 201, 233-234; numbers needed for survival 93-95
power, as a value 280
Presbyterian 206
press, freedom of 25, 84-85, 164-65, 193, 225-226, 227
Princeton University 21
propaganda 28, 82-83, 124, 247
psychological testing *see* testing of individuals

public health 209, 233, 241
public opinion 25-26, 78, 99-100, 116, 121-124, 145-146, 161, 212-215, 305-306; *see also* world public opinion
public opinion polls 84, 145, 170-171, 244
Putnam, Robert D. 171, 213, 289, 311, 314

Q
Quillian, Robert D. 156

R
Rand Corporation 240
rectitude, as a value 282
religion 32, 44, 45, 70, 104-115, 124, 148, 155, 199, 204-210, 302, 306-308
Renshon, Stanley 154
respect, as a value 280
Rich, Meghan 260
Roman Empire 114
Rothkopf, David 179
Rowley, H.H. 111
Royal College of Engineers 56
Russia 54, 145, 151
Rwanda 19, 146

S
Sachs, Jeffrey 21
safety, as a value 281
Sage, Russell 274
Saint James Episcopal Church 209
Samoa 197, 319
San Salvador 155
sandwich families 204
Sayers, Dorothy ix
Schell, Jonathan 323
Seabright, Paul 168
Serbia 146
Sheehy, Gail 323
Shils, Edward A. 104
slavery 4, 19, 122

Smith, Adam 293
social capital 290
social organism, definition 37-38
social work 219, 267, 276
society, definition 13; *see also* world society
Sokka Gakkai International 155
Somalia 43
Soviet Union 75, 82, 92, 142, 151, 160, 181
Spain 17, 18, 151, 158, 181
Spiro, Peter 159
sports 136, 218-219
Stalin, Joseph 142
Strand, Kerry 260
Sutherland, William J. 14
Sutton, Francis X. 324
Sweden 164
Switzerland 153, 155, 243

T
Talleyrand, Charles Maurice de 121
Tamil Tigers 172
taxes 26-27, 171, 214-217, 223, 240-243, 251
Taylor, Charles 154
Temple Israel 209
Ten Commandments 104-107
terrorism 4, 24, 28, 152, 167, 172, 178-179, 250-251
testing of individuals 30, 255-256, 258-259, 291-292
Thessalonians 107-109
Tierney, Kathleen 130
Tocqueville, Alexis de 311
traditional governance 23, 91, 120, 138-140; definition of 131
Treadway, David 268
trust 24, 148, 167, 169, 171
Turkey 151
Turnbull, Colin M. 15

U

Unitarian 207
United Nations 20, 28, 97, 151, 152, 154, 158, 159, 164, 172, 173, 245
United Nations Convention Against Corruption 154
United States 28, 120, 155, 156, 184, 249, 311
University of Chicago 53,
University of Michigan 145, 244, 260, 319
University of Minnesota 200
University of North Carolina 261

V

values, list of 278-285
Verba, Sidney 119
Viet Cong 172
violence 3, 18-19, 28, 167-168, 172, 289; *see also* war
volunteers 47, 56, 93, 138, 172, 277

W

war, as unprofitable policy 18-20, 166, 181, 248; as reasonable strategy 18, 167, 218; research on 296-97; *see also* violence
Warner, Steve 307
Watch and Ward Society 122
wealth, as a value 280
Weber, Max 275, 306
well-being, as a value 279
Wells, Spencer 14
Women's Christian Temperance Union 122
Wood, Michael 214
Wooldridge, Adrian 152
World Bank 245
world public opinion 183
World Social Forum 153
world society 13, 21-22, 24, 148-185, 191, 222, 243-244, 305
World Trade Organization 166
World Values Survey 145, 163, 244, 283, 305, 319
Wright, Robert 18, 35

Y

Yagnob 14

Z

Zakaria, Fareed 325

0-595-32933-0

Printed in the United States
23373LVS00007B/27